DIPLOMACY AND GLOBAL GOVERNANCE

DIPLOMACY
AND GLOBAL
GOVERNANCE

THE DIPLOMATIC SERVICE IN AN AGE OF
WORLDWIDE INTERDEPENDENCE

THOMAS NOWOTNY

TRANSACTION PUBLISHERS
NEW BRUNSWICK (U.S.A.) AND LONDON (U.K.)

First paperback printing 2013
Copyright © 2011 by Transaction Publishers, New Brunswick, New Jersey.

This book is printed on acid-free paper that meets the American National Standard for Permanence of Paper for Printed Library Materials.

Library of Congress Catalog Number: 2011003368
ISBN: 978-1-4128-1844-5 (cloth); 978-1-4128-4958-6 (paper)
Printed in the United States of America

Library of Congress Cataloging-in-Publication Data

Nowotny, Thomas.
   Diplomacy and global governance : the diplomatic service in an age of worldwide interdependence / Thomas Nowotny.
        p. cm.
   Includes bibliographical references.
   ISBN 978-1-4128-1844-5
   1. Diplomacy. 2.   International relations. 3.   International organization.
I. Title.
   JZ1305.N69 2011
   327.2—dc22

                                                              2011003368

Contents

Acknowledgments

I write this book as a tribute to all those—and to those diplomats in particular—who have promoted and supported politics that have carried the world forward over the last 70 years into an era of unprecedented wealth, welfare, and relative peace.

Their work is still incomplete. By now, it even seems threatened by backsliding into a past dominated by sterile and disruptive power plays, by mutual distrust and hostility, and by a failure to tackle those tasks that can be accomplished by common action only.

I write this book in the hope that we will summon the resolve to stem such a reverse into a tragic past and that we will be able to shape the tools of governance indispensable in a very interdependent, and thus fragile and risk-prone world.

I owe thanks to goddess Fortuna, for the luck of having lived in places and at times that have encouraged a positive outlook on human prospects. And I owe thanks to the good fortune of having been involved in, or close to, political efforts to improve on the dismal record of human history in the first half of the 20th century.

I wish to salute all my colleagues in the diplomatic service who have not fallen into the trap of careerism, posturing, and complacency, and who are tenacious in advancing global cooperation.

Above all, I wish to thank my wife—a prominent diplomat, and warmhearted and generous as a spouse and companion. I don't recount how often she went over my notes and the ever-changing manuscript of this book. Her help was essential.

I am aware that the book does not easily fit one of the usual categories. It is not simply a handbook for practitioners. It is not just one of the overly numerous memoirs by ex-diplomats. And it is not one of the many academic writings on a changing world order. So I am grateful to the publisher for taking the risk of publishing something for a still uncertain market. I hope that readers will find it worthwhile to follow me in roaming over these three distinct areas.

It is necessary, I believe, to tie together these three accounts. Practice and theory are intertwined. Even when not aware of it, hands-on practitioners are nonetheless guided by some ideas on how things work in general. They are guided by some theories on international relations. But on its turn, theory that looses sight of actual practice will become useless at best and counterproductive and dangerous at worst. When pursuing political goals one thus has to deal both with practice and with theory at the same time. This is what the book aims at.

1

Introduction

When was the last time you read a book on utopia—a book about a possible, bright future for mankind? You are not likely to find one in bookstores. Utopias are not in fashion. Yet books that predict a bleak future are in ample supply. As are films about the last ones from the human species roaming the garbage dump earth would have become.

Social scientists are fully in this trend. They promote it with dire predictions:

- A "population bomb" would be about to explode, making for standing room only on the earth's surface and dragging us all down into misery.
- We would soon, very soon run out of essential raw materials and thus soon witness a collapse of the world economy.
- Anarchy would spread over the globe as gaps in wealth continue to widen and poorer states descend into chaos.
- A sizeable part of humankind would perish after global warming, having overshot a "tipping point," accelerates in an unbridled fashion.

The predominance of such stark scenarios should surprise in light of recent history. It does not support such pessimism. On the contrary, developments over the last 70 years make it difficult *not* to believe in human progress. People lead longer lives. Fewer children die at a young age and fewer of their mothers at childbirth. A bigger share of the world's population can read and write. Famines touch an ever-smaller percentage of humanity. And, last not least, we have obviously progressed in the political organization of human societies. The number of democratic states has grown. Wars between these have become rare. Where wars between states still occur, they seem to be symptoms of the past and not a pointer to the future.

Why should such positive trends *not* continue into the future? Why must optimists who believe in the continuation of such progress bear the stigma of being perceived as naïve and uninformed?

Indeed, there are weighty arguments against such optimism and against the notion that the future would resemble the past. The massive growth in the global population and the even more massive growth in overall wealth needed and created a dense interdependence between humans, societies, cultures, and states. This interdependence makes for great complexity, and complex systems are fragile. Also, with the growth of the global economy and of the earth's population, limits have become visible that would inhibit a simple continuation of past practices. That is something new. Never before has humankind been faced, for example, with the fact that its economic activities will raise dramatically the temperature of the globe.

It would therefore be unwise to simply ignore the pessimists and, in looking back on past progress, assume its continuation as inevitable. Such further progress is not preordained. It is contingent on political support and direction. Progress would stagnate or become reversed if politics would fail in that task; if humans would lack will and capacity to organize politically in order to influence the course of events.

True—the challenges for such remedial, corrective political action are now greater than they have been in the past. But even when minor in comparison with present ones, such challenges had existed in the past too. We have not been carried forward in these last 70 years by some powerful, broad current of an abstract "progress" that would have worked in absence of human intervention. Global/international politics had shaped the last 70 years of our history and made them the success they were.

So as to demonstrate the relevance of politics, consider how affairs could have evolved in the absence of political guidance; or with the wrong political guidance:

-    What if the American-Soviet confrontation would have gotten out of hand; or would have been pushed to its extreme by suicidal politics?
-    What if institutions such as the United Nations, the International Monetary Fund, or the World Trade Organization (previously GATT) had not been created?
-    What if after World War II the nations of Europe would have relapsed into mutual hostility just as they did after World War I?

- What if the recent world economic crisis would have resulted in a wave of protectionist trade policies and thus in the reversal of globalization?

All these things have not happened. They were avoided because global/international politics pushed events into another direction. Progress was possible because it was supported by politics. It would not have occurred in absence of such politics. And why shouldn't politics do for the future what it has done for the past?

One possible obstacle, already mentioned, is the greater complexity brought about by global interdependence; and the emergence of massive new challenges of a nature unknown before. Yet these new obstacles make solutions not only more difficult, they also make them more urgent. And—if we exempt the eventuality of the earth being hit by a major meteor—none of these challenges is of a nature to escape the countervailing force of politics.

We still might object that the very basis of global politics has shifted, so much so that its past record has little to say about its future reach and potency. That is true also. In these last 70 years, global politics—or the "global regime" had largely been shaped by the United States (and to a much lesser degree by Western Europe). That era of exclusiveness is drawing to a close. The United States, Europe and Canada produced 68 percent of the world's wealth in 1950. By 2003 this share had dropped to 47 percent, and it will have declined further to a mere 30 percent by 2050.

Other regions and/or states of the world will come to share the till now exclusive American and the European capacity to shape the global regime. These other regions and states might hold on to some of American/European values and goals. They will not share all of them. In addition, these states and regions will not be the only ones to emerge as new "actors" on the global scene. They will be joined by potent actors of a new type, such as transnational corporations or international non-governmental organizations. Things will be complicated further by the blurring of traditional divides between internal and external politics, and by a greater diversity of both the objects and the subjects of global political action.

To quote the prince in Guiseppe Lampedusa's book, *The Leopard*: "if we want things to stay as they are, things will have to change." If we want progress to continue, we will have to continue to shape it by politics. We will have to do that with greater efforts, but also with new concepts and new tools. Many of the past concepts and tools have become useless. They need to be replaced by more fitting ones.

For me these reflections of global governance, on its past record and on its necessary overhaul, are nothing abstract and merely academic. I am a citizen of Austria and had been Austrian diplomat until my retirement from the service. Internal and external politics had accompanied and prompted Austria's decline in the first half of the 20th century—just as they, on the other hand, had facilitated its stupendous development after World War II.

Between the two wars, the external policies of other countries, as well as the external policies of Austria itself had a major and negative impact on its economic social and political development. Dismal, dysfunctional internal politics fed on this negative influence from abroad and fed into it on its turn.

In retrospect, the disintegration of the old Austrian/Habsburg Empire must be seen as having been inevitable. The empire was destined to disappear sooner or later. That would have occurred even without the shove of World War I. But it was not inevitable and it was a conscious political decision that implicated the Austrian monarchy in the outbreak of this war, thus accelerating its own demise. Neither was it inevitable that after this war, international politics failed to substitute for the by-gone order in Central Europe a new, organic, and more cooperative one. This was an option not taken and that failure complemented the general failure of Western Allies, which, relishing their victory, impeded a solidly based economic and democratic development among the vanquished.

Internal politics among the latter became erratic, polarized, and murderous in the end. Negative trends were accentuated by the world economic crisis of the 1930s, when the leading economic powers could not agree on joint actions to counter the downward trend in production and consumption. States withdrew into self-sufficiency and protectionism. Globalization was brought to an end. Narrow, confrontational nationalism and egotism came to dominate. A new arms race escalated. No agreement was found to challenge in a timely fashion an ever-more threatening Hitler. Germany, with its insane visions of glory, dreamed of imposing, by military means, dominance not just over Europe, but over the world as a whole.

Austria was implicated in these developments, both as a victim and as a perpetrator. Civil war and the slide into authoritarian rule had weakened it internally, while its foreign policy had failed to gain it outside support. It became the first country to fall prey to Hitler's aggression; and with astounding speed, the vast majority of Austrians then came to support the German war efforts together with the associated cruelties up to the horrors of the Holocaust.

My first childhood memories were those of hours spent in bomb shelters; of the pervasive, silent threat of Nazis to my conservative Catholic family; of rumors about concentrations camps where bodies of slaughtered humans were mined for the gold of their teeth and for the hair of their scalp.

Miraculously, we had escaped. The years of terror, years of hunger, and winters of unheated apartments were followed by years of progress. Food became available. Heating oil replaced the wood in stoves. My father could in the end even buy a car. Austria was spared the fate of Germany, which was divided into a communist East and a democratic West. The foreign militaries left Austria in 1955 and, gradually, democratic practices became internalized and routine.

These developments did not present themselves as a natural and inevitable return to normalcy. Even when young, even when caught in the self-centered turmoil of youth, I was aware that politics had propelled these positive developments. Unlike in pre-war years, Austria's major political parties did not perpetuate their murderous antagonism, but joined forces to rebuild the country and to strive for its full independence from foreign occupation. Rebuilding was helped in a decisive manner by the US Marshall Plan assistance. Relations with neighboring states were normalized even at the cost of emotionally and politically onerous concessions. The country seized every option to participate in international and European cooperation. It aimed at being a "net-producer" and not a "net-consumer" of international security. As a consequence, it had its share in softening the East-West confrontation into mere "détente" and thus had a hand in the ultimate "opening up" of Central and Eastern Europe.

On their turn, international politics largely favored Austria's march to prosperity and democratic consolidation. They made disappear on the European continent age-old enmities, substituting the rich rewards of cooperation for the high costs of rivalry and power politics. The United States could guarantee stability and effective defense against the Soviet threat. Expansion of international trade found support in newly created international institutions and European integration found support in organs created specifically for that purpose. Democratic proceedings and respect for human rights became anchored not just in international consensus, but in Europe, also in highly effective, operative agreements.

Austria now ranks among the wealthiest countries of the world. Other indicators of well-being also show it in a positive light: unemployment is low, life expectancy and literacy are high, corruption is less than the European average, government and administration are effective.

Frequently this rise has been described as a "miracle," as if it had been brought about by mysterious forces and not by human efforts. But wealth and democracy do not maintain themselves without continuing efforts; without a never-ending struggle against the erosion and decay that inevitably threaten human constructs such as politics and the economy.

I came of age in this period of Austria's rapid economic and political advance. It instilled in me an appreciation of the positive potential in humans and in human society; and an appreciation of those politics that had facilitated the realization of such potential.

It is difficult, in retrospect, to clearly analyze all the motives that made one decide on a professional career in preference to other ones. I do believe though, that the realization of the positive potential of politics, of their decisive impact on society and life, did have an influence on my opting for a career as diplomat and for my becoming engaged on the liberal-left side of politics. After a stint of work at an institute for empirical economic research, I took the entrance exam for the Austrian diplomatic service.

My first foreign posting was with the consulate general in New York.[1] This was in 1960s. New York was an exciting place. But it also resounded with the unrest of that period. Protests against the US engagement in Vietnam had become massive and shrill. These were the times too, of the civil rights marches and of cities burning. Nonetheless, US power still seemed unchallenged and the "American way of life" was accepted as an ideal over much of the globe.

Back in Austria for the consecutive five years, I became private secretary to the Austrian head of government Bruno Kreisky. Kreisky, a moderate Social Democrat, is still widely regarded as one of Austria's most successful politicians, owing this repute also to his international role. He was prominent in launching the so-called "Helsinki process" which bolstered peaceful coexistence between the two rivaling superpowers. And he is best known for his efforts to promote peace between Arabs and Israelis.

When returning to my original turf in the diplomatic service, I was sent as counselor to the embassy in Cairo. Prospects for a lasting Arab-Israeli peace opened as the Egyptian President Sadat switched alliances from the Soviet Union to the United States and established diplomatic relations with Israel. This decision of the Egyptian leader was symptomatic too, of the by-then evident failure of the Non-Aligned Movement that had sought to establish a potent, political, and ideological counterweight to the groups dominated by the United States and by the Soviet Union respectively.

From Egypt I moved to New York—this time as head of the consulate general—while my wife, also a diplomat, became political counselor at our mission to the United Nations. This was a period of renewed East-West tensions, of the hostage crisis in Iran, of the United States supporting insurgent movements in Nicaragua and, increasingly, in Afghanistan. Many of those US foreign policy decisions reflected the ascendency of the US neoconservatives. Their ideological hegemony was to last for another quarter of a century.

Having returned to Austria in 1983, I resumed work at the Ministry of Foreign Affairs as head of a department for Council of Europe matters and for political planning,[2] while it became the turn of my wife to work for the head of government. For ten years she held the position as foreign affairs advisor to the Austrian chancellor. Europe continued its economic and political renaissance and Austria started negotiations for membership in the European Union. The Soviet empire collapsed. In Austria, postwar consensus and postwar political structures began to crumble with a parallel rise of populist/right-wing political parties.

I took leave from the diplomatic service when my wife was appointed ambassador to France in 1992, three years after the former Soviet satellite states had shed the yoke of communist domination. It was in the obvious and urgent interest of Western Europe to assist them in their economic and political consolidation. I applied myself to this task in Paris at the OECD Center for Co-Operation with Economies in Transition. Continuing in the same field when my wife was made ambassador to the United Kingdom, I was appointed senior political advisor to the London-based European Bank for Reconstruction and Development—a bank specifically created to assist formerly communist countries.

In the years since my entry into the Foreign Service, I thus had been witness to the consolidation and integration of Europe; to the demise of the Soviet empire; and to the first symptoms of a weakening US position in the world. Equally if not more relevant to the world was, I believe, the rapid economic and political rise of Eastern and Southern Asia; accompanied by a waning power and declining relevance of some institutions that had girded the post-World War II order, such as the International Monetary Fund, NATO, or the Organization for Security and Cooperation in Europe. Austria's position too, had been transformed profoundly through its membership (since 1995) in the European Union. It affected both the content and the tools of its external politics.

After Paris and London came a second, shorter interlude in Austria. In the Ministry of Foreign Affairs, my wife reached the highest civil service rank as head of the section for European and for economic affairs. I myself had quit the Foreign Service for good and became employed by a semi-public bank that promotes economic innovation and small and medium enterprise. I also devoted myself with renewed energy to academic work.

Four years thereafter we returned to the United States—my wife as Austrian ambassador and I still in my capacity as consultant of this promotional and development bank. The mood in the United States had darkened since our last stay. The terror attacks on the World Trade Center and on the Pentagon made the US public painfully aware of no longer being invulnerable. The American dream was fading, with a growing divide separating the few super-rich from the rest of the population. The supreme military power neoconservatives gloried in had proven useless, as it could not extract the United States from the deepening quagmires in Iraq and Afghanistan. Military dominance had not created the "unipolar world" of a "new American century." The economic and moral foundations of the "shining city upon a hill" had become eroded.

We witnessed the dusk of an era. But we witnessed not just the end of that era in which US politics and much of European politics too, had been shaped by neoconservative ideas and policies. Changes were more basic. Something new is about to replace the international structures built in the aftermath of World War II. In history, these long 60 years after World War II had been unique. The old European empires had vanished with the Soviet empire being the last to disappear. Hundred new, independent states had emerged. The world population had doubled. The world's wealth had tripled. Two superpowers had misspent resources on a senseless arms race and a vain struggle for exclusive dominance over the world. Surprisingly, all of those dramatic developments and shifts in power had occurred without a major war, such as it had accompanied similar "tectonic" shifts in past centuries.

Those relatively peaceful 60 years are also part of a longer stretch of history that lasted from the beginning of the 16th century until our times. This was the era when either the Western or the Eastern side of the Atlantic, or both sides together had dominated world affairs. Their wealth and their military power had set these two shores of the Atlantic apart by vast margins from the rest of the world. That other part of the world survived powerless and poor. Both sides of the Atlantic dominated not just by military and economic muscle. They also were able to establish a world regime that conformed to their own interests and values, and which had been accepted by the rest of the world not least because the lack of an alternative.

The power of the Atlantic region is shrinking. The relative decline of Europe is now followed by the relative decline of the United States. Their common values, their belief in democracy and markets were still unquestioned through the 1990s. Now they are under assault. No longer may we assume that in the future, others will see them as central to a stable world order. We must fear that this end of an era and transition to a new one will be accompanied by uncertainty and conflict.

The present challenges cannot be met by missiles, nuclear weapons, and not even by regular armies—well equipped though they might be. A different perspective and different tools are needed for preserving the "global commons," for the promotion of "global goods," and for the suppression of the "global bads." The search is still on for consensus, methods, and institutions to tackle these tasks.

Clearly though, any more stable new world order would have to be constructed with the participation of new players and with new tools. In this endeavor, what is the role of diplomacy and of diplomats?

The public is ambivalent about diplomats and diplomacy. Among insiders, diplomacy might be seen as a noble pursuit. But such positive sentiments are not widely shared. It is not obvious what the profession is about. What are its products? A carpenter uses his tools to make a table. A lawyer writes briefs for the court. A prima donna uses her beautiful voice to sing an aria. But what do diplomats produce? That is not so obvious.

A negative tinge is added to such doubts by the suspicion that diplomats do not stick to rules others are bound by. They are suspected of having lesser loyalty to their state than other citizens. If they want to solve problems in relations to another state, they have to "think with the head of the other." They have to understand the motives of the other side. They even have to show empathy with their opposites. Using that base of understanding and empathy, diplomats will seek solutions acceptable to both sides of a conflict. Doing that, they will have to abandon some of the claims their countrymen believe to be well justified and non-negotiable. The public will therefore suspect them of having mixed loyalties, of not being really and unconditionally one of them. It might regard them as potential traitors.

The public also resents the discourse of diplomats as obfuscating and duplicitous. The public hankers for clarity and certainty. It has little patience for what diplomats see as "constructive ambiguity. If someone is said to have been overly "diplomatic" in a controversy, what is implied is the reproach of his having not given clear answers and of having escaped into evasive word games. But such avoidance of the firm and definitive is sometimes useful. In a world of flux and uncertainty, where future events and future policies cannot be predicted, avoiding a clear "yes" or "no" is often the better policy.

Such an attitude will not resound positively with a public that expects messages to be precise, that yearns for speedy decisions, and which, in conflicts with other countries often prefers confrontation and escalation, as this flatters its vanity and shores up its sense of identity.

The lifestyle ascribed to diplomats also creates resentment in a public that has to fund that lifestyle with the taxes it pays. The average taxpayer does not spend his late afternoons at receptions and other social events. Only rarely will he don a dinner jacket. He will have to pay parking fines that he suspects diplomats are exempt from. Resentments like these have only a small basis in reality. In reality, most diplomats do pay their parking tickets, and otherwise are rather gray and hardworking. Theirs is not the money-drenched, glittering lifestyle of the high flyers in finance, sports, and entertainment, whose pictures grace the society pages of newspapers.

The public image of diplomats is certainly far removed from the grayish sobriety of their frequently tedious work and existence. This sometimes resentful public image therefore does not enlighten us on what diplomats actually do. But then, what is this work truly about? How is it connected to politics, which—as we have seen—have the capacity to steer the world into disaster, or on the other hand, may set it on a course toward firmer peace and greater wealth?

In times past, diplomats used to have a very prominent and sometimes even leading role in dealings between states. But while the world since has been transformed, diplomacy seems to have remained the same—at least in its outward appearances. The form of its official transactions, its hierarchies, its rules of protocol, all of these still are largely those that had been agreed upon by the nations of Europe in the 17th and 18th century.

This raises the questions as to whether under present conditions, the traditional diplomatic intercourse between nations is still that relevant, or whether it has become an empty ritual and—in some cases—even detrimental to world order.

Various definitions are being offered on what the words "diplomacy" and "diplomat" imply. Most of these definitions still assign to diplomats the role as the main, or at least as the privileged "gatekeepers" at the borderline that separates internal politics from the world beyond national borders.

Until quite recently this claim for an exalted role of diplomats was still upheld widely. In a book, *The Evolution of Diplomacy*, written in 1950 by the British diplomat Harold Nicolson and considered a standard text, traditional diplomacy is being assigned *the* central function in shaping relations between states; as is evident from the following quote:

> An ambassador must always be the main source of information …and above all interpreter regarding political conditions …in the country in which he resides. *In every democracy … power rests with three or four individuals only. Nobody but a resident ambassador can get to know these individuals intimately.*… It must always be on his reports that the governments base their decisions on what policy is practicable. The ambassador remains the *chief channel of communication* between his own government and to that to which he is accredited …he remains the intermediary who *alone* can explain the purposes of one government to another.

Those are extreme claims. Yet that extreme claim and that self-image of diplomats still found its expression and legitimization in the 1961 "Vienna Convention on Diplomatic Relations." The convention sanctioned a view according to which international political transactions would be done by diplomats mainly. Yet at that time already, this postulate had become mere fiction. It is significant that the diplomats that drafted this convention failed in framing a similar convention on multilateral diplomacy. Attempts foundered upon questions of privilege and protocol—questions taken too seriously by traditional diplomacy. Evidently, it was easier to stick to a fading role model of an increasingly marginal traditional, bilateral diplomacy than to adapt the practices to the by far more prominent role of multilateral diplomacy.

My personal experience with diplomacy and at the margins of diplomacy, as well as my academic interest in the subject, oblige me to conclude that traditional, bilateral diplomacy cannot and should not maintain claims for such a decisive and near exclusive role in global governance. Holding on to outdated notions on the tasks and tools of their profession threatens to make diplomats not only redundant; but it even could make them into obstacles on the way to arrangements that would better serve the world.

Such new arrangements are called for by the worldwide interdependence that has created a complex global system and complex subsystems. As all complex systems, these too are susceptible to sudden rupture and even to sudden collapse. Political intervention is therefore[3] needed so as to keep these systems in a steady state. That task is not an easy one:

- Because *the global interconnections have become direct and massive*, with events and decisions in one part of the world having direct repercussion in other ones. What happened in American agriculture 400 years ago had little impact on the rest of the world. If the United States today were to use agriculturally produced ethanol to fuel all of its transport system, it would have to devote two-thirds of its farmland to such a production. That would result in worldwide famine.

- *Because differences in life condition now vary more widely than ever before,* with concomitant wide differences in the nature and aim of national politics. Two hundred years ago, the average income in China was still rather close to the average income in Great Britain—then the wealthiest nation on earth. By now, the per capita income in the wealthiest states (such as Norway or Luxembourg) is 200 (!) times that in the poorest states, such as those in sub-Saharan Africa.

- *Because a cleavage exists between the challenges, tasks, risks, and threats that are global in their nature;* and the local, state-bound methods of conferring legitimacy to actions intended to address such global issues. It is evident that one single state has little sway in countering a worldwide economic depression or in thwarting the threat of a global pandemic that is bound to affect its citizens. Appropriate actions have to be taken on a worldwide level. Nonetheless, such worldwide measures have to be accepted as legitimate. And it is states still that may confer that legitimacy upon these global actions even if such global actions are urgent and necessary.

Those cleavages are hard to bridge. Bridges have to be built nonetheless. That is the task of global politics. To accomplish that task, statesmen[4] need specialists that help them, just as static and mechanical engineers help builders in constructing bridges. Look over the shoulders of statesmen assembled at summit conferences and at similar events, and you will discern such diplomatic mechanics active in the background: preparing decisions; seeking consensus, editing text; preparing for the follow up, etc.

It is worthwhile to reflect upon why, among many others, diplomats are still so prominently engaged in this work. Perhaps, we might wonder, there is something in their tradition and their professional ethos that pre-selects them for such tasks. That ethos and tradition has found expression in some rituals, habits, and role models that no longer are functional and that add little to global governance. Yet that ethos and these skills may also be channeled into other, more productive employs.

But for that to happen, diplomatic services will have to adjust. As the pressure to do so has been intense, most of them have done so. Yet much distance is still to cover. Success in such reforms depends on substituting a new worldview for the one that informed traditional diplomacy; and it depends, last not least, on diplomats altering the image they have of themselves and of their accepting a new role in global governance.

Much has been written on globalization and on how it has changed relations between states. Numerous books describe the traditional techniques and tools of diplomacy: instructions on how to draft official notes, on the seating order at dinner tables, on duties and privileges of diplomats, on how to conduct negotiations, etc. But less has been said about what connects these two spheres—about what links this new global order with the realm of diplomacy. In this book, I will try to cover this area in between. I will look into the relationship between diplomacy and a world transformed by interdependence.

I will start out by reflections on my own experiences in the diplomatic service. They provide a lesson on what diplomatic services no longer are and no longer should claim to be:

- They are no longer the sole and no longer even the most important source for information in country A on conditions in country B. At best, they can provide just a small part of such policy-relevant information.
- They hold no monopoly in communications between country A and country B; and no monopoly even in communications between the administrations of these two countries.
- They have no monopoly either, in official negotiations between the two countries. In most cases, embassies in particular, have no substantial function in such negotiations.
- They have a limited impact on the perceptions held by the public in country A on country B.

Routine diplomatic activities often turn in the void of a self-enclosed, self-referential system. In their aim to outcompete the diplomatic services of other states, and in their search for empty prestige, they may not just fail to promote a common good; they even might impair it.

That is not to imply, that even traditional, bilateral diplomacy would have been emptied of all tasks and functions. The political relevance of embassies has certainly shrunk. Yet their workload has grown in line with the expansion of trans-border flows of goods and persons. Consulates are even more affected by this heavier workload than embassies.

Embassies also retain a certain, politically relevant symbolic function in affirming the political individuality of their home country. One cannot conceive of a state without an embassy at the United Nations, just as one cannot conceive of a state without its proper flag.

Nonetheless, the redundancies and dysfunctionalities of the present setup are obvious and they do not result mainly from bureaucratic inertia and the failure to depart from established routine. They are the necessary outgrowth of the whole worldview that has shaped international relations over the last centuries and up to the most recent times. According to this view, the world system would be based on a competition of nation states, with one state's gain being the other state's loss. With no overarching authority in place, we would still live in global rulelessness; that is in a state of *anarchy;* in a system being determined by the relative distribution of power; and with such power defined primarily in military terms. In that sense, wars and military power would be the sole true "currency" in international dealings.

By now, the vacuity of such a worldview should have become obvious. Military might has proven impotent. Wars have brought losses even to those who won. Among wealthy, democratic states, they thus have ceased altogether. Anarchy, the inevitable conflict among states, and relative military power can thus no longer be seen as the constitutive elements of the present world system. It is based on cooperation, in absence of which that system of global interdependence could not be maintained.

The transition to this new system is not complete, and even less is the change to a new mode of thinking about relations between the citizens and the states of this world. Yet nonetheless, this transition is made urgent by the heavy weight of those numerous issues that can be tackled only by joint action among all those, that are able to have an input into such "global governance."

Prominent among those actors are the international organizations. They are more than mere reflections of the frequently discordant interests of their member states. Most of them have scope for action independent of these their members. These official international organizations have been joined by international non-governmental organizations of various size, agendas, and bearing. In the fields of their respective interests, the more prominent among them may now impact on global governance more strongly than a good number of states. In a still limited way, yet increasingly, national parliaments too, have entered the fray, sometimes with policies deviating from those of the executive part of their government.

Both the activities of non-governmental organizations and the new international role of parliaments reflect the blurring of the border between internal and external politics. This blurring is inevitable as interdependence makes "foreign" events impact on internal ones; and—vice versa—makes "internal" events impact on foreign states and societies. The intermingling of external and internal politics is facilitated by the spread of democracy, with local and global public opinion restricting the once unencumbered decision-making by the traditional foreign policy elites.

The mingling of internal and of external policies has led to a certain "delocalization" of political processes. Once, these used to be imbedded in a specific, clearly defined geographic location. They no longer are. Delocalization and global interdependence is driven by the globalization of information and the globalization of the economy; with transnational firms as the most effective promoters of this process. These firms have become powerful agents of global governance; not just influencing the decisions made by other "global actors" such a states or international organizations. They have become political agents themselves as they themselves set global rules and enforce them. Lording over all of these new global economic actors are the financial markets with powers to bully any firm or state they choose to bully.

With all those new actors with their widely different interests, and in the absence of anything close to being a world government, one should assume chaos to ensue. It does not. Intense interdependence can persist because of a dense net of formal and informal rules. They are effective even in absence of one all-powerful enforcer. We have thus to revise traditional notions on how politics steer social/economic processes. It is not done exclusively in the former, top-down manner of national or international law being defined and enforced by states. Over vast stretches those methods have been supplemented by the more flexible instruments of "global governance," with many "actors" participating and with many different tools being applied.

This is not to say that states have become less powerful both internally and in their input on this "global governance." While they have lost some influence and functions, new ones have accrued. Overall, the number and scope of tasks incumbent upon states have increased instead of becoming smaller. Not only have states assumed many new tasks in relation to their own citizens, but in cooperation with other states, they have now also to deal with worldwide problems that are urgent and that they did not have to deal before—such as climate change or nuclear proliferation. Yet over and above that, states retain a central function in global governance because they are irreplaceable in providing the ultimate political legitimacy to global rules and regimes. They are indispensable also in their function of enforcing many of these rules.

This is where a modern diplomacy comes in. It can no longer be guided by the image of an international system defined by the competing claims of mutually antagonistic, fully independent nation states. Its style and ethos should not be geared toward signaling the uniqueness and separateness of their states. It should be geared toward the commonality of most problems that need to be addressed in global governance. The whole administrative setup will have to reflect that change of underlying philosophy.

Diplomatic services will have to jettison their claim for having a monopoly in international/global politics. They will have to learn to share that task with other official and non-official actors. They will have to adjust to democratic scrutiny and to the requirements of transparency. And they will have to adapt to the diversity of both of the issues that have to be dealt with; and to the growing diversity and some widening cleavages among states and societies. In their internal setup, they have to shift emphasis from traditional, bilateral diplomacy toward multilateral diplomacy, with the first becoming subservient to the latter.

A diplomatic service that can adapt to these new circumstances is a national asset, as it provides citizens of a state with an effective voice in global affairs. The chances are good that most diplomatic services can adapt and that they will be effective in the new setting of global governance. This is because many of the traditional diplomatic virtues retain their positive function in the more fluid and uncertain settings of global interdependence: empathy, precision, patience, tolerance, and the capacity to search for common ground are not less, but more important in today's world.

Notes

1. I also served, at the same time, as the deputy head of the Austrian Information Service in the United States.
2. "Political planning" is the somewhat misleading translation of the German designation of the department as "Grundsatzabteilung."
3. A truth brought home dramatically by the recent failure of the world economic system to self-stabilize (as academic economists would have had us assume).
4. I beg the reader to excuse my use of this gendered expression.

2

Not Living up to Its Claims: Obsolete, Irrelevant, and Sometimes Dysfunctional

Blind Eyes, Deaf Ears, Mute Mouths: Cairo, 1975–1978

I was posted at the Austrian Embassy in Cairo from 1975 to 1978; and, in absence of the ambassador, was in charge of the embassy for a year. Egyptians are seen as industrious, warm, welcoming, and agreeable. The need of living closely together on that narrow strip of fertile land seems to have made them so. Yet in the 1970s, this was not a happy place. There was a pervasive sense of decline and futility, with proverbial Egyptian tolerance, patience, or apathy slowly giving way to a creeping mood of repressed resentment, anger, and rage.

Egypt had had a parliament long before all European countries had established one. At the time between the two world wars, a wealthy middle class had put the country on the first promising steps of industrialization, and women had been participating in public life since the early 1900s.[1] Cairo had also been the center of Arab learning and publishing. Its newspapers had circulated through the Arab-speaking world, as did the films that were turned out in great numbers.

As we arrived in Egypt, outspoken intellectuals had been silenced. Ever since the deposition of the king, the country had been ruled by the military with heavy reliance on the secret services. Democratic institutions like parliament and elections were sham. They were tools of the rulers and not checks on them. Private enterprise had been suffocated by a lumbering, inefficient bureaucracy. The nationalized heavy industry stagnated. Vast resources were misspent on the military, which nonetheless had not saved the country from humiliation in three consecutive defeats by Israel. In the meantime, the population had vastly expanded, straining the ageing infrastructure and overwhelming the existing education and health system. Yet, even with all of these deficiencies and dysfunctionalities, Egypt remained a key player in the Arab world and—of course—also in the Arab-Israeli conflict.

Bruno Kreisky, the Austrian chancellor, had a keen interest in this conflict. He saw long-term European security threatened by instability on Europe's southern flank in the countries on the other shore of the Mediterranean. It was obvious that greater stability in the region was contingent upon a resolution of the Arab-Israeli conflict, and especially on a deal involving and being accepted by the Palestinians. Kreisky thus became the first among European statesman to advocate a two-state solution for this problem—with Palestinians living in their own state, side by side with Israel.

In Europe and in the United States, this was not a very popular policy at that time. Kreisky was heavily criticized for it and for his advocacy of negotiating with the "terrorist Arafat." At any case, it was central to these efforts to keep Egypt engaged. Kreisky had been in Egypt himself as the leader of a delegation of the Socialist International. As I found out later—he remained in contact with Egyptian leaders by backchannel communications through someone in the office of the Egyptian president.

Yielding to precedent, custom, and convenience, our lifestyle had become somewhat neocolonial, with many servants, horses in the desert, late afternoons spent at the swimming pool of the "club," and dinners with upper-class Egyptians and colleagues from other embassies. Yet we saw ourselves as not being the old type of diplomats enjoying such frivolities. We thought ourselves to be utterly modern and up to the challenges of a new time. We made some efforts to break out of this cage of a pleasant but irrelevant existence. We took lessons in Arabic so as to be able to at least read the headlines in newspapers. We traveled through the country. And we sought and maintained contacts with Egyptian intellectuals. But while some of them were in opposition to the Sadat regime, this was nonetheless a group with interest in Europe and in the Western world mainly. When cultivating these contacts, we ignored the more relevant and potent opposition. The opposition to truly pose a challenge to the government arose from a base we knew little about. It arose from the mosques in the slums of cities, and in villages sidelined by a wave of superficial modernization.

One day, rioting broke out. The noisy city fell silent. From the balcony of our apartment we saw smoke wafting upwards and heard the occasional clatter of automatic weapons. I later drove through the eerily empty streets of the city center. Noticeable at once was the fact that the wrath of the population had turned against symbols of Western culture: against shops selling Western fashion; against billboard advertising films with pictures of unveiled blondes. In all places, yellow color had been used in defacing such Western symbols. The yellow color is of religious significance in Islam. The uniform use of this color made it obvious that the defacement of Western symbols had been inspired and/or coordinated by one single group.

I had become witness to a defining moment. The religious-fundamentalist opposition had not yet attempted to seize power via a strategically planned rise of the masses. But it had felt strong enough to openly challenge the regime. The revolt had demonstrated the explosive power of repressed anger and resentment. Ministries of foreign affairs and chanceries in Europe would have to take note of this turn of the tide, as it was bound to affect not just Egypt, but also much of the southern rim of the Mediterranean and the Middle East. Any European embassy in Cairo should have felt compelled to reflect on the implications of the events and communicate to headquarters what should have been alarming conclusions: regardless of whether Marxist, nationalist, or capitalist concepts had guided them, Arab countries had failed to modernize. Instead they were about to revolt against modernity and thus to raise hurdles to their integration into an increasingly globalized web of mutual dependence.

Did the Austrian Embassy send such an alarming report? No—it just repeated in some Tele-Text cables, much of what the ministry back in Vienna could have learned even earlier from international wire services.

Neither did I report that, according to the attorney of the embassy, the Muslim faction had taken control of the Egyptian association of lawyers. I also failed to report that female students at the Cairo universities increasingly felt obliged to don the Islamic veil and to shun the presence of their male colleagues.

We were friends with several journalists, among them one who wrote for a major Austrian daily. Unlike us, he was fluent in Arabic. He mentioned, as a by the way, a blind Muslim preacher who drew full crowds with his hate-filled Friday sermons. Several years later I recognized this preacher as the man who had instigated the first bombing of the New York World Trade Center. This observation of our journalist friend never entered into any of our communications with the Austrian Ministry of Foreign Affairs. Driven by the ambition to "improve bilateral relations" to the regime in place, we failed to see and evaluate events that could negatively impact on these relations. Or if we saw them and gave them their proper weight, we failed to report or otherwise act on them.

Following diplomatic routine, we were blind even to some negative repercussions this routine was bound to have in the Egyptian public. Most of the diplomatic corps participated in charity events organized by the wife of President Sadat. These charities benefitted war veterans and poor children. Yet, notwithstanding such charitable intent, Mrs. Sadat—half English, light-skinned, unveiled, and expensively dressed—had become the object of vicious hatred among a downtrodden population that increasingly found sustenance in a rigid and aggressive version of religion.

Mrs. Sadat's charities took the form of auctions of goods, many of them provided by embassies. It was no secret among us that the main revenue came from the sale of hard liquor at high prices—prices that nonetheless were still below the black-market prices for these beverages. We diplomats thus offended the sentiments of the majority of the population twice: first by associating with the reviled Mrs. Sadat, and second by trading in a substance held by Muslims in the same regard as cocaine is held in the United States or in Europe.

We took care not to trouble relations to our host country even at instances when that host country tread on our toes. Years before I arrived, money had disappeared from the embassy's safe. A colleague, who then had been counselor, had been made responsible and his career suffered accordingly. Then, on my watch, a short article in one of the papers reported on the sentencing of a high-ranking secret service officer for having lifted money from the safes of embassies, to which he had access due to his position and training. We never had even thought about that eventuality before and never had suspected the secret service of such misdeeds.

Only gradually did we learn another fact though it should have been rather obvious. At regular intervals, the Egyptian staff members of foreign embassies had to show up at secret service headquarters so as to report on the work and the personal lives of the foreign diplomats they were serving. When we finally became aware of something so ill hidden, we did not protest to Egyptian authorities. Neither did we pursue the matter of the secret service officer who had broken into our safe. To raise such issue would just have caused embarrassment and might have negatively affected the "good relations" we sought to promote. And yes—as many of our European colleagues—we saw ourselves as effective, modern representatives of our craft.

What lessons to draw from looking back at the years in Egypt?

- I never had, and never would have the same access to the president's palace as the Austrian head of government Bruno Kreisky, deeply involved, as he was, in the search for Middle East peace. My blissful ignorance was in no ways detrimental to his efforts, but, on the contrary, quite functional. Some channels of communication have to be short and secret. In many such cases, involving diplomats might just jeopardize the secrecy and clarity of such direct communication.

- The styles and settings of diplomatic life facilitate and smooth access to certain groups of persons in the host countries. This lifestyle reflects the legacy diplomacy still carries from its origins in the aristocratic and upper-bourgeois couches of society. That preselects the persons a diplomat will have contact with in his host country.

- Yet communications even with this select group are often ritualized and inconsequential. Controversial topics are shunned in order not to "rock the boat" or to raise disapproval. *Faites aimer la France* was the priority task the French foreign minister Talleyrand assigned to his diplomats at the beginning of the 19th century. Diplomats of all nations have taken it to heart. Their goal remains gaining sympathy for their country. Their aim is to improve relations.

- Information arising from other than diplomatic channels is often, or even in most cases, more timely, complete, and relevant.[2] Information distributed via free media also profits from what I would call the *Wikipedia advantage*. Once information has been published in a public media, it will be corrected or completed by others if needed. This is not the case for the "eyes only" dispatches of diplomats. As few see them, there are also only few in a position to correct or update them in the light of new information coming from other sources. The US economist J. K. Galbraith, who had served as his county's ambassador to India, once mocked such reporting as "the least recognized form of art."[3]

- Assuming as their main task the creation of goodwill in their host country, diplomats are tempted to lose sight of the interests of their own country; and even of simple reality.

New York 1964–1969 and 1978–1983: What Compensation for
Jews Expelled from Austria

I was posted at the Austrian consulate general in New York from 1964 to 1969; and then served as its head from 1978 to 1983. It was part of my duty to remain in contact with citizens and ex-citizens of my country. Many of the latter were Jewish who had managed to escape the Holocaust. The circumstances of their escape had been harrowing. Their start of a new life in the United States had mostly been difficult.

Jews had formed a sizeable part of the Austrian population and especially of the population of Vienna. It had been these Jews mainly, who had made for the former cultural glitter and the intellectual prominence of the Austrian capital. They were expelled after Hitler had invaded the country in 1938 and after Austria had become part of Germany.[4] Austrians fully participated in the nastiness and cruelty that accompanied this expulsion. Later on, they fully participated in the inhumane treatment of those that could not escape; and in the terror of the concentration camps.

Some of the most notorious Austrian villains in this drama were punished after the war. Some of the property that had been taken from the Jews was restituted. But this restitution was not done in a magnanimous manner. No great efforts were made, for example, to return all of the art that had been seized. The loss of intangibles—such as living rights in rent-controlled apartments—was not compensated for.

Shortly after Austria regained its full independence in 1955, a general settlement of claims by Jews was reached with the *Claims Conference* that had acted on behalf of the Jews from Austria. Negotiators on the Jewish side then declared the issue closed. No further claims would be made. Yet the sums paid out to individuals from an Austrian compensation fund ("Hilfsfond") were paltry.

Jews from Austria could thus rightly claim not being compensated fully for the injustices inflicted upon them; for the suffering and the destruction of careers and livelihood that this expulsion entailed. Yet in view of Austrian officialdom, it would have been up to the Germans, who had occupied Austria, to pay such full compensation.[5]

During my first tour of duty in New York I met with a group of Jewish refugees from Austria. Their goal was to prompt Austria to grant to its former Jewish citizens compensation as magnanimous as the compensation given by Germany to its former Jewish citizens. I reported to the Ministry of Foreign Affairs on the claims made by this group, but there was no response either from the Ministry of Foreign Affairs; nor from the Ministry of Finance, the latter being the office in charge of compensation to war victims.

Also, during my first tour of duty in New York it fell to me to arrange for a meeting of this group of refugees with the Austrian minister of foreign affairs then on a visit to the United Nations. The meeting was a disaster. It contributed to a worsening of relations between Austria and this diaspora of Jewish ex-Austrian citizens living in New York. The minister haughtily dismissed their arguments and simply pointed to the agreement with the Claims Conference, which, in his eyes, had settled the matter once and for all. He made his argument without the simplest sign of empathy, ignoring the moral dimension of the case. A record on that meeting was inserted as a short paragraph in a report on the New York visit of the minister. The Ministry of Foreign Affairs never reacted and neither did the Ministry of Finance.

It should have been our duty at the consulate to keep this issue in focus, to follow it consistently, and to prompt the Austrian authorities to also take a closer look at the questions thus raised anew. Clouds were gathering. But our reaction at the consulate was halfhearted; and found no echo anyhow.

Our limited and inefficient role became obvious in a second incident with more immediate consequences for Austria. As consul general in New York in the time from 1978 to 1983, I became friend of a freelance art critic of the *New York Times*. Jewish, she had to flee Vienna still a child, leaving behind in the well-appointed apartment a drawing by the famous turn of the century artist Gustav Klimt. On a visit in Vienna, she noticed that drawing at the "Albertina" museum and wanted to claim it. The museum refused and the issue came to the courts. The courts dismissed her petition as she had failed, in their eyes, to prove that the drawing she had seen in the "Albertina" was identical with the one that had been left behind when she was forced to leave Austria. In its dimensions, the drawing in the "Albertina" would differ by a few centimeters (I do not recall the exact figures) from the dimensions she had reported for the drawing left in the old apartment.

Incensed, my friend started a campaign via a prominent art journal, raising—well beyond this specific case—the general question of art in Austrian museums that had been expropriated from Jews. The affair escalated and dragged on with much damage to Austria's reputation and was resolved only 15 years later.

What conclusions to draw from these incidents?

-       In diplomatic services, the flow of authority and information is
        such as to enshrine and protect the status quo. Diplomats become
        engaged in defending it. Scarce attention is given to new issues
        that emerge on the political agenda.
-       To the extent that diplomatic missions do report, these reports
        frequently do not echo in their Ministry of Foreign Affairs and
        do not spur it into action.
-       The loop between the diplomats abroad and the Ministry of
        Foreign Affairs at home is mostly a closed one. Other authorities
        in the home country tend to be excluded. This even may happen
        where such other authorities have the main and final say on a
        question.
-       Much if not most of the information that is politically important
        and that should be acted upon is being transported not via dip-
        lomats but via media and via other channels. The information
        concerning the art seized from Jewish Austrian citizens had also
        first been carried by public media.[6]
-       Diplomatic representatives are rarely directly involved in truly
        important negotiation between two countries. Neither the Aus-
        trian Consulate General in New York nor the Austrian Embassy
        in Washington was involved in the subsequent negotiations to
        accommodate the Jewish claims.[7]
-       In the diplomatic service, work routine and work-culture is
        geared to the conduct of relations between states. The service
        adapts uneasily to the necessity of dealing with non-state actors
        such as the group of Jewish refugees from Austria that demanded
        a more generous compensation for their sufferings.

Not Involved in Crucial Decisions: To Devalue or
Not to Devalue the Currency

Before exchanging its currency, the schilling, for the euro currency
of the EU, Austria had "pegged" its schilling—that is tied the external
value of the schilling—firmly to Germany's currency, the mark. Germany
was Austria's main trading partner both for imports and exports. When
this was done in the early 1970s,[8] the question of this "pegging" had
been discussed widely. The advantages of the "pegging" were seen in a
general lowering of so-called transaction costs and in preventing major

fluctuations in the external value of the Austrian currency. Disadvantages were seen in the possibility that the external value of the schilling could rise steeply in tandem with the external value of the German mark. This would have impacted negatively on exports and economic growth. One also feared the possibility of a sudden, unplanned unraveling of the "peg." That would have had consequences more severe than the more gradual changes in the external value of a currency that are common in a regime of flexible, "unpegged" exchange rates.[9]

When I came to New York as consul general, the "pegging" to the German mark had been in place for several years already. It came under strain, however when, unlike Germany, Austria decided to counter a recession with an expansionary fiscal policy. The balance of Austria's current account turned negative as a consequence. That led some to speculate that the whole "pegging" might become untenable and that the demise of the arrangement would be accompanied by a drastic devaluation of the schilling.

It so happened that previously I had come to know the desk person of a Wall Street firm that did the political risk assessment for Austria. I had been helpful in providing few minor details for an earlier report. Now I was contacted by the same desk officer and confronted with his view that the schilling would be devalued in the next few days. I had some good arguments to counter that view: the consensus on the advantages of the "peg" had become firm in Austria in the meantime. The deficit in current account was not structural, but a recent and temporary one, caused by a divergence in the German and the Austrian macro-economic policies. I believe that I could persuade that Wall Street analyst and keep him from publishing his prior view on the demise of the schilling/mark peg. I do not know if that made any contribution to the passing of the crisis of confidence in the Austrian schilling. If so, this contribution was certainly a very minor one.

What lessons from this incident?

-      Next to London, New York is the second most important global money market. For diplomats stationed there, it should be a prime duty, one should assume, to keep contact with key players in the capital and money markets; and also be in contact with experts assessing political risks. Yet when departing for New York, I did not receive any instructions to that effect, nor had my predecessor provided me with a list of relevant contacts in Wall Street. My acquaintance with the analyst doing the political risk assessment for Austria came about by mere accident. It just as well might not have occurred.

-   An unwanted, imposed devaluation of a currency is a major calamity. I am certain that the Austrian Central Bank in particular, was aware of the danger and was watching the situation very closely. I assume it to have been on the phone constantly with all international players that could impact on events. But even in such situations, diplomats are not in the loop. The official representative of Austria in the key capital and money market, New York, was not in the loop—and he never will be.

-   Tacitly thus, the diplomatic service has acknowledged that, in some fields, it simply is not a player. That is the case even if issues are as central to the well-being of a nation as unwanted changes in the external value of its currency. In the Austrian Ministry of Foreign Affairs, there is no one to deal with such questions. There is no desk to deal with international monetary affairs. In fact, I would have vainly looked in this ministry for someone who could have provided me with added arguments in my discussion with the analyst who predicted the devaluation of the Austrian schilling.

Diplomats Blocking the Wheels of Global Cooperation: Paris 1993–1997

While my wife was ambassador to France from 1993 to 1997, I worked there at the Organization for Economic Cooperation and Development (OECD).

Its history, its actual and its potential function make the OECD a unique institution. It was created in conjunction with the postwar US aid for Europe. It multilateralized this aid and thereby promoted intra-European trade. Preying open the closed postwar European economies, it initiated European integration. One might rightly wonder if it would have come about without that US support. Yet with that task accomplished, the OECD's mission changed and membership was expanded so as to include major non-European, democratic, and wealthy countries, such as Japan and Australia (and more recently, Korea and Mexico). Not just the membership of the OECD was thus expanded, but so was its agenda.

The OECD is organized as are most such international institutions. International civil servants work in the secretariat of the organization.

The secretariat is headed by a secretary-general, who is being elected by the member states. Over and above that, member states participate in decision-making on two levels:

-       by an annual meeting which is attended by members of governments; and
-       by regular meetings of a Council that monitors and gives directions to the work of the Secretariat. At the OECD, this Council meets once a month.

Members of the OECD Council are mostly diplomats. Many of them are generalists, not specialized in any of the issues OECD deals with. These issues are many and diverse. One of the most important tasks is the harmonization of statistics so as to make them internationally comparable. In absence of statistics that are based on common criteria, member countries would not know where they stand in educational achievement, in the creation and distribution of wealth, in agricultural policy, in matters relating to the health of the population and the cost of the health system, etc. By its very nature, this task of making statistics internationally comparable calls for solid and reliable linkages among those specialists and higher civil servants that compile these statistics in each of the OECD member countries. The OECD functions as the catalyst and curator of such a network.

The same holds true for other OECD activities: protection of the environment, labor market policies, industrial policies, fiscal and tax regimes, migration, corporate governance, oversight and regulation of financial markets, etc. Here too, OECD gains its function and competitive advantage as the facilitator of networking between experts in its member countries.

The OECD has also moved beyond that. Not in terms of international law, but in fact it has become one of the most powerful actors in global governance. A minor part of that is done via the traditional tool of international treaties (such as the OECD treaty that governs the transboundary disposal of noxious waste). Yet many of the tools employed by the OECD are not clad in the form of such treaties. Nonetheless they are equally—if not more—binding. The OECD has pioneered[10] and mastered the tools of peer reviews, of benchmarking; and of ranking countries by various indices.

In this role as global actor using new tools of global governance, OECD does not act via diplomats, but via experts gathered in and around the OECD. Diplomatic generalists are not such experts. They even will find it difficult to precisely understand all of the issues experts work on. Nonetheless, the diplomatic generalists who sit on the OECD Council do not shy from administering and micromanaging the OECD Secretariat. They impose themselves on experts while having scant knowledge on what the work of these experts actually implies. Instead, they are guided by the traditional ethos and by the traditional concepts of their profession. If they care about it, the promotion of international networking among specialists is not their top priority. Their prime aim is to promote what they perceive to be the "national interest" of their home state. They will persist in such efforts even if they thereby damage the organization they are posted at.

Let me recount three examples for this pernicious tendency:

Given the staffing of the OECD Secretariat and given the highly technical nature of much of its work, it is evident that the administrative head of the organization—the secretary-general—has to be:

- one with a past professional career that has made him at least aware of the work of the OECD, its vast variety and its political relevance, with some understanding of the tools and techniques used for analysis and policy proposals;
- an able administrator;
- of some international standing, well-respected and open to dialogue.

When I started work at the OECD, its secretary-general was the former, very senior French civil servant J. C. Paye—a model of efficiency and quiet tact though not a political heavyweight. He might not have been the optimal choice for this position, but he was a good one. The term he had been elected for drew to an end. Member countries and their diplomats had to decide on a successor. A core principle in deciding on a candidate is the need of this position to "rotate" between persons nominated by countries of North America, by European countries, and by the other member countries of the organization. As J. C. Paye had been proposed for his position by the European member countries, the United States started to lobby against a prolongation of his term and for the installation of a new secretary-general from North America. The prolongation of the term of J. C. Paye was being opposed by the United States not because Mr. Paye would have failed at his job, or because the United States could propose a successor better qualified. In fact, the persons they finally nominated—a Canadian—was rather ill suited for that important position.

A battle between European and American diplomats ensued. It was resolved by a compromise. J. C. Paye would serve a further half of a term, and his successor the remainder of the term. Evidently, such a solution of creating first a lame duck leader and then his short-term successor is not in the interest of an organization in need of continuous and firm leadership. The less-than-optimal solution found was the result of a battle between diplomats, each of them fighting for what they saw as their national interest in having a secretary-general from their region of the world.

Any big private organization, such as a big transnational firm or an important foundation will use a more rational method of selecting a leader. It will first establish a list of criteria a candidate would have to meet. It would nominate a committee to cast a wide net in the search of suitable applicants. In most cases, it will employ specialized head-hunters. Background checks will be done. Candidates will be further screened in hearings.

Not that the OECD did not go through similar motions. But they were faked and they did not affect a decision already taken before. This charade was unavoidable, as taking another course would have implied a diminished role for the diplomats on the Council of the organization. Understandably, not only from their position but also from their profes-sional self-image, they refused to yield such influence to outsiders—to outsiders such as professional headhunters who unlike them, were not closely bound to this or that state.

Two further observations: the US decision against a prolongation of J. C. Paye's term was taken without the United States being yet in a position, at that time, to propose an alternative. And second, the term of the Canadian successor to J. C. Paye was prolonged later on, though it had become evident by then that he was not really qualified for that leadership position.

I remember two other instances of diplomats of the Council injecting, to ill effect, narrow national political predilections into the working of the organization. In the early 1990s, unemployment had risen danger-ously in most of Europe. This made for a hot issue in political and ideological terms. Anglo-Saxon countries with a then-more favorable labor market situation began to lecture the continental European ones and tried to entice them into more "flexible" labor market policies—with the term "flexible" usually standing for the disempowerment of trade unions.

In such a situation of ideological and political battle, it is useful to search for a common base of agreed-upon data. The OECD was well prepared to provide them. Its highly regarded Directorate for Employment and Labor not only furnishes statistics that are internationally comparable. At that time, it also had done some solid studies on the implications and consequences of the "flexibility" that some of the OECD member countries regarded as the best instrument in the fight against unemployment. Yet, one such study of the OECD Directorate had demonstrated that greater or lesser "flexibility" did not make much difference in explaining unemployment.

In the eyes of the Anglo-Saxon member countries and of some of their ideological camp followers, this automatically disqualified the Directorate on Employment and Labor from directing an intended flagship study on unemployment. In the OECD Council, these "Anglo-Saxon-Plus" countries prevailed. The task of preparing this flagship publication was given to carefully chosen outsiders. These outsiders came up with the results that met the expectations of those who had installed them. Unlike the OECD Directorate on Employment and Labor, the outside experts concluded that enhanced "flexibility" on the labor markets would provide the most potent medicine in the fight against unemployment.

Unfortunately for the OECD, this intended flagship publication on unemployment was not well executed. Other institutions had done a technically superior job; for example the International Labor Organization in Geneva. This was detrimental to the standing of the OECD and its reputation as a source of objective analysis.

As mentioned, I had worked at the OECD at its Center for Co-operation with the ex-communist countries ("Countries in Transition"). This center had financed a study on industrial policies recommended to the Czech Republic. The study proposed policies in wide use at other OECD countries. It did *not* recommend picking this or that industry as a winner. The recommendations were on financial instruments, on education and research, on the overall structure of the tax system, etc. At a time that the study had already been printed but not yet been distributed, the Czech ambassador intervened on behalf of the then Czech prime minister Vaclav Klaus—a politician of notoriously short temper and of a quasi-religious trust in markets. I do not actually know, but doubt, whether Prime Minister Klaus had actually read the study. I believe that he was incensed by the title alone. In his view, countries should abstain from having an "industrial policy" and leave the development of industry to markets exclusively. To its shame, the Secretariat of the OECD caved in to the demand that the study not be distributed. It was pulped. Its author was reprimanded and demoted. On the premise of this incident having become more widely known, would any country in the future seek OECD guidance on industrial policy?

The Czech diplomat who intervened on behalf of his head of government, was he aware of the damage this intervention could cause to the credibility and reputation of OECD? And if so—would he have cared? Given that his career was dependent on his standing with his head of government and with other Czech authorities, one would have to assume that he never considered objecting to the instructions received from these authorities: namely to make disappear a reputable study of the OECD just because it ran counter to the ideological predilections of Vaclav Klaus.

Evidently, diplomats feel comfortable in representing what they see as a narrowly defined national interest even when that is to the detriment of some higher common goal an international organization was set up to serve. And they see themselves as the true masters of the game with other diplomats being their sole legitimate counterparts. Outsiders are not welcome. They are being pushed aside or ignored. In the long run, this position is untenable and will detract from the relevance of diplomacy as well as from the status and practical value of diplomats. If their worldview and their daily work cannot accommodate the other actors that now populate the field of global relations, these other actors will bypass them, causing diplomats to lose mission and status. The tendency of traditional diplomats to act as representatives of a self-enclosed, self-referential group might ultimately assign them to decorous irrelevance.

Notes

1. There also was an opera house (in fact Verdi composed *Aida* for its opening).
2. Evident in the case mentioned above of the Austrian journalist who reported on the hate- and rage-filled prayers of a blind sheik who later instigated the first attack on the World Trade Center in New York.
3. Let me add that other forms of information offered to rulers are even more dubious: namely the reports of secret services, which do not easily lend themselves to the same reality check as reports in newspapers or even as diplomatic dispatches. An apt quote from Patrick Moynihan 1998 "Secrecy is for losers. For people, who do not know how important the information really is."

4.   To be precise: according to the official legal line, which has also been accepted by other nations, Austria would have continued to exist as a subject of international law during the German occupation between 1938 and 1945, but—due to that occupation—it would have been unable to act as a sovereign.

5.   This was the Austrian position at the time I worked in New York. This attitude changed only later on, in the 1990s, when Austria conceded that there was still a moral debt to pay and that it would be obliged to provide at least some added material compensation.

6.   In this case of the restitution of art—by specialized magazines.

7.   The issue was resolved—decades later—in negotiations by high-ranking diplomats acting on both sides: on the Austria side my friend the former UN ambassador Ernst Sucharipa; and on the US side Under Secretary of State Stuart Eizenstat. The main question in this context is, however, why the issue had not been tackled earlier. Why had diplomacy not preempted a clouding of US-Austrian relations; and had not brought an earlier remedy to the Jewish victims of Nazi terror in Austria?

8.   The discussion had been very acute in the ruling party, and in the government between Chancellor Bruno Kreisky and his minister of finance. The latter, favoring the "pegging," prevailed; but this was to the detriment of his later political career.

9.   As had the unraveling of the "peg" that had tied the Argentine currency to the US dollar.

10. The OECD has pioneered, *inter alia*, the most important tool of international economic comparison, namely the standardized national account.

3

Traditional Diplomacy and Its
Operative Functions

"Diplomats are like swans which, to the outside observer, glide unperturbed and elegantly over the water. But under the surface they are paddling like mad."
—A European ambassador in Washington, 2007

The accounts from my experience in and with diplomacy might be mere anecdotes. But it is difficult to ignore that these accounts clash with the notion that diplomats still hold that elevated and powerful position they had claimed in the past. The diplomatic service is neither the exclusive nor even the widest channel of communication between states. Most of the information that flows between states does so without the intercession of diplomats. By necessity, diplomats know little about the content of these vast flows. They are unaware even of many pieces of information that are politically relevant in relations between two states. Nor are diplomats the exclusive agents to shape these relations. Some of the more important political transactions are done in direct communications between heads of governments. Other politically relevant transactions are frequently handled by persons who are not diplomats.

Nevertheless, even traditional diplomacy still does have some useful function:

1) Embassies and consulates are administrative anchors in foreign countries. They act as all-purpose service organizations for official, semi-official, and frequently even private institutions of their home country. But now, some of these institutions have established their own contacts in other countries and see no reason why *not* to bypass embassies. This holds true, in particular, for private enterprise. Only rarely will it need the help of diplomatic or consular representations. Not only private

institutions, but some public or semi-public ones too, will tend to use their own channels of communication when dealing with partners in other states. Secret services, for example, have notoriously stuck to their own ways and contacts, leaving embassies in the dark even when dealing with political touchy issues. Ambassadors are mostly ignorant about their doings. In a like manner, ministries of finance operate over their own channels of international communications and contacts. So do central banks, which are expressly exempt from any obligation to coordinate with governmental institutions. Other line ministries, regional governments, larger cities, all now cultivate their own version of international relations. Increasingly, they do so in direct contact with their foreign partners.

2) This trend of activities shifting away from embassies and consulates will, however, be compensated for, and will even be overcompensated by the increasing volume of trans-border transactions and contacts; and by the growth in the number of institutions that are obliged to exit from a purely national cocoon and enter the global arena. Inevitably, much of that will involve embassies or consulates. These will have to assist co-nationals in finding their way.

3) This makes for a growing workload of embassies and consulates. It burdens them with additional tasks that lack glamour, that are routine, but which they cannot escape. Meetings have to be arranged. Briefings have to be prepared. Persons in the embassy's host country have to be informed on who is going to visit them and about the issues these visitors are likely to raise. Frequently it is then also up to the diplomatic staff to provide written documentation on what has been said in such meetings. Even much of the nitty-gritty cannot be unloaded from the embassy: the reservation of hotels and meeting rooms, the pick up at the airport, the provision of interpreters, etc.

4) To provide such services, embassies (and to a lesser degree consulates) should be able to know who is truly in charge and who might be helpful. They have to establish a relation of mutual trust with such insiders. That calls for socializing and for the hosting of events like dinners and cocktails, which a skeptic, taxpaying public interprets as empty and expensive frivolities.

5) Consular work[1] has expanded even more rapidly than this routine work of diplomats. The trend is bound to continue. Globalization

is contingent on a vast expansion of international travel and on a massive rise of foreign direct investment (FDI) with firms going international not just in sales but in production too. Criminal activities also have expanded beyond the borders of single states. Crimes like drug smuggling or human trafficking are international by their very nature. The ensuing tasks and challenges have to be tackled in international cooperation. But they also add to the workload of consulates: passports lost, travelers falling ill or dying, foreign documents that need to be certified or translated, kidnappings for ransom. Nationals facing courts in a foreign country need lawyers; should they land in jail, consuls have to safeguard their humane treatment, etc.

6) Consular officers extend the services of the sending state into the receiving state. Their work grows not just because of globalization, but also because the volume of services provided by states has expanded. States now are active in fields they did not cover some decades ago; such as public old age and health insurance and child welfare. With the increased international mobility of persons, the services of their state have to follow them unto the territory of other states. Consulates have to provide or at least mediate such services. Add to that, the many trans-frontier transactions that had been ungoverned in the past but which now are subject to state oversight and control. International travel is the most prominent of these activities. In the 19th century, no visas were needed for travels within Europe. This has changed, as the increased mobility of persons had to be balanced by greater precaution against the entry of terrorists, of other criminals and of illegal immigrants fleeing poor countries in search of better paying jobs. Some of this consular work might be outsourced. Some of it might be shared by several states pooling their resources. But this will lift only a small part of the consular workload. It will continue to become heavier.

7) As a rule, both diplomats and consular officers become involved in case a major disaster happens in their host state. This involvement will vary in its nature according to:
   a) whether this disaster is large-scale and mainly touches the population of the receiving state; or
   b) whether it mainly touches the own nationals that happen to be in the host state.

There is a clear tendency for enhanced international cooperation in response to large-scale, natural or man-made disasters
that strike a country. Special institutions and plans are now
in place (for example, not only within the European Union,
but also within the United Nations) to permit a rapid response
with each participating country being assigned specific tasks.
There was a swift and coordinated international response, for
example, to the disaster of the tsunami that struck the coasts
of Southeast Asia in December of 2004. Such international efforts are frequently complemented by efforts rendered by or via
consuls and diplomats. In the aftermath of the Tsunami disaster,
Austrian diplomats were on site to assist in the search for, and
help to Austrian victims. When New Orleans was flooded in
2005 several Austrian consular officers were sent down from
Washington with the twofold task of facilitating the work of
an Austrian relief team[2] and of assisting Austrian victims.[3] In
the same line of duty, within hours the Austrian ambassador
in Bangkok was on the place where a plane carrying Austrian
vacationers had crashed in Thailand in May 1991.

8) In the past, negotiations had been defined as the main task of
diplomats. As we have seen, this is a task now increasingly
shouldered by experts. Indeed, how should diplomats have the
know-how to negotiate the substance of very technical agreements such as on veterinary control; on double taxation; on the
protection of the privacy of personal data in the Internet or on the
mutual recognition of patents? The number of such international
treaties has grown exponentially. More than 50.000 of them are
now accounted for in the official UN register.[4] While diplomats
will usually not negotiate the substance of such treaties, they
will frequently be involved in the run up to such negotiations,
as well as in their follow-up and implementation.

9) The diplomatic task of reporting has not become wholly
superfluous. It still might happen that diplomats gain access to
information that is not available to others. This will be the case,
when they have been specifically charged with carrying back to
their home country a message that has been entrusted to them
for that purpose by authorities of the receiving state. In order
to keep open the options for negotiations, and in order to shield
such negotiations from the pressure of public opinion, it will
be prudent, in many instances, to keep secret such exchange of

information via diplomatic channels. But there is a place for diplomatic reporting even next to this function (that is already closer to negotiating than to reporting). At rare instances, diplomats may convey back to their home country information that is freely accessible in principle; that is not widely circulating nonetheless; and which is of specific relevance to their country. It is one of the tasks of diplomats to sieve the vast flow of information for such rare items; or to search for them actively in personal contacts.[5]

Serendipity

My sister—a US fashion designer—has a country house in central Vermont, a six-hour drive from New York City. Staying there over a long weekend, I had gathered the newspapers from the local general store; next to the Sunday edition of *The New York Times* was the weekend edition of *The Burlington Free Press*—a major Vermont daily. Having taken due time to dig through the two pounds of *The New York Times*, and having nothing else to do, I also perused the Vermont paper. My attention was caught by an article on a corporation called Space Research. Its headquarters straddled the Vermont border between United States and Canada.

Space Research had been founded with the vision of using high-powered guns instead of rockets to put satellites into orbit. The firm did not succeed with that project. But it had managed to develop artillery pieces with an ultra-long range. In countries that had not yet gotten hold of tactical missiles, such artillery pieces could substitute for them. South Africa was one of the potential customers. At that time, around 1980, South Africa was still ruled by the apartheid regime. This regime was under international sanctions, which banned arms exports to South Africa.

Space Research, intent on exporting its guns to South Africa, was thus looking for alternative locations in countries it thought less strict than the United States in enforcing international sanctions against arms trade. According to *The Burlington Free Press*, the owners of Space Research must have thought neutral Austria to be such an apt location. The paper alleged that Space Research had been sold to a prominent Austrian, state-owned corporation—a technological leader in the production and shaping of steel, and one of Austria's most prominent exporters.

So I learned from the local paper, *The Burlington Free Press*, that this important and state-owned Austrian company was about to break stringent international sanctions against ostracized South Africa. For Austria, the negative fall-out from such a breach of international solidarity could be substantial.[6] I therefore clipped the article and sent it with comments to my former boss—the Austrian head of government, Bruno Kreisky.

I had no response and after a few weeks called a secretary of Kreisky to inquire as to whether use had been made of the information I had provided. It had. The Austrian chancellor had summoned the chief executive officer of the Austrian national steel company, who assured him that there was no substance to the article. They would have no deals with Space Research. With that, the case was closed as far as the chancellor's office was concerned.

But—as I am tempted to say: of course—the article in *The Burlington Free Press* had been correct. The Austrian state-owned steel firm had indeed purchased Space Research. It had begun to produce these long-range guns itself. As it turned out a few years later, it also had sold them to states in the Middle East that at that time were also under an international arms embargo. Investigative Austrian journalists brought that to light. A major scandal ensued. Several members of government had to resign.

So, does my experience with an article from *The Burlington Free Press* prove that, as a rule, diplomatic reporting continues to have political relevance? No—it does not! It only points to the very exceptionality of instances when this still might be the case.

- My observations were not communicated via the usual channels and to the Ministry of Foreign Affairs, but to the head of government instead. This is a channel of communication usually not available to diplomats.
- Had I sent the report to the Ministry of Foreign Affairs instead, not much would have been done with it. I assume that a diplomat in the ministry would not have had the authority to summon the head of one of Austria's biggest and most prestigious companies.

- How frequently does a diplomat posted in New York sit on a porch in Vermont to read the local newspaper? This cannot be seen as part of his professional routine.[7]
- No diplomatic skills or training are required for noting in a local newspaper an article of obvious relevance to a specific country. The only qualification required is interest in the subject and knowledge of the interests of the various parties involved. Diplomats might have part of that knowledge; but so would others like arms producers and arms dealers, groups then engaged in the fight against the South African apartheid regime, competitors of the Austrian state-owned steel company, etc.
- In the 30 years since this incident, other channels of communication and information; and other ways for searching for content have become more prominent. The dots I came to connect by reading a small local paper can now be connected by those millions of persons skilled in the use of the Internet.
- It finally says something about the credibility attached to diplomatic reporting that the chief executive of a prominent firm could feel safe in discrediting its content.

The other remaining function of diplomatic reporting is the one of setting in its context information that is widely available. This is the task of evaluating the consequences for the home country of events or processes that are being reported in the various public media of the host state. Diplomats are not the only ones engaged in such an evaluation. They have ample company. It is still growing. Such evaluations and assessments are being done by think tanks; in academia; by experts for political risk assessment in financial institutions; and—increasingly—by what might be called free floating diplomatic advisory services such as the highly regarded International Crisis Group.[8] Foreign services are thus well advised to use the information and assessments provided by such groups, and to compare them with their own, in-house, evaluations.

10) "Public diplomacy"—relations with the public of a host country—have already been part of traditional diplomacy. It will continue to have its place among the present tasks of diplomats.

But I am a bit skeptic about assigning it too prominent a role. We will deal with that specific issue in one of the later chapters.

11) In a later chapter, I will also deal more extensively with what has turned into the most relevant political function bilateral embassies still retain. It is their work complementing and supporting multilateral diplomacy—that is the diplomacy transacted by several states together—mostly in using special international organizations for that purpose. The negotiating position of each participating state is contingent, of course, on political/administrative processes within this state. Reporting on them, and—if possible—influencing them has become the principle task of bilateral embassies.

12) Roughly US$ 100 billion are being disbursed each year as Official Development Assistance (ODA) from the rich to the poor countries.[9] Donor countries differ in the way they organize and administer this assistance. Some countries have special ministries in charge of this assistance; and/or they have a special service to run the programs in the field. In other donor countries, that assistance is being administered by the ministries of foreign affairs; and executed by diplomats in the field. But even when run by separate ministries and by separate corps in the field, diplomats of various ranks will become involved in such tasks too.[10]

13) On rare occasions, diplomats may still do more than such mundane and routine things. On rare occasions, they might come to impact on the course of political events and change their direction. In their book on (US) career diplomacy, the authors Harry Kopp and Charles Gillespie provide one example for such exceptional cases. In 1975, shortly after the autocratic Portuguese government had been toppled in the *revolution of carnations*,[11] a US career diplomat—Frank Carlucci—had been appointed ambassador to Portugal. The quickly succeeding post-revolutionary Portuguese governments had drifted leftwards. There was fear that the NATO country Portugal might end up as a communist state. In their book, Harry Kop and Charles Gillespie describe this as a concern of the then-US Secretary of State Henry Kissinger. They hint at his having toyed with the idea of instigating a counterrevolution like the one that the United States had instigated in Iran with the effect of reestablishing the rule of the shah by removing the left-leaning Iranian Prime Minister Mossadeq.[12] US Ambassador Carlucci warned against such a

project. Speaking perfect Portuguese, he was in daily contact with all-important political players in Lisbon and concluded that there was no danger of Portugal turning toward the Soviet Union. Carlucci was not afraid of personally bringing this message to Henry Kissinger, and—should that be necessary—even to the US president. In the end he prevailed and thus prevented the United States from sliding into a foreign policy adventure with an uncertain and likely very negative outcome.

In crucial moments and on occasions, in *hinge moments* when events might turn into one direction or another, diplomats sometimes do have a chance to shape events. The chance is certainly greater for diplomats from large states like the United States. But two of my former colleagues from the Austrian diplomatic service have also been able to impact, in their host countries, on the course of politics. Like Carlucci, they could do that in the fluid situation of a state being on its way from dictatorship to democracy.

One colleague was ambassador in Chile at the dusk of the Pinochet era of right-wing, authoritarian rule. It was in the residence of this Austrian ambassador that forces of the democratic opposition could gather for the first time. Another colleague acted in a similar fashion in Spain, which—after the death of the dictator Franco—was on its way to democracy. It was feared that high-ranking military officers might impede this process in the event the left-leaning Socialists should become dominant in a post-Franco government. The Austrian ambassador to Spain was the first to bring together the military and the Socialists, who could thus establish that it would be possible to live with one another.

But these are the rare exceptions. Overall and on the average, the role of traditional diplomacy is clearly not the role that it had been assigned in the past. By now this role is mostly routine and administrative. When active in the field of bilateral relations, diplomats are not the all-powerful gatekeepers at the barrier that separates internal politics from external events. Representing their own country in another state, they are not the exclusive eyes and ears of their state in that foreign country. Their scope of independent action is limited and their impact on relations between the two states is mostly minimal. In that sense, the traditional discourse on the role of diplomacy is not only erroneous, but also misleading, as it directs attention and resources away from more fruitful employ of diplomats, and from the contribution to global governance rendered by a modern version of diplomacy.

Notes

1. In most countries the diplomatic and the consular services had been separate up until the end of the 19th century. Nearly everywhere, they are merged by now. This too signals a growing weight and a growing consular workload.

2. It is specialized in water purification.

3. It is a bit disconcerting that European citizens now tend to request such assistance under all circumstances and without regard to their costs. As it seems, they have come to expect that all and even minor inconvenience can be unloaded upon the state and its representatives.

4. One of the causes of this rapid increase is the equally rapid increase in the number of states. It doubled since World War II.

5. That might, for instance, be information on the likely outcome of a vote in the US Senate that could affect trade relations to countries the United States regards as rogues. Or it might be information on the position a fellow European Union member country on an issue of high relevance to Austria (such as tolls on heavy duty road-transport.)

6. In view also of the fact that, at that time, Austria had been non-permanent member of the UN Security Council; that is member of the body charged with the enforcement of UN sanctions such as those against South Africa.

7. Neither is that within the reach of most of those "clipping services" that are used by embassies and consulates. The "clipping service" I used as a consul general in New York (my fief extended to Vermont) did *not* bring to our attention the article from the *Burlington Free Press*.

8. Only a few diplomatic services will surpass this group in the quality of the information and evaluation it can offer on the developments in critical spots like the Kosovo or Georgia.

9. There is a moral imperative behind such assistance. It is exactly for this reason that one should not ignore the fact that notwithstanding a track record of now 50 years, the results of development assistance have been disappointing. Evidently, it is difficult to change countries from the outside—even with large-scale financial assistance.

10. Not necessarily by working with the government of the host country. There is a growing tendency to bypass central government when providing development assistance; especially in cases where central governments are inefficient, ineffective, corrupt, not very legitimate or simply nonexistent for all practical purposes.

11. In order to signal their peaceful intents, soldiers had stuck carnations into the barrels of their guns. Hence, the name given to this revolution in Portugal.

12. I myself can attest from the little could gather in the office of the Austrian chancellor, that those musings of Henry Kissinger were not merely abstract. He seriously seems to have considered the overthrow of the new democratic regime in Portugal.

4

Diplomats as Symbols

The actual function of diplomacy and the traditional role model of diplomacy diverge. This is because the role model was formed in times and circumstances that differ from present ones. As we have seen, traditional diplomacy nonetheless still retains some of its practical functions. It also still retains an important symbolic function. States use flags and national anthems to signal a claim for a distinct political entity.[1] They also use diplomacy.

Many events and trends that deeply impact *within* states, originate from *outside* the state. They have to be dealt with in cooperation with other states. But that interdependence and that need for cooperation has not detracted from yearning for local identity. Citizens of a state mostly cherish the notion of forming a politically distinct group and of having this distinctness affirmed by outward symbols like flags and anthems; and having this identity secured too, by other trappings of membership in the club of independent nations. Diplomats are such symbols. Affirming the separateness and identity of their states is one of their functions. Their existence and their rituals serve that emotional need. They bolster the cohesion of a group formed by its support of, and dependence on the political institutions of a state.

Ambassadors present letters of accreditation to heads of state. The ceremony is the same for countries big or small. In the United Kingdom, the same gilded coach fetches the ambassador of Liechtenstein and the ambassador of the United States to this ceremony with the queen.

Some may find proof in that for the utter dysfunctionality of such diplomatic traditions. Treating Liechtenstein and the United States in an identical manner must seem out of tune with reality. Nonetheless, that seeming dysfunctionality hides some sense and purpose. Peace and cohesion in the world is enhanced, if small states too, are given symbolic assurance of their being accepted and recognized as separate political bodies with distinct identities; if they are given a seat at the common table of all nations.

By now, many institutions, many actors weave at the web of global interdependence. Many share in the tasks at the helm of global governance. But among them, states are still the most prominent. States still are those actors that have the most solid base of political legitimacy. Among the many global actors, they are still those best able to infuse, on their turn, political legitimacy to global governance. Symbols like the ceremony at the presentation of the letters of credence are there to confirm them and assure them in this role.

National flags are another such symbol. They can be used for sending symbolic messages. They are the letters, so to say, in a symbolic language. Flags can be hissed and lowered, can be dipped or flown half-mast. Messages thus sent are widely understood. The British public reacted with anger to the failure of Buckingham Palace to lower the flag to half-mast on the death of Princess Diana.

Like flags, diplomats can also be used for sending coded but well-understood messages. Embassies can be opened or closed. Diplomatic recognition may be granted to, or withheld[2] from a state. Ambassadors can be sent, can be withdrawn or may be called home for consultations. Diplomats may, or may not mark with their presence an event in their host country. Foreign ambassadors might be summoned to the Ministry of Foreign Affairs to receive a stern remonstration on something that had displeased their host country, etc. It is useful to have such a symbolic language. It sends a message that is fairly clear, but avoids causing damages that other expressions of displeasure, such as economic sanctions, might entail.

The mere fact of using the diplomatic channel for communications has also a symbolic significance. Using the diplomatic channel for sending messages puts that message on a specific political level. A message sent that way is defined as being more than just a simple piece of information. It is the suggestion, offer, or demand to start a political process.

It was well-known, for instance, that the United States was displeased with what it regarded as too comfortable economic relations between Austria and an Iran bent on the acquisition of nuclear arms and therefore under increasing international pressure. Reports on this concern of the United States had appeared in Austrian newspapers. Some of these articles might even have been planted by US authorities. But the issue gained a wholly different dimension when raised with the Austrian Embassy in Washington.

Why did the United States use the embassy to convey a message? We can exclude that it was simply meant to provide information to Austrian authorities; as such information had become available by other channels already. We can also exclude the possibility that this was meant as an invitation to the Austrian ambassador to start, himself, negotiating the matter with the United States. If lucky, the Austrian ambassador might have been furnished with some speaking points on that issue by the Austrian Ministry of Foreign Affairs beforehand and might have dutifully delivered them in response to the US remonstrations. But these remarks could certainly not be construed as being part of true negotiations. In theory, ambassadors are plenipotentiaries, fully entitled to speak and negotiate on behalf of their state. In reality, they do not have such power as they lack both information and authority for binding negotiations.

So, in this and in similar cases, what is the meaning and the intent of communicating via embassies? Using this form of communications one state alerts another one to the fact that the first country considers an issue to be open and relevant in the relations between them. Sending a message that way implies the expectation of receiving a substantial answer from an authoritative source; it implies the demand that exchanges continue and change into negotiations until a mutually acceptable solution has been found.

The resident ambassador will become involved in such later negotiations on rare occasions only. He will have helped in setting negotiations on their course. The substance of the issue, however, will be dealt with later by experts from the two nations and at bilateral meetings or conferences. In most cases, the ambassador will no longer be involved.

Notes

1. States and their citizens cling to minor, even petty symbols of identity. Austria did so, for example, in its negotiations for membership in the European Union. German is the official language in Austria. Yet there are differences in the names used for potatoes, which are called "Erdäpfel" in Austria, but "Kartoffel" in Germany. For what Austrians call "Paradeiser" (i.e., paradise-er), the Germans use the word "Tomaten." Germans use the word "Konfitüre" for what Austrian call "Marmelade." Austria made some efforts, and successful ones at that, in having these differences recognized in the accession treaty to the European Union. Such efforts might seem disproportionate. Obviously though, they reflect a deeply held desire; namely the desire to be seen, and to see themselves, as different from their bigger, northern neighbor even if this neighbor uses the same language.

2. This is rarely a wise thing to do. The withholding of a diplomatic recognition to a state—or a regime—will not make that state or regime disappear. Withholding recognition is meant to signal a negative attitude. But it is exactly in these negative settings that the diplomatic channel of communication is especially relevant.

5

Confirming Identity through the Narrative on Foreign Policy

"In the affairs of man, wounded pride and xenophobia often triumph economic reason. Why else would Russia terrorize its gas customers? Or Britons demonize the European Union? In a rational world, China would not stir up Japanophobia and rich Saudis would not help Islamic extremists abroad."
—The Economist (November 7, 2009)

The speeches exchanged on the occasion of ambassadors presenting their credentials to heads of state[1] follow a predictable pattern. They start with some flattering remarks on the receiving state and on its government and then proceed to a characterization of relations between the two countries. It is not necessary in this part of the speech to stick too close to reality. Where relations are anemic they still can be termed "fruitful." Troubles in these relations should be hinted at only; or mention of them should be avoided altogether. The speeches usually end with the rendering of the foreign policy philosophy of the state the diplomat represents.

In this their last part, such speeches are akin to general-purpose speeches ambassadors are likely to deliver when invited by a "Lions Club" or "Rotary Club" to explain the foreign policy of their country. Such speeches can never abstract completely from the actual situation, from actual problems, from parameters for foreign policy action actually available. But the description of such basic data and constraints is not the main purpose of such speeches. They serve to project an image. They are there to establish and confirm the identity one seeks to establish for a country in the eyes of the world.

The foreign policy narrative of the two succeeding administrations of US President George W. Bush provides the perfect, if somewhat extreme, proof. Its purpose was to establish an international image of the United States in conformity with the image the administration also wanted to project back to US voters. This was the image of the *"manly"*[2] United States, so very different from the irresolute, *feminine*, Europeans. Unlike them, the sole surviving superpower would not shy from toppling regimes (regime change) in rogue states, like Iran or North Korea. It would stand ready to take up arms even in defiance of world opinion— ("who is not for us is against us"). It could proudly disdain as ephemeral the soft power of other countries, be they allies or opponents.

Next to compensating for the personal insecurities of President George W. Bush, such a narrative also had the effect of compensating for growing internal problems and tensions in US society, such as those arising from the misery of blue-collar workers and from stark inequalities in income. Not just US politicians, but political leaders in many other countries too, had found it expedient to divert attention from internal problems, and weld together a fracturing society by going in search of (foreign) monsters to kill;[3] and by inflating problems in international relations into mortal threats to be thwarted by resolute action.

Still, there also was another incentive for the Bush administration to "militarize" foreign policy. The economic[4] power of the United States is in decline. Its military power, though, still has no equal. It is overwhelming.[5] It is therefore tempting to assign to this asset a central function in foreign policy. The US administration thus could project to the world and to its own citizens the image of a country of still unsurpassed strength.

The foreign policy narrative of President George W. Bush thus made a virtue out of the fact that overwhelming military power had become the main asset the United States held in comparison to other states. In its narrative on foreign policy, the George W. Bush administration defined military prowess as central to all external policies and as the basis of the US position in the world. In this too, the United States is not the sole one tempted to define as crucial the advantages it has in relation to others, and to ignore or belittle the shortcomings it has as compared to others.

This tendency to use the discourse on foreign policy as means to affirm the political identity of a country is therefore not unique to the United States. It is fairly ubiquitous. I remember, for example, a dinner-table speech delivered by the Algerian President Boumedienne when on a state visit to my country. The speech was endless, making guests wait for 20 minutes or so before they could dip their forks into the hors d'oeuvres. But the truly remarkable thing was the content of the speech. It was as if it had emerged from a time capsule that had been reopened after having been sealed in the 1960s.

The main issue to be discussed at the state visit was the purchase by Austria of natural gas from Algeria.[6] But that issue was not touched upon in Boumedienne's speech. Instead, he dwelt at length on Algeria's role in the Non-Aligned Movement; on its aim to escape from neocolonial bondage; on the virtues of a "Third Way" between capitalism and socialism, etc. Like Austria, Algeria is a rather young state. The need to distance itself from its former colonial master, France, translates into a discourse filled with reservations about European ways. The rhetoric of a "Third Way" in politics and the allegiance to the vast Non-Aligned Movement satisfied that need, and also provided an anchor for the identity of a young country with a young and restless population. Yet the foreign policy options that Boumedienne's speech referred to had long since disappeared. At the time of Boumedienne's visit to Austria, the Non-Aligned Movement had already withered into insignificance. The "Third Way" in social and economic policy had proven a mere rhetoric construct. When Algeria had tried to make more of it, it had prompted political stagnation and economic decline.[7]

What then are the reasons for a rhetoric so far removed from reality? States use such rhetoric to define what they are or what they wish to be. They use it so as to affirm their identity. They use it to define to the world and to their own citizens what makes them differ from others and what makes them unique.

The Austrian Tower of Babel in New York

When I was consul general in New York, I tried to sell the building of the Austrian Cultural Institute. The Institute is financed by the Austrian Ministry of Foreign Affairs and is staffed by Austrian diplomats. It is located on a narrow plot (21 feet wide) on East 52nd Street, between 5th Avenue and Madison Avenue. I had three good reasons for proposing the sale.

One was the fact that the narrow building with its narrow rooms was ill fitted to accommodate larger audiences.

Second, I was motivated by the chance to use the high proceeds from a sale in order to purchase long-term accommodation for *all* of Austria's New York offices in a single building: the Mission to the United Nations, the Consulate General, the Cultural Institute, the Information Service, the Trade Commissioner, etc. Uniting them under a single roof would have provided ample synergies.

The third motive, though, was the most potent one. The whole idea of having such a building seemed utterly misplaced. It made sense, of course, to promote cultural exchanges between Austria and the United States. Many such exchanges are organized on a commercial basis by agencies that arrange for concerts, exhibitions, lecture trips, or theater performances. There is ample space for exchanges that cannot be arranged on a commercial basis, but which need to be promoted by the state.

Such non-commercially financed cultural exchanges projects should best be organized in cooperation with local partner institutions. This cooperation would provide Austrian artists a wider US audience than which could be accommodated in the narrow confines of the Austrian Cultural Institute. This is why the institute seems to have become an obstacle to this reach for a broader US audience. The need to fill its premises kept it from joining forces with those US organizations that could have guaranteed a far wider public to Austrian art, music, and science.

My efforts to sell the Austrian Cultural Institute building failed, because the foreign minister considered them to be too ambitious. The Republic thus kept the building. As the inadequacies of the old, Tudor-style structure became more obvious, a decision was made in the 1990s to tear it down and to replace it, on the same site, with an ultra-modern Austrian Cultural Forum. The competition for the design of the new building was won by a US architect of renown. He had been forced to leave Austria in his youth and was better known for his theoretical writings than for the few buildings he actually had designed.

The new building is spectacular. With a slightly slanted and sculptured façade, it rises 24 stories from its narrow base. After a phase of architectural sterility that had marked New York City in the 1970s and 1980s, this was indeed a welcome, new, and eye-catching architectural landmark.

Design tricks could somewhat compensate for the disadvantages of the narrow building site. A succession of absolutely remarkable directors has managed to do the near impossible: namely to have such a foreign institute accepted as one of the regular venues for memorable cultural activities in New York.

And yet rational arguments still cannot justify the high construction costs and the high operating costs of this extravagant structure. The building's costs were exorbitant if priced per usable square feet. They set a record even for New York. The true hitch, however, is that the structure is not owned by the Ministry of Foreign Affairs, but by an Austrian special purpose agency that owns and runs public buildings. As a consequence, the Austrian Cultural Forum has to pay to this corporation a high rent. Costs for maintenance are high too. The two expenses add up to a sum several times greater than the whole budget of the Cultural Forum to finance the activities in this building, as well as for its activities in the *rest of the United States.*[8]

What has prompted this extraordinary disregard for practicality? Austria is dotted with symbols of a rich past. The capital Vienna still radiates the grandiosity of an empire that ceased to exist in 1918. Those witnesses of the past suggest a continuity of identity that in fact does not exist because, in reality, Austria is still rather young as a state. An "Austrian political identity" began to consolidate in the time after World War II only. This identity was fragile at the beginning and in need of support and arguments. Austria needed such arguments to ease a break with a great past, and for retaining a respected place in the family of nations. Culture was used as such a crutch to sustain the claim for continued international relevance. Austria might be a small state, but in the realm of culture it still would continue a presence as a "major power." Highly visible symbols were needed to sustain that claim. What better place to implant them than in New York, the cultural capital of the world? What better tools than architecture to suggest a continued cultural relevance also in modern times?

So this is the symbolic value of the extraordinary and extraordinarily expensive building in New York. It is wasted money in a sense, but it is still better spent than money expended by other nations on symbols like battleships and nuclear weapons.

As the main purpose of such a foreign policy discourse is the one of affirming a political identity, it is not very well suited to provide direction to the actual foreign policy, as it abstracts from constraints imposed by history, geography, and by the actions and interests of other states.

But that is not to imply that this discourse does not have its effect on foreign policy. It does and mostly with the effect of adding an element of irrationality to this foreign policy.

Throughout its history, the United States had largely defined itself through its foreign policy. Several narratives on a truly fitting US foreign policy stand next to each other. All of them have in common that the United States would be the Non-Europe; that they would differ fundamentally from the "Old Continent." But beyond that commonality, the narratives on the international role of the United States are contradictory.

-   According to the isolationist narrative, the United States would and should stand alone, in no need of allies and unaffected by enemies.
-   The second narrative is on the *manifest destiny* of the United States to become and remain a superpower, ready to take on any opponent.
-   A third narrative is intended to define the United States as the *shining (sic) city upon a hill*,[9] for other nations to emulate and destined to lead the world into a better future by its example.

It is obvious, that these three distinct foreign policy narratives not only impact upon the external relations of the United States They also impact on their internal politics. The most acrimonious battles in US internal politics were about these conflicting narratives:

-   whether or not to have colonies;
-   whether or not to join the League of Nations;
-   whether or not to enter World War II on the side of the United Kingdom;
-   whether or not to define communism as a mortal challenge;
-   whether or not to wage pre-emptive war against the Soviet Union ("roll-back");
-   whether or not to accept defeat and withdraw from Vietnam; and
-   whether or not to invade Iraq.

The options so discussed had, of course, serious and widely differing consequences. But that alone does not explain the ferocity of these political battles. The battles were emotional because they revealed irreconcilable differences in what one aspired to be; irreconcilable differences in the national identity one sought to define for the own citizens and for the world. Should one aspire to be the manly, aggressive warrior?

Or should one aspire to a mission of bringing peace and prosperity to the whole world? Or should one leave the rest of the world to its devices and retreat into the bastion of the continent state? These questions proved of utmost relevance in internal US politics. Frequently, they have decided the outcome of elections.

Foreign policy and foreign policy discourse have an important symbolic function. They bolster the search for a distinct national identity. In many instances they connect but loosely to the foreign policy choices actually open and to concrete material interests of a state.

Notes

1. In order to save time, one had done away with this charade in Washington. The speech the foreign ambassador intended to deliver is deposited in writing with the US Department of State, as is the intended answer by the US president (written anyhow, in the Department of State).
2. The "gendered" nature of this discourse is obvious, and it mirrors to the equally gendered discourse of the Islamist terrorists, who, on their turn, castigate Americans for being "unmanly" and soft sissies. Robert Kagan's now-notorious characterization of the United States as the warrior god "Mars," and of Europe as the love goddess "Venus," puts such gendered stereotyping into a nutshell.
3. Quote from the second US president, John Quincy Adams.
4. As confirmed by the onset of the world economic crisis in 2008. It had its origins in the economic weakness of the United States, long-hidden to ill effect by the large-scale import of foreign capital.
5. According to SIPRI, a Stockholm-based research institute, the United States accounts for nearly half of the world's military expenditures.
6. That enters Austria via a pipeline laid through Italy after having crossed the Mediterranean.
7. I could add to these two specimens of a foreign policy discourse the one dominant in Egypt when I served there at the Austrian embassy. At that instance, Egypt's previous dream of being the leader of the Arab world had already proven futile. The fusion with Syria had created the United Arab Republic. But by the mid-1970s, the construct was based on nothing more than a common flag and a few functionaries without function. So another discourse was needed so as to suggest to Egyptians and the world the unique and powerful role of a country actually adrift both economically and politically. It was found in a regress to time-worn and not very plausible "geo-strategic" concepts. Egypt would gain prominence as the strategic crossroad between the three continents of Africa, Europe, and Asia. That would provide it with a three-dimensional "strategic depth." Such concepts are based on the discredited notion of the supremacy of military power and the defining role of geography.
8. The need to fill the house in New York also detracts from the need to devote greater attention also to other US regions less saturated culturally than New York.
9. Quote from the first governor of Massachusetts.

6

Co-dependent: Discourse and Reality

"[T]he ideas of economists and of political philosophers, both when they are right and when they are wrong, are more powerful than is commonly understood. Indeed, the world is ruled by little else. Practical men, who believe themselves to be quite exempt from any intellectual influences, are usually the slaves of some defunct economist. Madmen in authority, who hear voices in the air, are distilling their frenzy from some academic scribbler of a few years back. I am sure that the power of vested interests is vastly exaggerated compared with the gradual encroachment of ideas."
—*J. M. Keynes, in the last paragraph of his* General Theory of Employment…"

Social science uses the term *epistemic communities* for networks such as the one constituted by the global network of diplomats. Epistemic communities are groups held together by the use of common language and of common symbols. The common language in these communities would *construct reality*. It would constitute reality.

While such explanations cannot be dismissed roundly, they provide but limited insight. This "constructivist" approach does not provide an answer to the basic question as to why these specific networks come into existence and why they manage to persist. It abstracts from the social, economic, and institutional factors that condition the emergence and functioning of such networks.

At first sight, that question seems purely academic, a question to be pondered just by those who write articles in learned periodicals that are never read by persons actually shaping international politics. But the issue is of more than academic interest. The question as to why a certain epistemic community comes to prevail over another one, this question has implications for the practice of diplomacy.

Natural science has an advantage over social science. The reality it describes cannot be altered by that description. The science of geophysics and of astronomy has established that the earth is a globe. If a group of dissident scientists claims the world to be flat, that will not change the spherical nature of our planet.

It is different in social science. Its definitions and concepts reflect back on the object of its studies. The social science of international relations might claim that nations are mutually aggressive by their very nature and that the expansionary instincts of one state are curtailed by the countervailing power of another state only. If such teachings become accepted, then each state will adjust its policies to such a worldview. It will invest in military power, triggering even heavier such investments by its neighbors. Jointly, they will *create* the world of balance of power and deterrence that had existed before in their heads and as a mere theory only. In social science, and in the science of international relations in particular, perceptions do not just reflect reality. They also shape reality. In these fields, a theory is not merely "correct" or "erroneous" in an academic sense. Such theories have political implications.

The following is thus the salient question: Can *any* theory become dominant at any time? Or are there limits to such arbitrariness? Are there reasons as to why one such epistemic community comes to replace another one? For if social reality could be shaped by arbitrarily chosen theories in any direction whatsoever, then sheer fashion or accident would decide the nature of the global system and the basic rules that govern it.

It is not very likely that history would roll the dice in such a way. It is not likely that any discourse could come to prevail at any time; and that this discourse that came by happenstance could then transform reality according to its own rules. We rightly regard such conclusions as not plausible and even absurd. Obviously, the international system is not that malleable. For a *certain time*, the nature of the dominant discourse might be the strongest factor in shaping the global regime. But over a *longer stretch* of time, the economic, social, and institutional conditions that prevail will assert themselves and will cause the demise of an older epistemic community and the rise of another, newer one.[1]

For the longest part of the time since *Homo sapiens* came into existence about 200,000 years ago, an international system as such did not exist. Mobility and intercourse was too limited for that. Humans moved around and survived in small groups, not unlike the groups of hunting and gathering primates they were related to by a common ancestry. We thus should assume that these groups too, were territorial, defending their realm against intruders that could compete for food or access to females. Such clashes would have been limited by the limited capacity of these groups to roam farther and thus to extend the base of their subsistence.

That changed with the rise of agriculture (10,000 years ago) with the construction of irrigation systems, with the invention of sea going vessels, with the use of horse and of other draft animals. The base of food production expanded. Products and raw materials could be exported and imported over longer distances; as could be armies. This was the first era of empires with the Roman Empire being the most well-known and the Egyptian the one that survived for longest.

In Europe, the dark Early Middle Ages that followed saw a fragmentation of such vast networks. Later on, some rebuilding occurred with the establishment of the feudal system. Emperors or kings stood at its top. But their reach was limited. Effective power was mostly held by their feudal vassals, each of whom ruled over a limited territory. These territories still had scant economic and social relations to other, similar ones.

From the High Middle Ages on, a process of slow, but then accelerating innovation set in: in agriculture, in transportation and navigation, in the exploitation of the energies of wind and water, in metallurgy, and at last but not least in the building of public institutions and by the steady advance of rational thought over superstition and religion.

This advance was accompanied by the consolidation of nation states as armies of mercenaries came to supplement and then to replace the armies of feudal knights. Dukes and Kings monopolized power, wrenching it from the feudal lords and from the proto parliaments (the "estates") that had limited it up until then; and clawing it back, too from the emperor that still had somewhat limited their authority. By the 17th century that development resulted in a new European political system. By then, the rulers—the *sovereigns*—had gained unquestioned, supreme power over their territories. They only could expand it with the certainty of thereby causing war.

The international system thus established has been termed the "Westphalian" system; the term referring to the "Westphalian peace," that ended the disastrous Thirty Years War in 1648. It sanctioned the supreme dominance of the territorial rulers and reduced the role of the emperor ("Holy Roman Emperor") to the one of a mere figurehead.

The nature and scope of *global commons* was still limited then as were the interests that these sovereigns had in common and felt compelled to protect jointly. At that time, the global commons basically encompassed just the freedom of the high seas and a set of other rules than facilitated that minimum of transaction amongst states that was necessary even at those times—for example, rules on the status and function of emissaries, and some first rules on fighting wars.[2]

The limited nature of the global commons provided little scope for *positive-sum games*—that is for games in which all would be winners.[3] This was an era of *zero-sum games* or even of negative-sum games, as implied by the ever-present risk of warfare and the concomitant need to ward against it by ever-larger and ever-more costlier armies and navies. These were the times of few common interests; of the unquestioned primacy of nation states; and of the undisputed authority of "sovereigns" ruling them. These were the times and circumstances that accompanied the emergence of diplomacy as we know it.

Diplomacy as it was then created reflected these circumstances of its birth and legitimized them. It legitimized the absolute power of the sovereign; his decision to go to war if he saw fit; and the use he made of his diplomats. The *dominant discourse* on international relations and the dominant discourse on the nature of diplomacy were conditioned by the situation of Europe in the war-torn 17th and 18th centuries.

Why and how did this discourse become dominant? That did not happen overnight. It was preceded by a century-long battle over an alternative and older discourse. This was the discourse that endowed the emperor—or king—not only with worldly powers and legitimacy, but also with a spiritual/religious one. This discourse therefore sustained his claim to a dominance not curtailed by any geographic boundaries. Wars over territory are limited in their reach and ferocity. Not so wars over spiritual values and religions with their claims to unlimited, universal validity.

In the centuries before the Westphalian Peace, this old discourse on the religious foundations of political power prevailed. It did so even as the basis for this discourse had become precarious in the real world as the Reformation and the wider spread literacy and the new prominence of science had splintered the common religious base.

Yet even in the face of such developments, the old discourse on the spiritual/religious foundation of political power had persisted for quite some time. Nonetheless, the cleavage between discourse and reality had made this old discourse dysfunctional as it legitimized the religious wars that ravaged Europe in the 16th century and in the first half of 17th century. The old discourse was abandoned only in the latter part of the 17th century, superseded by a new discourse based on the philosophy that informed the Westphalian Peace.

The transition to this new Westphalian discourse therefore took time and was troubled. Already at the beginning of the 16th century, the discoveries and the expansion of world trade had resulted in the first wave of globalization, with German banks financing silver mines in Latin America and Portuguese vessels fishing cod from the banks off the coast of North America. An international authority—the pope—had ruled on the division of Latin America between Spain and Portugal. Yet the rationality of such arrangements did not prevail. It ceded to the irrationalities and violence caused by conflicting claims for universal spiritual/political/religious dominance.

In that sense, the new Westphalian Discourse brought a clear improvement. No religion would be dominant, but the firm rule of a single sovereign with absolute powers over a clearly marked territory.

To return to the notion that we introduced at the beginning on this reflection on the use and function of political theories and concepts: in the long run, a dominant discourse can remain dominant only if it has a function in making things plausible; and if it motivates actions that do not detract from a common good that can be claimed at a certain point of history. The discourse on the earth being flat could not remain dominant after the circumnavigation of the globe. By then, the flat earth discourse had ceased to be useful. Another discourse proved better suited in guiding action. The new Westphalian Discourse too, corresponded to the reality of the then absolute reign of the territorial masters; and it was useful in terminating the uncertainty and the conflicts caused by the discourse it replaced.

Since the 17th century, when this discourse came to dominate and to instruct the notions on how to conduct international relations, the world has changed again. These changes were profound. We therefore may rightly assume that the Westphalian discourse has to be replaced, on its turn, by a new one, better suited to provide a functional basis for global governance.

A discourse is mostly prescriptive with the inherent mission to actually guide action. Nevertheless it has to be based on generalizations concerning the nature of relations between states and societies. We will address that part of the question in the following chapter.

Notes

1. The discussion on whether ideas shape reality; or reality conditions and forms the theories—this discussion is an old one. It is well known from the intellectual battle between Marxists (theories are shaped by reality; they are but the "super-structure" of reality); and Max Weber who believed in the priority of ideas. But the same questions had already been raised by the "nominalists" in the Middle Ages. I do not believe in this stark dichotomy of an "either-or." The two spheres

are interrelated. But as I believe and as I will point out, over the long run, reality will prevail. That might take some time though and "the long run" might be long indeed.

2.   Codified by H. Grotius "Mare Liberum" 1609 and "De jure belli ac pacis" 1625.

3.   One such exception was the positive-sum game of banning piracy that benefitted all seagoing nations.

7

Beyond Its Usefulness: The Enduring
Dogma of "Realpolitik"

"The political future of countries such as Georgia, Moldova and the Ukraine will be decided not by strategists in Moscow or Washington, but by people on the ground.

In the twenty-first century the power of attraction trumps that of coercion... contrary to the view of the Russian leadership... (according to which) the world is composed of sovereign empires competing against each other over zones of influence."
—*Dimitri Trenin, 2009*

Diplomacy will have to adjust to the changes in the global system. It will have to adapt its tools to these changed circumstances. But as a prerequisite for such a changeover, it will have to scrutinize the worldview that underlies and informs its work. My personal experience in and with traditional diplomacy leads me to assume that it still is largely wedded to a worldview which does not easily accommodate and support the interdependence and cooperation required by globalization.

That should not surprise. It is frequently the case that—for a limited period at least—a certain discourse, a certain theory may prevail even though it is ill fitting to circumstances. In sciences[1] that deal with political issues, such failure to adapt or correct a prevailing theory may have pernicious consequences. As we have pointed out, the theories of social science do not just reflect reality. Inevitably, they also shape reality. The failure to adapt the discourse on diplomacy to the realities of global interdependence therefore constitutes more than a mere intellectual failure. It would be a failure with vast practical consequences, as it would keep us from dealing effectively with the present reality of a world of six and a half billion humans who are interlinked in a dense net of interdependence. The failure to adapt theoretical concepts underlying diplomacy would turn world order back to one in which states and societies lived isolated from another. Diplomatic action based on a theory that is no longer fitting would make for a political reversal into a past, these theories still reflect.

The possibility of such a reversal is real even in our times. It is true that we may diagnose a trend toward tighter international cooperation if we take the long-term view that spans centuries. Yet if we narrow the period under observation and look at the more recent past only, we will see that this long-term trend has not been continuous.

Both economic interdependence and international cooperation had intensified in the latter half of the 19th century. International trade expanded. Travel and migration was not restricted. An international peace-movement had found wide support. Much progress was made in humanitarian international law. A book published in 1910 defined as an *illusion* the notion that nations could again revert to war.[2]

The outbreak of World War I showed that such optimism was premature. This war had no winners. It caused irreversible damage to Europe. It ran counter to basic material interests of all who started it and fought in it. All of that should have been obvious at the time already when armies were mobilized. But the ideas and ideologies of military power prevailed. They depicted as necessary and inevitable a disaster that could have been averted. The war was not caused by the clash of basic, and mutually irreconcilable real interests, but by misplaced, retrograde ideas on what international relations are about.

The tragedy of World War I brought a sputter of efforts to reconnect with the ethos that had informed the prior phase of growing global interdependence and cooperation. But such efforts were burdened by the legacy of embitterment, suspicion, and hostility the war had left. The inability to envision and trust in a world of safe interdependence left states without effective remedy against the World Economic Crisis of the 1930s. Ties connecting states were weakened or undone. World trade declined. Efforts failed to safeguard peace though disarmament and through the League of Nations. International politics were again guided by the fear and distrust of others; and by the conviction that what counted in the end was military might and the willingness to actually use it. A new war ensued.

Figure 7.1 World Trade, 1929–1933 ($ bn)

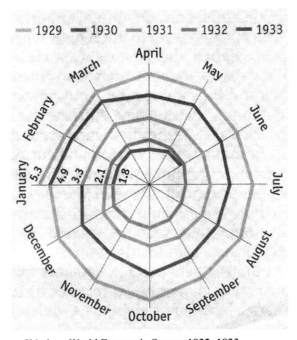

Source: League of Nations World Economic Survey 1932–1933.

Unlike after World War I, the lessons taught by this new disaster were absorbed. During the war still, it was decided to base the order of a post-war world on firmer institutions and to ground it in a political/ideological concept that enhances cooperation between nations.

The United States took the lead in these efforts and supported them though their own example as a *benevolent hegemon*. The unprecedented growth of the world's wealth would not have occurred without that US acceptance of interdependence and that US readiness to trust and cooperate. This trust and readiness—on its turn—would not have existed had it not been based on a worldview other than the one that had facilitated in the 20th century the disaster of two all-out wars.

One would assume that the obvious success of that political philosophy would have shielded it against being questioned and undermined. But that was not the case. Under President Ronald Reagan already, the United States began to distance itself from that function and self-image of a benign hegemon, there to sustain a world system of interdependence and cooperation. In the years between 2000 and 2008, that withdrawal became more marked under President George W. Bush. The system of cooperative global governance became endangered by no longer being politically anchored in the support of the strongest among the nation states, as the US abdicated leadership on core issues. The United States even openly rejected the very notion of global regimes constraining their freedom of action.

Up till then, for example, the United States had promoted efforts to limit the arms race, or to deal at least with those dimensions of that arms race which were most destabilizing such as nuclear proliferation, the militarization of outer space, or the "vertical proliferation" of weapons of mass destruction, with ever-more complex expensive and error-prone arms system being set against each other.

While less convinced than Europeans of the notion of international law setting limits to sovereignty, the United States had, up to then, gone along with initiatives to create and codify international law and to expand its rule. The already meek support for such efforts muted, however, into outright opposition under President George W. Bush, as highlighted by his administration's ruthless campaign against the International Criminal Court, tasked to persecute the most heinous crimes against humanity.[3]

Progress in the liberalization of world trade came to a standstill. Obviously, the United States did no longer wish for globally binding agreements on trade. They preferred to remain master of the game by sub-stituting bilateral agreements for globally binding ones. The United States would always be able to dominate such purely bilateral agreements, but could not be assured of retaining the same capacity in multilateral agreements in which it would have been just one of many actors.

The United States even felt uneasy with the one alliance it was destined to dominate. In going to war in Iraq, the United States ignored NATO and sought support instead in an ad hoc and rather brittle *coalition of the willing*. When a visiting European statesman tried to convince President George W. Bush of the advantages of multilateral approaches, he was hushed with the US president reminding him: "*You know Mr. ..., we Americans do not like to have our hands tied.*"

But whatever the inclinations and preferences of President George W. Bush, the fact is that the "hands of Americans are tied" already. Just as other states, the United States too is enmeshed in a web of interdependence. Like them, the United States will not be able to reach its goals in absence of support by other actors. Powerful as they still might be, even the United States cannot simply opt out of this system. Whatever their political rhetoric on global trade, for example, the fact remains that like other wealthy nations, the United States depends on it. At the risk of otherwise committing economic suicide, they have to participate in free trade and would have to support it if it became truly endangered.

The United States is deeply preoccupied with the threat of Iran acquiring nuclear weapons. The chances are slim of keeping Iran from getting them.[4] Yet even such slim a chance of success exists only if the United States can establish, and merge into a broad international consensus on how to oblige Iran to change course. Such a broad consensus would constrain Iran more firmly than any isolated US campaign.

Military power alone will not provide the United States with means to impose its will on the other six billion inhabitants of the globe. Yet between 2000 and 2008, the United States behaved as if all those limitations to its will and power were nonexistent. As the United States was still unrivaled in military power at the dawn of the 21st century, it should not surprise that it was inclined to play on that strength and that it chose to define the world and its place in it in terms of military power.

That US strategy was based on the notion that nations compete against each other and are inherently hostile to another. This, in turn, shapes the view on how to achieve security in this *anarchic* system of competing, mutually hostile nations that are not bound by any higher authority. In a system so defined, security could only be gained by the capacity to be stronger, in military terms, than any other actual or potential rival. That world view found expression in the US Security Doctrine of September 2002 and in the double goal—expressed in this document—of retaining that supreme military power; and of denying any other nation—or combination of nations—the chance of ever drawing even.

The document is not based on lessons from recent history. In fact, it blatantly ignores them as if the failure of US military power in Vietnam would not have occurred; or as if its strong military power would have prevented the demise of the Soviet Union. The US security doctrine of September 2002 is a *religious or ideological* document instead. It decrees the true faith and does not bother whether that faith is anchored in reality. What are the main articles of this faith?

-   Inevitably and by their very nature, states have to compete against each other.
-   Security is therefore defined as prevailing in that competitive game in which the gain of one state automatically translates into the loss of another one.

-   To prevent others of gaining the upper hand, the United States must see to it that no power stronger than the US itself will emerge.[5]
-   History had dealt the United States the necessary cards for this game, as it had made it the sole surviving superpower at the dawn of the 21st century. Proper politics would permit to hold on to this exalted position for the rest of the century ("The New American Century").
-   Military power would offer the most important, the strategic instrument for maintaining that role at the top of a *unipolar world.*

The September 2002 US Security Doctrine thus fatefully ignored what till then had truly made for a dominant US position:

-   First, this leading position was not primarily based on military power, but on economic strength and on other forms of US presence in the world.
-   Second, this position was due to the fact that most others did not feel threatened or bullied by the United States, but saw the US influence as something basically benign.[6]

As the Doctrine of September 2002 makes evident, the foreign and security policy of the George W. Bush administration was in clear break with such traditions. No rational motives can justify this break. It is folly, in particular, to define it as a necessary response to the September 11, 2001 terror attacks on the Pentagon and on the World Trade Center. Military power could not have prevented that attack; nor has the subsequent massive use of military power in Afghanistan and in Iraq lessened the danger emanating from Muslim terrorists. On the contrary, it has heightened it.

What If....

What would have happened if the United States, instead of organizing a massive military posse in pursuit of a nebulous enemy, had openly suffered its wounds as the innocent victim of outrageous cruelty? Even the most Islamic of all Muslim states would have found it difficult not to show sympathy and not to join the United States in seeking punishment of the perpetrators.

Policies enshrined in the September 2002 US security doctrine not only failed to promote US interests,[7] they actually ran counter to some important US security interests better preserved by joint efforts rather than by unilateral action. More than other nations, the United States should, for example have a stake in preventing an arms race in outer space. Such a race would result from the development and the stationing of anti-satellite weapons. More than any other nations, the United States is profiting from satellites orbiting in outer space. These orbiting satellites would be seriously endangered by anti-satellite weapons. The actual use of anti-satellite weapons could furthermore create clutter in the orbits used by satellites, thus inhibiting both the military and the civilian use of that part of outer space.

The Law of the Sea Treaty provides another example for the United States putting ideology ahead of its true interests. The US Senate had failed to ratify that treaty though it would have favored the United States, surrounded as it is by oceans and dependent on maritime traffic.

The rupture in the tradition of acting as a benign hegemon came about not because it was forced upon the United States. It was brought on by an intellectual revolution spearheaded by US neoconservatives. They prompted a return to outdated ideas of past centuries, imposing policies, and concepts on a world they were not fitted for.

The notion that the best protection of national interest is power, and especially military power; the notion that others are competitors at best and enemies at worst; the notion that in the end, nothing could rein in the full independence of states; the notion that international organizations do not have a nature of their own, but are mere forums for their member states—these notions found their most extreme expression in the foreign and security policies of the G.W. Bush administration. Yet these notions on the alleged true nature of the global system still inform much of traditional diplomacy.[8] Somewhat arrogantly, those providing the intellectual underpinning of this worldview call themselves *realists*, relegating dissent to the realm of irresponsible dreaming.

In Europe, the French President Chirac basically shared such a worldview with his call for a *multipolar world* in which the military power of the United States would be balanced by other, countervailing and competing power centers such as Europe or China.

One should assume that statesmen from the more liberal Left were not wedded to such theories on the nature of international/global relations. But according to my observations, at least two prominent leftist European Social Democrats did not conform to that assumption.

French president François Mitterrand had broken a long period of political dominance by the national-conservative Gaullists. Yet his foreign policy philosophy did not differ that widely from the one of his predecessors. When asked for his view on the basic mechanism of international relations, Mitterrand replied in pointing to the Greek historian Thucydides—the patron saint of the *realists*—who in his *Peloponnesian War* had depicted this war as the inevitable consequence of a rupture in the balance of military power between Athens and Sparta.

The prominent German Social Democrat and Chancellor Helmut Schmidt based some of his key foreign policy decisions on a similar worldview. One such decision allowed for the stationing of intermediate US nuclear missiles on German soil. The Soviet Union had triggered this decision by stationing such weapons on its own territory and on the territories of its European military allies. Helmut Schmidt concurred with assessing this Soviet move as a one-sided break in the balance of military power. It would destabilize this balance, which would have provided the base for Europe's relative security in the postwar era.[9]

One may excuse that politicians had stuck to such a *realist* interpretation of world order up to the end of the Cold War. It is surprising though, that politicians, hailing either from the political "Left" or from the political "Right" would still stick to such an outdated philosophy at the dawn of the 21st century, in a world that has been transformed profoundly and as the benefits and constraints of global interdependence have become so very obvious.

Prime example for this persistence of a dysfunctional philosophy is the Russian ex-president and now Prime Minister Vladimir Putin with his aim to reestablish an extended zone of Russian influence and dominance over his neighbors. He renews a reliance on the military and on the secret services. He disdains world opinion, and perceives of trade not as a vehicle for common benefit, but as a tool to extort political concessions from trading partners.

Its membership in the European Union and its decline as a major power have not completely erased all vestiges of *realist* principles from the foreign and security policy of the United Kingdom. It is full of reminders from a past that no longer can be recovered. In relations to its partners in the European Union in particular, the United Kingdom sometimes behaves as if it still could act in its historic role as arbiter of European conflicts; as the one to tilt the balance between them in one way or another. A *realist* interpretation of the world and a hankering after-lost influence also misleads it into believing that it could act as a go-between the United States and the European Union, having alone among the EU states a privileged relationship to the United States.[10]

It would be misleading to characterize realist concepts a simply "wrong." They guide action and thus create a reality. They create the realty that they had assumed to be in place already. If the United States defines its presence in East-Central and Eastern Europe in military terms by using NATO membership as the principal lien to the ex-communist countries, it will create a region in which such membership and military considerations in general become the ordering principle of external relations. Russia uses its (starkly reduced) military power and its clout as provider of prime energy to clobber its neighbors. Doing that, it might transform the regime in that part of the world back into one depicted by realists and as it existed in the 19th and in the early 20th century.

Being more of a prescription than a description, the *realist* concept of world order has a normative function and norms cannot be judged in terms of empirical data. What we can say, however, is that a policy based on the *realist* view fits ill into the present world, as it endangers its cohesions as its runs counter to the requirements imposed by interdependence and globalization.

What has all of that to do with diplomacy? Statesmen might be guided or misguided by theoretical concepts underlying their actions. But diplomats are not statesmen. They are supposed to merely be their passive instruments. That supposition is a bit misleading though, because diplomats, while obeying their political masters, still have some leeway in their actions. It is misleading also because diplomacy as such is still being colored by the outdated, nonfunctional concept of *realist* theory. It still is imbued largely by the notion of a world order determined by the competition of states.

Much in traditional, diplomatic tradition and routine projects a desire to outdo others and to prevail against them. From time immemorial, buildings have been seen and used as symbols in the competition for influence and prestige: from the pyramids in ancient Egypt, to the palaces of European royals, to the sky-scrapers of transnational firms that now dot cityscapes. The embassies and residences of diplomats cannot compete in height with these show pieces of corporate power. But they try to make up by the lavishness of the exterior and interior, and by the names of famous architects who have designed them. In those residences, dining tables cannot be long enough so as to demonstrate the capacity to feed the maximum of guests—just as medieval kings bragged about the number of vassals they could host at their banquets. No costs are shied even when they are unrelated to the size and wealth of a country or to the actual, practical function these buildings have to serve.[11]

Since the invention of the horse-drawn carriage, vehicles have also been symbols in the competition for power. The limousines of embassies all have to be big, expensive, and black of course. In Washington, no ambassador dared to use a simple Chevrolet or Toyota.[12] Black Lincolns or Cadillacs were de rigueur even for diplomats of states mired in poverty.

One might be tempted to regard as frivolous but not very consequential such competition of diplomats for visibility and prestige; wouldn't it reflect their more general disposition to perceive of their work as a zero-sum battle for position and influence. Which of the colleagues has been most successful in arranging for the highest number of mutual visits between countries? Whose name has been quoted most frequently in local media? Which of their home countries has gained most in the foreign trade with the country they are posted in?

Multilateral diplomacy with its more direct link to global governance is a more modern and timely version of diplomatic work. That does not inoculate it against tendencies to engage in fights for empty prestige and vain victories. Even multilateral diplomacy is still distracted in its function by such zero-sum battles. It is quite common for sharp and vicious battles to erupt in the competition to fill positions in international organizations, even if such positions have no more than symbolic significance. Whether a diplomat from this or from that country is elected as chairperson of this or that committee or sub-committee of the UN-General Assembly does not change the course of events and does not very much affect the actual work accomplished or not accomplished in those committees. Nonetheless, battles for such positions of mere symbolic weight matter a lot to diplomats. An inordinate amount of energy is being invested in such competition. Obviously, diplomats still see a higher purpose in such strife where others might just detect an absence of political content and consequence.

As Lord Keynes reminded us at the end of his seminal book, political actors are inevitably being guided by theories on what their work is about. They might not be aware of following such ideological mentors. But follow they do nonetheless.

The virus of "Realpolitik" is capable of infecting the lifestyle and work of diplomats. It may create wrong parameters for success or failure. It will damage serious efforts of global governance. A diplomat driven by an ambition to outdo others and to prevail against them will not be very apt in building bridges to these others. He or she will not be very apt in gaining the trust and cooperation that would be needed for combining forces for joint efforts.

Competition for symbolic victories might discredit diplomacy in the long run as such strife is useless, expensive and not in the common interest of arriving at a more substantial and solid form of global governance. But nonetheless, that merely symbolic competition is less dangerous still than a competition fought by the military.

Notes

1. We may—and should—wonder, of course, as to whether the canon of teachings on international relations really constitutes a form of *science*. The question is probably a mute one because we cannot escape the need to generalize, that is, have theoretical generalizations about the past and about the past relations between states and societies, so as to have instruments for guiding political action.

2. Angell N., 1910. *The Great Illusion; The Relation of Military Power in Relation to Their Economic and Social Advantages*, London.

3. And that only under the provision that authorities in the state concerned would fail to do so on their proper account.

4. Also slim are the chances of preventing Iran from obtaining enough fissionable material to be ready to assemble nuclear weapons on short notice.

5. It is for this end that the United States, under President George W. Bush, tended to weaken the cohesion of the European Union by playing on diverging preferences of its members; and by encircling both China and Russia with a string of military bases and by forming tacit alliances with the smaller neighbors of these two big countries.

6. In terms of political science: if they had felt threatened by the United States, other nations would have "balanced" US power, instead of "band-wagoning," that is instead of joining up with it.

7. The damage done to true US interests is most consequential in the economic realm. As was inevitable, the relative economic position of the United States weakened with the rapid economic rise of other states—especially those in East Asia. That trend was enhanced by wrongheaded US policies, such as permitting an indefinite and massive current account deficit. The wrongheaded emphasis on military power, and the waging of unjustified wars, further accelerated the relative economic decline, with the US administration being unwilling to fund armaments and wars through taxes and savings. Financing military spending with money borrowed from abroad helped turn the United States into a debtor nation.

8. At instances, the Bush administration had deviated from those concepts and was not as "realist" as old school diplomacy would have stipulated. Old-fashioned diplomatic "realists" would not have shown the same missionary zeal to expand the realm of democracy, regardless of costs and risks involved. They would have been more prudent with adversaries and circumspect, in particular, in entering a war without clearly a defined strategy and without a predefined exit. Yet, as mentioned, on a majority of issues the US neo-conservatives did agree with

old-school realists. They agreed on the supreme importance of military power; on the basically anarchic nature of international relations; on the notion of an insurmountable wall separating internal from external policies; on the unlimited power of the "sovereign" in the case of war; and on disrespect for international organizations. Therefore, the ideologues of the George W. Bush administration were not wholly unique in their philosophy on international relations. They were unique only in the extremes to which they went in applying this philosophy.

9. As I had noted before, I had been private secretary to one of these prominent European Social Democratic statesmen, namely Austrian Chancellor Bruno Kreisky. He did not share all of the theories underlying the foreign policy of Francois Mitterrand and of Helmut Schmidt. In many instances, his foreign policy philosophy seemed far removed from the basically pessimistic one of these two Social Democratic comrades of his. Unlike the so-called realists, Kreisky did not believe that in Europe's East, military power alone, would forever sustain communist regimes that had lost legitimacy with their citizens. (Repeating the saying that "you could do all sorts of things with bayonets; but you cannot sit on them.") His support for the "Third World," and his campaigning for a separate Palestinian state also seem based on another than a realist philosophy of balance of power and military might. Nonetheless, he still saw the underlying structure of the world system as being basically "bipolar" and defined by the confrontation of military alliances, one led by the United States and one by the Soviet Union. Much of Kreisky's attention on the "Third World" was motivated by the aim to keep this part of the globe from becoming a battlefield between "East and West," adding uncertainty to the otherwise rather stable stand-off between the two blocks.

10. More than anything else that conceit had motivated the fateful UK decision to break ranks with its European partners and to actively support and even encourage the US decision to go to war in Iraq. Prime Minister Tony Blair paid a heavy political price for this misguided decision.

11. The renewal of the lease for the residence of the Austrian ambassador on the London Belgrave Square—due in 2025—is likely to cost more than half of the whole budget of the Austrian Ministry of Foreign Affairs.

12. Not even the Japanese ambassador.

8

The Role of the Military and the Response to Threats and Risks

"Diplomacy without arms is like music without instruments."
—*Frederick the Great, king of Prussia*

"We have learned, a little late no doubt, that for states as for individuals, real wealth consists not in acquiring or invading the domains of others, but in developing one's own. We have learned that all extensions of territory, all usurpations, by force or by fraud, which have long been connected by prejudice with the idea of 'rank,' of 'hegemony,' of 'political stability,' of 'superiority' in the order of the powers, are only the cruel jests of political lunacy, false estimates of power, and that their real effect is to increase the difficulty of administration and to diminish the happiness and security of the governed for the passing interest or for the vanity of those who govern...."
—*Talleyrand, the "prince of diplomats," at the Congress of Vienna*

The *realist* vision of world order is based on a pessimistic view of human nature and on a pessimistic view of the political organization humans set up to organize their collective life. Both would be conflict-prone. Relations between them would be defined by this proclivity. Organized human groups would tend to wage war against each other. That tendency would prevail even among advanced and complex human groups such as modern states.

And over the millennia, war between human groups had indeed been the quasi natural state of affairs. That holds true for the roving gangs of plain Indians in North America as much as for the European nations of the 17th and 18th century.

As wars threaten the very existence of states and of its citizens, it is inevitable that guarding against the enemy and being victorious in a confrontation with an enemy becomes the foremost task of states with their diplomatic representatives devoting their attention to this challenge mainly.

That was the case at least up to the recent past. Over the last decades though, this proclivity for warfare seems to have waned. While the number of states has increased, the number of wars between states has declined. Among wealthy, established democracies wars have ceased altogether.

This is due to three factors mainly:

a)   Wars have become expensive.
b)   Their outcome has become unpredictable.
c)   They promise no material gain.

Waging War No More ...

a)   *Wars have become expensive.* In a sense that is not really new because they have always cost a lot. Fielding an army or equipping a navy has always strained finances of states.[1] But in the past, wars left more or less intact the economic and other physical infrastructure of states. Wars were fought among soldiers and did not directly threaten the lives of a major part of the civilian population. Now they do. In fact, more civilians die in such wars than soldiers.[2] The very notion of wars being fought along frontlines had to abandoned. The enemy country and its population and not just enemy soldiers have become the targets. The damage thus caused is heavy. It is not on one side either. Both sides in a military conflict have now the capacity to strike the hinterland of the opponent. A growing number can do so with weapons of mass destruction. Among the nations involved in World War II, only the United States emerged relatively unscathed—because it is an island—continent which then was still unassailable by enemies. Due to the evolution of military technology, the United States now has lost that privileged position. It has become target not just of nuclear weapons but also target for less sophisticated weapons—as the September 11, 2001 terrorist attacks have proven.[3]

b)   *The outcome of wars cannot be predicted.* In fact, since 1913 all wars had an outcome different from the outcome expected by the one who initiated warfare. The relative size and wealth of opposing states, the size of their armies, and the quantity and quality of their weapons once had permitted plausible predictions as to who would be the winner and who would be the loser. But recent wars have shown that such predictions are no longer possible. A smaller opponent, with fewer resources and fewer and less sophisticated arms might nonetheless prevail; thanks to tenacity, flexibility,[4] ruthlessness and the support of the local population. Expensive, big arms can now be countered by simpler and cheaper ones that have become widely available. Aircraft can be downed by shoulder held surface-to-air missiles. Tanks can be destroyed by rocket-propelled grenades. The very complexity of sophisticated weapons-systems makes them vulnerable to attacks carried out with simple tools. Nor is this vulnerability reserved for sophisticated weapons systems now used on battlefields. Essential infrastructure of highly developed, war faring countries is also exposed to disruption or destruction by opponents less advanced in their economic and technological development.[5] Wealthy countries find it difficult, for example, to effectively shield against cyber-attacks, capable of disabling resources as strategic as electric grids or communication facilities.

The fog of war has become denser still. It has become impossible to calculate the balance between means and ends; to establish realistic strategies; and to define and locate allies and enemies. A tool is useful only if one can be certain of its serving the intended purpose. When using a hammer, I can be certain that it will do what I wish it to do and drive in a nail. But if I now seize the tool of warfare, I can no longer be certain of reaching what I want to reach—namely a victory that merits its name.

c)   *Wars promise no gain.* The wealth of states used to depend on what could be extracted from their territory. With productivity unchanged over centuries, wealth could be expanded by an expansion of territory only. As such expansion necessarily reduced the territory of another state, it automatically implied war. If successful in such a war, the resulting increase of territory brought greater wealth to the state that started the hostilities. Today, territory is no longer the basis of a nation's wealth and status.[6] Wealth and status depend on the nature and quality of its economy, which in turn depends on the economic culture, on the use and management of information, on the ability to innovate, and on the capacity to link to suppliers and buyers.

Invading armies may be able destroy this basis of wealth. But
they cannot conquer, appropriate and use it.

Superior military power thus does not automatically translate into
military power; and victory does not automatically translate into heightened international status. The status of the United States has survived its
defeat in Vietnam, but the status of the United Kingdom has not outlasted
its victory on the side of Allies in World War II. North Korea fields one
of the world's strongest armies and has acquired nuclear weapons and
missiles to deliver them. Nonetheless, it will sooner or later cease to exist
in its present form, vanquished not by a hostile army but by deficiencies
of its political and economic system.

In view of the uncertainties and risks connected with an open engagement in war, states have sometimes fought war through proxies. In
most cases, that too, did not bring the desired results. The United States
has not gained by its support of the MLPA in Angola or by its support
of the Contras in Nicaragua. Pakistan's backing of the secessionists in
Kashmir has backfired, as has the US assistance to the Ethiopian troops
in Somalia. The United States has also come to regret the help it once
provided to the Afghan Taliban in their fight against Soviet occupiers.
Now they have to fight the Taliban themselves.

These then are the reasons for wars between states having become rare.

The Notion of "Democratic Peace"

Wars between democracies have become very rare. As the data
assembled for the last century demonstrate, mature democracies
do not wage war against each other. This seems mainly due to the
fact that those developments that make states desist from war are
most advanced in those countries that also have become wealthy.
Wealth, in its turn, favors democracy. All truly wealthy countries
are democracies.

Internal Wars

Violent armed conflict between states has become rare. But it still
occurs *within* states. While the number of violent *interstate* conflicts has
decreased, the number of violent *intrastate* conflicts has grown.

Figure 8.1 Intra- and Interstate Conflicts of High Intensity, 1945–2008

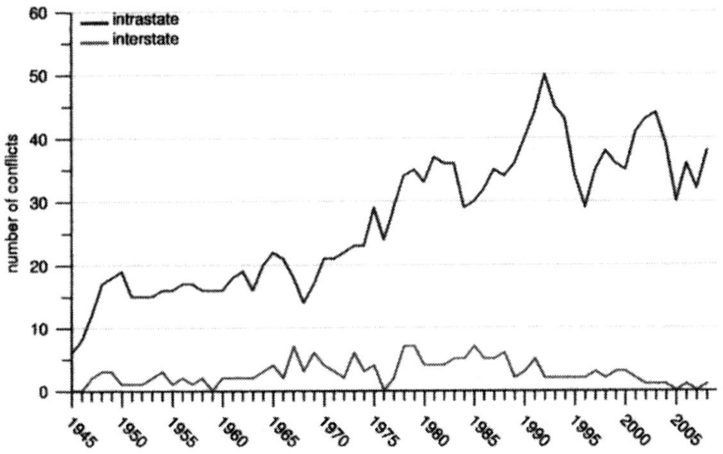

Source: Heidelberger Institut für Konflikt Forschung.

It has proven impossible to smother such internal violence by limiting the supply of arms that are used in it. These are small weapons mainly: assault rifles, machine guns, grenades, homemade explosive devices, and even machetes. More persons are killed by these weapons than by all of the more advanced weapons used by regular armies. There are 1000 million small arms in circulation; among them 70 million Kalashnikov assault rifles. The police and even the military are outgunned by all those arms in possession of private persons.

Figure 8.2 Who Owns Firearms?
(in Millions)

Category	Low total	Average	High total	Proportion
Law enforcement	26	26	26	2.5–3.5%
Military	150	200	250	20–25%
Civilian	570	650	730	73–77%
Global total	745	875	1,000	

Source: Small arms survey 2007.

These *small weapons have become the true weapons of mass destruction*. Even if international agreement could be found[7] on stemming the flow of such weapons to combatants in internal wars, such agreement would be difficult to enforce, as any look at the arms bazaar in Peshawar/Pakistan, or any visit to an US gun auction would make obvious.

Being merely intrastate instead of interstate has not made these conflicts irrelevant to the rest of the world. Most violent and large-scale internal conflicts have international repercussions. They tend to involve neighbors; especially where states are weak, borders porous, and identical ethnic communities live on both sides of such borders. Even faraway countries might become infected by the seeds sown by organized violence within a weak country.

Civil war in Afghanistan proves the point. Neighboring and nuclear-armed Pakistan has been pulled in. As a consequence, it has to fear for the safety and unity of its own territory. Central Asian neighbors are affected too, through the mobilization of their own religious fanatics. The conflict provides a safe haven for the recruitment and training of terrorists, who see much of the rest of the world as their field of action. Last not least, this intrastate war has enabled Afghanistan to become the world's prime supplier of opium,[8] the sale and use of which is associated with drug dependency and crime in faraway countries. The war in Afghanistan has even prompted the intervention of the North Atlantic Treaty Organization (NATO), ill equipped though it is for such warfare.[9]

Not all massive, violent internal conflicts are of a nature so as to *directly* threaten basic interests of outsiders. Yet even then, massive violent internal conflicts might damage the rest of the world in less direct ways. Some of these effects may be material such as those created by a massive flow of refugees that seek shelter in countries that are loath to take them in.

Some of these effects are not material, but are weighty nonetheless. An ongoing, massive violation of human rights, such as it occurs in intrastate conflicts, challenges the consensus on fundamental values that is indispensable as the basis for a common existence. Even citizens in distant countries and living under comfortable and safe conditions, instinctively feel that something of their own existence is at stake when nothing is done to stop genocide or the willed starvation of thousands of fellow humans. They feel under threat. This then motivates them to intervene in such violent internal conflicts. The international community, acting through the Security Council of the United Nations, has authorized such interventions by giving them a legal basis. It has agreed on a "responsibility to protect."

The Responsibility to Protect

Let us note here that the general acceptance of the "responsibility to protect" implies a fundamental change in the international regime. That regime used to be based on the notion of states being its exclusive objects and subjects. Now, individual humans have gained the status of being subjects of international law. They have gained the right of direct, unmediated access to the international community in order to seek protection if their own state fails to provide it.

Failing States

Massive, violent internal wars rarely erupt in wealthy states, but mostly in poorer ones.[10] Many of these poorer states are at the same time weak states. Some of them—like Somalia or southern Sudan—are on the brink of failure and disintegration.

Table 8.1 A Ranking of Failed and Failing States

Rank	Country	Rank	Country	Rank	Country
1.	Sudan	12.	Pakistan	23.	Sierra Leone
2.	Iraq	13.	North Korea	24.	Yemen
3.	Somalia	14.	Burma/Myanmar	25.	Sri Lanka
4.	Zimbabwe	15.	Uganda	26.	Republic of Congo
5.	Chad	16.	Bangladesh	27.	Liberia
6.	Cote d'Ivoire	17.	Nigeria	28.	Lebanon
7.	Democratic Republic of Congo	18.	Ethiopia	29.	Malawi
8.	Afghanistan	19.	Burundi	30.	Solomon Islands
9.	Guinea	20.	Timor-Leste	31.	Kenya
10.	Central African Republic	21.	Nepal	32.	Niger
11.	Haiti	22.	Uzbekistan		

Source: Fund for Peace/Foreign Policy magazine.

Not so long ago, one still tended to assume that, once set up, states would endure and consolidate. That supposition must now be revised as the number of failing states keeps growing. Why do so many states weaken and crumble?

Due to modernization, traditional social structures such as clans, families, and villages lose their binding power. The relative stability they used to provide vanes with them. Many states that had been newly created after the breakup of the colonial empires had not managed to create strong and efficient institutions. Until recently, that failure had, however been compensated for by the stability still provided by the traditional social structures. This era draws to a close as states would have to substitute for the weakening of traditional social communities and the loosening of traditional social control; and as many fail to do so.

Are some states also failing by their being inserted into the net of dense global interdependence? The answer is not straightforward, but it is mostly negative. An intense involvement in global economic exchange certainly causes massive tensions and dislocations—among them an unsettling and massive shift from rural to urban existence. Nonetheless, a wide interconnectedness with other societies and states tends to stabilize states more than it weakens them.

The table below reflects the findings from all empirical studies on the causes of internal wars. Some factors are shown to have particular relevance: Rising wealth—as it is brought about by a broad economic interchange with the rest of the world—strongly works against the likelihood of internal wars. We find that, on the other hand, a narrow economic interface with the rest of the world—as a consequence of the export of just one commodity such as oil—correlates strongly with the enhanced likelihood of civil war.

Table 8.2 The Causes of Civil War

	Strongly negative	Strongly positive
Neighbor at war		4
Mountains		3
Oil exports		6
Per capita GDP	9	
Secondary male school enrolment	4	
Trade as part of GDP	2	
Primary commodity exports as part of GDP		5

(Continued)

Table 8.2 *(Continued)*

	Strongly negative	Strongly positive
Peace years	11	
Inclusive, establish democracies	5	
Recent regime change or instability		7
Ethnic diversity		4
Ethno-linguistic fractionalization		6
Sanctions have neither a positive nor a negative impact.		

Source: Dixon J, 2009.

Peace-keeping, Peace-making, and Failing States

Interventions by outsiders may not be conceived to, or not be able to end hostilities between warring factions. But at a minimum, they aim to protect the civilian population. Yet even such limited goals of an intervention can be met only if some basic security is established, so that internally displaced persons can find shelter in camps, and so that humanitarian aid may reach those it is destined for.[11] Acting under mandates from the United Nations, multinational military forces try to create this minimum of security. The demand for such interventions and services is growing. At the moment, nearly 100,000 soldiers are serving under the flag of the United Nations in order to meet that demand.

Figure 8.3 Number of UN Peacekeepers

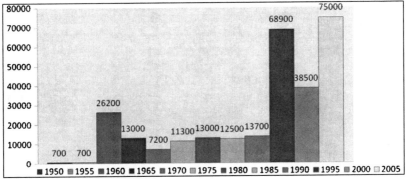

Figures include troops, military observers and police.

Source: Global Policy Forum

Such *peacekeeping, peacemaking* or *peace-enforcement* has become the obvious and most legitimate function of the military in wealthy democracies.

State-building

Peace enforced by outside intervention will not last in the absence of a functioning state to provide a minimum of government services—most importantly, internal security. Were those who intervened to withdraw before a state has become able to deliver these basic services, large-scale violence would return. The task of peace building is therefore likely to expand into the task of state-building. Police and the courts have to start functioning. Schools have to reopen. Infrastructure has to be rebuilt. Whosoever intervenes is thus in for a long haul. Those who assist state-building will have to devote massive financial and other resources to that task as their patience and persistence will be tested.

No one has of yet found a way to bridge an inherent contradiction that is bound to complicate interventions in failing states and that will complicate the subsequent task of state-building. On the one hand, stabilization and state-building cannot succeed without massive external help; and—if needed—without massive pressure from outsiders. But on the other hand, nations have to be built or rebuilt in a bottom-up manner. The resurrected polity must be anchored in the conviction and commitment of its citizens. Outside intervention cannot substitute for this conviction and commitment.

In Bosnia-Herzegovina, a bloody war between three ethnic groups would have rolled on, had not the United States and Europe decided to intervene. The Dayton Accords forced Bosnia's three ethnic groups into a tenuous compromise. By now though, these three groups have begun to chafe under the restrictions imposed on them by outsiders. They do not identify with the Dayton compromise and see it as something alien imposed on them against their will. They do not "own" that fragile peace which very well could vanish if Europeans and Americans would decide to leave and let the three ethnic groups become full masters in their own house.

From Thwarting Threats to Managing Risks

Security concerns have shifted. No longer do they focus on the intentions and military capacities of powerful, hostile, or potentially hostile states. They focus on problems that are being exported from weak, failing and failed states. Not the outward strength of states is the problem to be tackled. The challenge emerges from the inner weakness of states.

This is symptomatic of a more general reorientation of security policy. It used to be concerned with countering threats. It dealt with hostile outsiders, intent on inflicting harm. These outsiders once were mainly states. In more recent times, threats against states have also emanated from non-state actors such as terrorists or from transnational organized crime.

But if we look at what endangers human security at present, we will find that most of such dangers do not emerge from hostile intentions of states or groups. *We are confronted not with threats but with risks*. Many of them imply heavier damage to human interests than the threats that could be launched by hostile states, by terrorists, or by criminal groups.

To name but a few of those risks with the most serious implications:

-   A deep world economic crisis leading to a breakdown of the present system of global interdependence.
-   Unintended consequences of genetic engineering.
-   A pandemic which cannot be countered by any known vaccination.
-   An ecological collapse of some heavily populated regions of the world.
-   Global warming accelerating at an unanticipated pace, overwhelming the capacity to adjust.
-   A breakdown of internal order in China and its descent into anarchy.

None of these risks could be tackled by any single state acting alone. Many states would have to join forces. The military can do little to bring about such common action. That would be the task of diplomacy.

The Danger of Remilitarization

Globalization has created new risks. Yet while risk-prone, the new world order still is functional as it responds to the requirements of worldwide interdependence. Without that order of interdependence the world's population would not have doubled over the last 40 years. And the world's wealth wouldn't have expanded at an even faster pace. The vast majority of humans have benefitted from that world order. The rise of China and India would not have happened in its absence. But that does not imply that this world order of assured interdependence has become irreversible. It is a human/political construct. As such it can be replaced by another human/political construct. We cannot exclude such a reversal to other patterns and we cannot even exclude a return to the past pattern of national antagonism finding expression in the use of military power. Signals exist to warn us that this is a real possibility. These signals have become more ominous in the wake of the decline of the US/European hegemony over the world:

- One should have assumed for example, that big navies with their outsized battle ships would have become useless and would be on their way to extinction. Battleships are symbols and tools of power-projection. They should not have any meaningful function in today's world. In the Indian Ocean though, we are witness to an ongoing race to expand the navies and to secure for them faraway bases.[12]

- India and China are both destined to become important global players. The population of these two giant states is, however, easily given to bouts of nationalistic excess. At the same time, China and India invest heavily in their militaries. The foreign policy of these two countries will be decisive in shaping future global governance. The nationalist fervor in China and India, and the high military expenditures of these two countries might thus tilt the present world-regime of peaceful interdependence back to the one that existed in the late 19th and in the early 20th century.

- Russia seems to have settled again into the mindset that informed (or misinformed) security policies of imperial Russia and of the Soviet empire. Russia uses not just its status as an irreplaceable provider of oil and gas, but it also its military power, to gain the regional influence that it believes can be wrung out of its neighbors by the use of threats.

- In choosing such a course, Russia, China, and India might be comforted by the example of the United States. America reduced its excessive military expenditures only temporarily after the end of the Cold War and resumed expanding them in mid-1990s. It has to be seen—and is by no way certain—if the present US president can truly reverse this course, engaged, as he is, in escalating his *war of choice* in Afghanistan.

- War has not disappeared even in Europe, though the continent likes to present itself as the very example of a new world order in which wars have become impossible altogether. There is something very unsettling about the rebound of nationalism among the new members of the European Union and among the—growing—Radical Right. Potentially violent conflicts—such as the one in Cyprus; in Bosnia/Herzegovina or in Kosovo have only been frozen, instead of resolved.

In short, wars and the war-era might return. The disastrous consequences of the reversal do not wholly exclude that possibility. States might therefore be excused if they do not completely demobilize and do not retain from their military apparatus only the few elements that are needed for interventions in failing states and for dealing with humanitarian crises. They might be excused if they retain a downsized military apparatus as a kind of insurance policy.

The Present World Order: Not Established and Not Maintained by the Military

But even with that caveat and even if military do preserve some role in a state's security policy; it is obvious that in general, the status of the military in global governance is in decline. This is reflected in a steady reduction in the spending for the armed forces. On the average and in the wealthy states, they receive a steadily diminishing share of public budgets. The military face headwinds of other sorts too, as there is an overall and long-term trend to limit their sway and to lessen the impact of their philosophy and worldview.

With the evolution of modern industrial and postindustrial societies, wars have become too expensive, too destructive, and too unpredictable instruments for promoting political goals. The invention of weapons of mass destruction and the invention, use and further development of nuclear weapons in particular, has made that obvious and has heightened concern about the role and the ambitions of the military.

Contrary to their self-image as the ultimate arbiters and shapers of international relations, the military has actually little impact on those trends and developments that have transformed the world and that have established a new global order. The reemergence of vanquished Japan and Germany, the rise of China and India, is not due to military might.

The explosive growth of the world's population and the world's wealth was not promoted by military power. The doubling in the number of independent states came about because the militaries of the imperial powers were reined in by battle-wary politicians and told to cease fighting the independence movements. Where militaries were not so restrained and where they continued to fight independence movements—the French in Algeria and Vietnam, the Dutch in Indonesia—the European militaries found themselves on the losing side and had to withdraw ignominiously in the end.

In short, the outsize impact military had on the global system in the past came at a high price that discredits any claim to continue in such a leading role. This insight then is the motive behind present efforts to diminish the role of the military in global governance. The tendency might not be obvious in a look at present or recent events. But it emerges from a long-term view on the evolution of global governance.

About 150 years ago, nations set out to limit the suffering of combatants, by defining what could and could not be done to them in times of warfare. Somewhat later, similar international efforts sought to shield the civilian population from wartime cruelties. That was followed by attempts to limit the arms race (as for example the particularly wasteful naval arms race); and to altogether prohibit the use of certain kind of arms such as chemical and biological ones; and most recently—to limit the use of land mines. On occasion, such agreements were complemented by confidence-building measures[13] with the aim of creating transparency in military matters and disbanding the fog of distrust that induces each party to assume the worst, to prepare for the worst, and thus to promote the worst. Wars have even been outlawed by international agreement—as most recently by the Charter of the United Nations. That has not prevented the proliferation of internal wars, but it has—at least somewhat—dampened any remaining inclination of states to revert to war.

Cynics might belittle the effect of these and of other agreements to lessen the human suffering caused by wars and to dampen the arms race. But these cynics would have to ignore evidence that points to the restraining influence of such agreements. South Africa has given up nuclear arms it already had tested. Libya halted its efforts to build them.[14] Brazil and Argentina stopped developing them; and Sweden and Switzerland ceased toying with the option of potentially acquiring nuclear weapons. Ever since their use was outlawed, chemical weapons have been used but once, and that in an internal action by a bloody regime nobody wishes to emulate.[15]

One should not ignore the normative power of humanitarian concerns. But these alone would not have reversed the seemingly inborn tendency toward violent, murderous hostility between organized human groups. This turn to the better seems to be based rational assessment of self-interest eventually prevailing over darker instincts. Originally, states might indeed have been inclined, for example, to see as jolly useful the possession of nuclear arms. They might have lusted to obtain them. Nuclear arms do, after all, promise a lot of "bang for a buck." They seem to heighten the status of those who acquire them. They might frighten enemies and potential enemies into a tenuous peace that would have been threatened otherwise. But those gains are fleeting. If some nations are tempted into owning nuclear arms, they will prompt others to follow their example. Instead of the eight states that are nuclear armed at the present, there would be thirty, forty, or more states that have become nuclear powers. The risks of these weapons being actually used would increase disproportionally. Joining the nuclear arms race would therefore not add but ultimately detract from global security and from the security too, of single states.

The global regime once had been defined mainly in terms of military power and military security. The military largely shaped this regime. World War I became inevitable because military in general staffs were hostages to the time-tables for mobilization and did not leave room for efforts to avert the war, fearing that any delay of the mobilization would give undue advantage to the adversary. At that stage, diplomats were more the servants than the masters of the military, accepting, as they did, the military's worldview and acting as their mouthpieces.

Due to global interdependence, this old pecking order between the military and the diplomats is now being put on its head. The process of this reversal is uneven and slow. But if we take the historic perspective it is evident nonetheless. The military have less impact on truly important global developments.[16] Whereas 100 years ago, diplomats had been subservient to the military it now is the other way round. In promoting the interests of their states, politicians and their diplomats tend to set the priorities to which the military might contribute what they can.

Notes

1. In the early 19th century, the financing of wars against Napoleon had bankrupted the Austrian Empire.
2. When posted in New York, I had attended several seminars organized by Herman Kahn, the "theologian" of nuclear warfare. One of the questions he used to pose to his audience was on the number of civilian casualties a nuclear-armed state was willing to suffer when launching its own nuclear weapons in the certain knowledge that the opponent would retaliate in kind. Herman Kahn proposed—and the participants accepted—the likely threshold for the United States to stand at 20 million civilian deaths.
3. The absence of serious damage to the United States in World War II might partly explain that the United States—alone among the Allied nations—still stuck to the belief in the military as the most decisive and effective instrument in international relations. The angry shock after September 11, 2001 reflects a crude awakening from the dream of being invulnerable.
4. Two US carrier groups are stationed near the Straits of Hormuz—the maritime bottleneck through which much of the West Asian oil has to pass on its way to Western consumers. The passage is potentially threatened by Iran. US war games simulated the defense of the passage by the US Navy. They brought an unpleasant surprise to US admirals. A large number of cheap, small, and swift Iranian boats could easily overwhelm the behemoths of the US carrier groups.
5. A nightmare scenario for the United States: A simple "dirty nuclear bomb" (i.e., a bomb simply spreading highly radioactive material) being exploded in the narrow corridor between the Newark Airport and the Atlantic Ocean. It would shut a corridor of strategic importance channeling much of the US North-South traffic and also providing access to one of the biggest US ports.
6. There still are states that depend for their wealth on what they can extract from under their soil—such as oil or diamonds. That wealth is not just fleeting, it is "cursed." It stands in the way of developing a wider base for the economy. It also privileges authoritarian rule and corruption, as small groups can control the extraction of the raw material, and thus can control from above not just the rest of the economy, but politics too.
7. Put under pressure by the mighty National Rifle Association, the US government opposes international agreements that would restrain the sale of guns.
8. The base for heroin.
9. The outcome of that intervention is still in doubt, and—as of this writing—likely to be negative.
10. There are exceptions, such as the US Civil War in the 19th century and the wars in ex-Yugoslavia in the late 20th century.
11. Somalia may serve as an example for the fact that at times it is difficult to impossible to even establish these minimum requirements for effective humanitarian intervention.
12. China is about to establish a "string of pearls," that is of naval bases along its maritime supply lines in the Indian Ocean.
13. See the path-breaking agreements within the former CSCE—Conference for Security and Cooperation in Europe.
14. With assistance from Pakistan.
15. Iraq's former dictator, Saddam Hussein, used chemical weapons against the Kurds of his own state.
16. Not even in the United States. Recently, the US military were more prudent than gung-ho politicians when contemplating the eventuality of war. Instructed by previous errors and failures, they have generally counseled against too optimistic an assessment of the function of military power.

9

From Anarchy to Cooperation

"Economic self-sufficiency enables one to consolidate the independence of one's country and live independently.... [I]ndependence in politics and self-reliance in defense... ensures rich materials and cultural lives for the people."
—The North Korean despot Kim Jong-il (1985)
in an obviously not very sound counsel to his country

National security—defined in the traditional way as conditioned by military might and military relations—was at the core of traditional diplomacy. By now, non-military threats to security have become more prominent: threats through environmental degradation, through mass migration, through a global economic crisis, through international, organized crime, through the implosion of states, etc. Besides that, many issues have arisen that do not directly threaten national security (however broadly defined) but which have to be dealt with nonetheless. There has to be agreement on how to use the airwaves, on how to allocate fishing rights, on how to preserve biodiversity, on how to secure worldwide basic labor standards, etc. Most of such issues are being dealt with in an international context. They had not been dealt with by traditional diplomacy.

This traditional diplomacy was geared to mutually adjust what had been defined as *national interests*. The notion of a *balance of power* provides an apt metaphor for this traditional "game" of diplomacy. One side yields a bit, the other side gains a bit. But the sum of it all, the sum of what the game is about remains constant.

Today, this metaphor of balancing national interests, this metaphor of a zero-sum game, can no longer guide politics. We no longer live in a static world in which conflicting national interests nullify another. We no longer live in a world where a political action by one state is balanced, and has to be balanced through a countervailing move by another state. Common action is necessary so as to gain a *common good*, or so as to avert a *common bad*. A narrow pursuit of narrowly perceived "national interests" would not help us to reach that goal. It would impede such efforts.

Two examples to illustrate that point: at the time of this writing, the world is being shaken by a severe financial crisis that might very well result in a worldwide economic depression reminiscent of the one in the 1930s. National governments might be tempted to follow a narrowly conceived national interest by depreciating their currency so as to raise exports and to thus lower unemployment. They might feel tempted to curtail imports by raising tariffs.[1] As a result of such unilateral actions, the turbulence in the world financial and monetary system would increase. World trade would shrink. The narrow pursuit of a narrowly conceived national interest would result in the *common bad* of a deepening world economic crisis.

Overfishing threatens fishing stocks. In some places, populations of a specific species of fish have collapsed already. This was the case, for example, for the cod population at the Grand Banks off the eastern coast of Canada. This threatens to be the case too, for the Blue Fin Tuna in the Mediterranean. Other limits to fishing are being approached rapidly, especially in the Northern Atlantic.

Figure 9.1 Percentage of Oceanic Deep-water Resources in Various Phases of Fishery Development

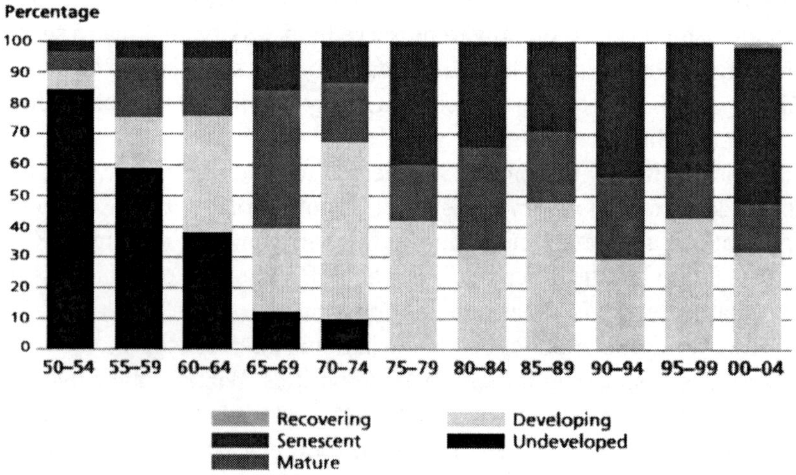

Source: FAO 2006 The state of world fisheries and aquaculture.

Assume now that there are no rules, that there is no effective common policy that would prevent overfishing. What would happen? Each fishing nation would try to get the largest possible piece of the pie as long as the pie is still around. It would be in the narrow interest of every fishing nation to exploit to the fullest extent possible the opportunities that still exist. Doing that, all of them would accelerate the destruction of the common base their fishing fleets rely on: namely a fish population sufficiently large to reproduce so as to keep its volume steady.

Many other examples could be cited to prove the same point. A narrow pursuit of narrow national interest that is contrary to the common interest of all members of the international community is finally not even in the national interest of each member of that community. In most cases, a common regime to safeguard common interests provides a better protection for national interests than policies that disregard this common good.

Which then are the mechanisms that make nations forego the unilateralist option and make them switch to common action for the safeguard of that *common good*? There is no supreme global lawmaker that could establish the rules for such common efforts. No global police exists, no global army that could enforce such rules against those who wish to dissociate themselves from such a regime.

At first sight, that absence of such global lawmakers and enforcers would seem to justify the traditional view of international relations and of the task of traditional diplomacy. In purely legal terms, nations are supreme. They confer tasks and competence on international institutions. States would be the ones to give orders and international institutions would be there to carry them out. If one sticks to mere legalities, no state could be forced to delegate this or that task to an international institution. In the end too, nothing could prevent a state to pursue a narrow national interest even if that were detrimental to all other states. If we look at the global system from a strictly legal and formal perspective, this global system would indeed be one of *anarchy*; with no one and nothing to rein in the free decisions of states, even at instances when such decisions result in damage to all.

But the world in its present state would not survive were it really that anarchic and rule less. World trade expands. Firms locate some of their production in faraway countries, being certain that the parts produced there will be delivered in time. We rely on ships and airplanes moving goods and people across the world in a predictable manner. In view of such regularity and predictability, the claim of the world being in a state of *anarchy* is patently absurd. Rules that assure a *common good* or that avert a *common bad* do exist. For the most part, they are being respected. Why is this case? How can that be when—according to a strictly legal view—anarchy should threaten at every corner of the international system?

As we have demonstrated with a look at the fishing regime, international regimes can endure only if there is agreement on the nature of a *common good*. Over and above that, states must be convinced that all—or at least most—of the other states will stick to rules that promote a *common good* or that prevent a *common bad*. Would the people of the world not be convinced of the functioning of such a system, they would not invest abroad, would not come to depend on the import of essential raw materials and of food produced in faraway countries, would not travel abroad. In absence of such trust, in short, the world would not be the one we know today.

But how and why did we get there?

The first part of the answer is obvious. The process of moving toward common, cooperative action reflects a necessity imposed by a changing reality. The area of *global common goods* is expanding, as is the area of threatening *global common bads*.

We can appreciate that by taking a look at the world as it was 1000 years ago, and as it basically still was at the time of the "Westphalian peace" in the 17th century, when modern diplomacy came to exist. By then, a famine in India did not affect agricultural production and agricultural markets in Britain. Wars in Europe had little echo in China. Tibetan monks had no following in Germany. Most of what happened in one part of the world did not affect the rest of the globe. The number of shared problems and challenges was miniscule. Few *global commons* existed. Incentives for joint global action were few.

That changed over the last centuries. Today, if China greatly increases its imports of oil, and if its emission of greenhouse gases rises dramatically, this has immediate and negative effects on the world market for oil; and immediate effects in accelerating global warming. Unsound practices of American hedge funds and of American investment banks led to their collapse. That collapse in turn ushered a worldwide financial crisis. Mad cow disease originated in Great Britain as processed animal carcasses were used to feed livestock. The plague then spread over a good part of the world where similar cattle feed was used. That resulted in deep problems for the global cattle industry.

In short, interdependence has grown. Action or non-action in one part of the world may affect other parts with both good and evil consequences. Common rules, common action thus become ever more necessary. Yet that urgency alone still would not solve the problem of exiting from a *negative-sum game*, in which each state just follows its immediate, narrow interest even when doing so adds to *common bad* or detracts from a *common good*. States might be perfectly aware that their behavior is damaging to the international community. Yet for making the change from such irresponsible to a more responsible behavior, a further element is needed. This element is trust; that is the trust that others will behave responsibly too. Such trust is acquired in a learning process. Institutions can promote and accelerate this learning process. Let us therefore look at the answers political theory offers on this question.

Persons and states can be caught in behavior that is not just detrimental to the common good, but detrimental even to their own best interest. They will persist in this behavior if they cannot be certain that others to whom they are connected and on whom they depend will also behave in a way that promotes a common well-being.

Social science has coined the term "prisoner's dilemma" for such a situation. The term derives from a complicated and not very life-like scenario. It deals with two prisoners caught incommunicado before their trial in two separate cells. Yet the dilemma it describes is a very common one and it is common especially in international relations. Let us therefore take an example from international relations to explain what this dilemma is about.

There is little intercourse between state A and state B. Though they are neighbors, both know little about another. They know little, especially about the intentions of this their neighbor. Are they hostile or are they peaceful? In absence of such information, both the state A and the state B must think it prudent to start arming. An arms race ensues, as each of the two states believes it will have to prevail over the military might of the other.

Each one of the two states involved would be better off, if there were no such arms race. Resources thus saved could be used to increase the wealth of the population thereby strengthening the legitimacy of the rulers. Stopping a competitive arms race would also preclude the emergence of a military caste which, in itself, might ultimately threaten and replace the ruler of the state. The internal political and social culture could adapt to more peaceful prospects making the society more cohesive and humane.

Nonetheless, the prospects of such gains would not stop the competitive arms race. For how could state A be certain that state B would follow suit if it were to cease arming? The consequences would be disastrous if state B were not to disarm too. State A would risk its annihilation. That is, it would risk costs higher than those associated with the arms race. So state A will remain locked in the arms race with state B.

How can the two states exit from that dilemma? That can happen only if sufficient trust can be established between these two states, if enough information is shared that can substantiate such trust in that the other will also behave in a positive manner.

Such information and trust is created by learning. What is being learned is that outcomes are different if the own strategy is either positive or negative. If I start out with negative expectations on what the other one is going to do, and if I base my own actions on these negative expectations, the other one will respond in kind with an action detrimental to my interest. I can learn from that experience that we both will be worse off as a consequence of my starting out with negative expectations on the actions of the other. If, however, I start out with positive expectations, I learn that the chances are good that the other one will also act positively. I learn that we both will have become better off thereafter.

We can assume humankind to be on the same learning curve. Humankind learned about the superiority of trust first within the bounds of the small roving gangs of hunters/gatherers. Later on, the realm of basic trust was expanded to members of tribes; and later still to citizens of states. We now are on the lengthy and troubled learning curve that expands trust slowly beyond the realm of states and gives it a global reach. *It is the prime task of modern diplomacy to expand this realm of trust.*

Institutions can help in that process of building and maintaining trust. They can help in exiting from the "prisoner's dilemma" into a *positive-sum game* of cooperation. Institutions can dispense *information.* One of the basic ingredients of the prisoner's dilemma is the lack of precise *knowledge* on the actions and intentions of the other. Institutions can provide such information. Institutions can provide for a *burden sharing* through a cooperative regime, assuring that no member suffers disproportionally and that a burden is distributed in an equitable manner.

International organizations are institutions that build and sustain trust in cooperation between states,[2] and that provide for a burden sharing that is seen as just. This capacity of international organization reflects the collective interest of their members to bolster a regime that is beneficial to the community of states and to punish a defection from such a "regime." We will look at these international organizations in one of the subsequent chapters. But first let us take stock, in more detail, of the profound changes in the way human life on earth has been organized.

Notes

1. At their meeting in November 2008 the members of the so-called Group of 20 (G-20) solemnly promised not to take any unilateral action that might endanger world trade. It is to be seen whether they will stick to that promise as economic prospects remain clouded.
2. This cooperation now increasingly also involves the new international "non-state actors" with their growing role in shaping "global governance."

10

Welded Together by the Economy: "All Politics Is Global"

"The bourgeoisie has, through its exploitation of the world market, given a cosmopolitan character to production and consumption in every country. To the great chagrin of reactionaries, it has drawn from under the feet of industry the national ground on which it stood. All old-established national industries have been destroyed or are daily being destroyed. They are dislodged by new industries, whose introduction becomes a life and death question for all civilized nations, by industries that no longer work up indigenous raw material, but raw material drawn from the remotest zones; industries whose products are consumed, not only at home, but in every quarter of the globe. In place of the old wants, satisfied by the production of the country, we find new wants, requiring for their satisfaction the products of distant lands and climes. In place of the old local and national seclusion and self-sufficiency, we have intercourse in every direction, universal inter-dependence of nations. And as in material, so also in intellectual production. The intellectual creations of individual nations become common property. National one-sidedness and narrow-mindedness become more and more impossible, and from the numerous national and local literatures, there arises a world literature."

—Karl Marx, The Communist Manifesto

The Great Transformation

When Karl Marx wrote this manifesto, the world he described was just emerging. Now it is a reality. Karl Marx was correct in his analysis. Today we can agree with his central thesis: namely that the economy and economic development underlie much of what occurs in other spheres such as politics or culture. This seems to hold true at least if we take a very long-term view of things and look at them in a historic perspective that spans centuries. It is the economy which, in the long run, determines the structure not just of national political systems but also of the global political system.

Over millennia and up to the beginning of the 19th century, the average per capita wealth of all inhabitants of earth had been rather constant. The Industrial Revolution then changed the economic basis of human life. Up to then, it had been provided by small-scale agriculture mainly. Productivity of human labor had remained roughly constant, with hard labor yielding the same low results. From the early 19th century on, the Industrial Revolution and the succeeding economic changes made for a steady increase in productivity. The world's average per capita wealth grew many times over. Even dramatic events like the World Wars and the Great Depression of 1930s are but blips in this long-term trend.[1]

Figure 10.1 World Population and World Per Capita GDP from the Year 1 to the Year 2000

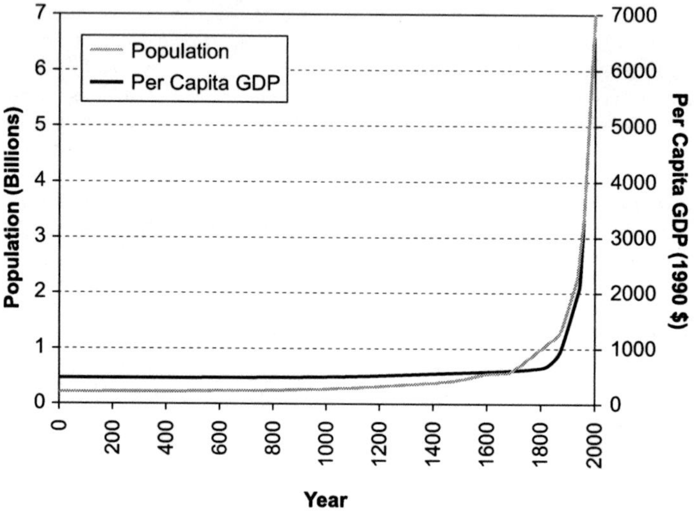

Source: Maddison, A., 2008. *Historical statistics for the world economy*: 1-2006 AD.

During the last decades, the pace of economic development has become even more rapid. Only half a century ago, wealth in the world was concentrated in a few spots, in a relatively small part of the earth's surface: in the Western parts of Europe, in North America, Japan, and Australia. The rest of the world survived in poverty. That has changed. India and China, as well as most of East Asia with its vast population, are on their way to become industrial-urban societies. The speed of that process is staggering. Most of Latin America has also begun to grow faster again. Its pace of growth might be slower than the one in East and South Asia, but it still is superior to the growth rate of the al-ready rich countries. The same holds true for the formerly communist countries of Central and Eastern Europe. Even some African states have surprised pessimists by growing faster than the world economy as a whole.

More rapid even than this growth in the overall wealth of the world has been the surge in the economic interchange between states. International trade has expanded at a higher rate than the production of goods and services. A growing share of a nation's economy is therefore in international trade, with increased dependency on imports and exports. National economic self-sufficiency is not advantageous. It even has become impossible.

Figure 10.2 World GDP and World Trade, 1950–2005

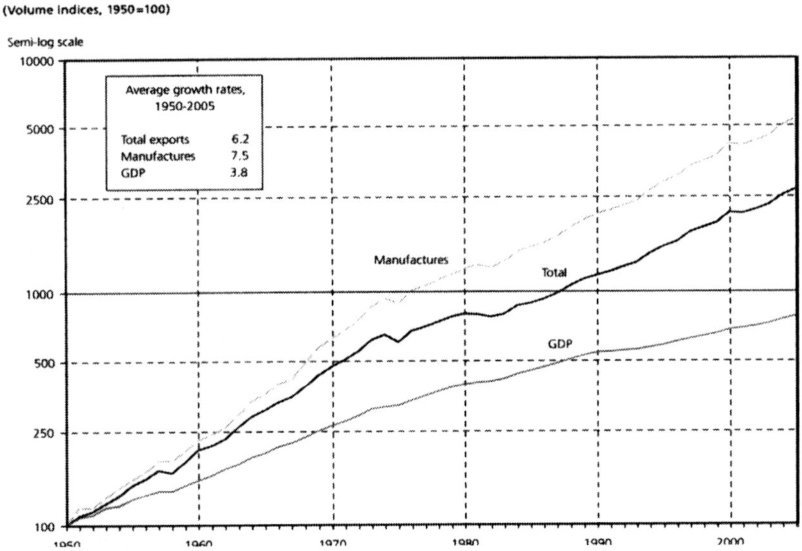
(Volume indices, 1950=100)
Semi-log scale
10000
5000
2500
1000
500
250
100
Average growth rates, 1950-2005
Total exports 6.2
Manufactures 7.5
GDP 3.8
Manufactures
Total
GDP

Source: WTO, International Trade Statistics.

Foreign Direct Investment (FDI)—that is investment made by firms in order to set up facilities in foreign countries—has expanded faster than the already fast increase in world trade. By setting up production in foreign countries, corporations have become transnational.[2] The supply chain for complex products like cars, airplanes, or computers is now long and spread over many nations. Even more than international trade, these foreign direct investments have made for a tightly woven interdependence between national economies. One should therefore wonder whether the notion of an economy being "national" is still a valid one.

That expansion of the world economy and the growth of interdependence between nations have come at some costs: scarcity of some raw materials; environmental degradation; explosively fast expansion of the world's population; human alienation; and insecurity. But nonetheless and overall, the balance is a positive one. Much human progress was associated with economic growth. A majority of humans have escaped from under the yoke of absolute poverty at the margins of subsistence. Life expectancy has risen. Literacy has increased. Hunger now affects a smaller part of the world's population.

Both the positive and the negative consequences of economic expansion are reflected in internal and in global politics. The very nature of politics has been transformed. The massive shift in the economic basis of human existence has made for a world order that differs profoundly from the one that existed before. Traditional ways of looking at it and of explaining it become misleading.

The structure of the global/international system used to be shaped by gradients in the capacity of various states to influence events beyond their borders. Some had greater, some had a lesser capacity to do this. They had greater or lesser "power." That remains true. States are still not equal in capability to affect events beyond their borders. What has changed, though, is that next to states, other entities also have acquired such power (and we deal with these new "actors" in later chapters). But the more profound change has been the change in tools used to affect events in other countries.

According to the traditional view and in accordance with the reality of the past, power was perceived as the capacity of one state to force another state to do something it had not intended to do. Yet the present system of global interdependence has not come to exist because one or several mighty states have forced others to do something against their will. The present global system of increased interdependence has come to exist because most of those involved have concluded that it suits them better than systems they had known before.[3] The structure of these previous global systems was defined by the capacity of one actor to impose his preferences on other actors even when those others did not wish to comply, but were forced to do so under the threat of negative consequences. The contemporary version of power, however, no longer depends on the ability of one state to force other states to do things against their will. The present system of global interdependence would not have come to exist if it this still were the case. We still would live in a world of mutually hostile states, each of them trying to frustrate and fight others and make their interest prevail under the threat of otherwise using force.

That change in the nature of power has not made states more equal. The capacity of states to affect events and decisions beyond their borders is still distributed unevenly. But it is no longer rooted in the capability and in the will to inflict damage on the non-compliant. Power nowadays is based on the position a state holds in the web of global economic exchange and interdependence. Its rank in the global pecking order corresponds to an uneven capacity to function as a node of economic interchange. It corresponds to an uneven capacity to move up in the value-added chain of production and to stay ahead in product-cycles and innovation.

The present version of power is therefore rooted in the capacity to impact on international relations by opening options others may also profit from. Frequently, this *relative power* will correlate with the volume of a state's economy. But this is not necessarily so. Some smaller economic entities with strategic functions—entities like Luxembourg, Singapore, or Israel—hold a prominent place in this new global pecking order.

No state is forced to participate in this system of mutual advantage and exchange. Like North Korea, a state might prefer to remain outside the system. But this is an uncomfortable option. It alienates citizens from the political rulers and it even threatens the long-term survival of such a state. Politicians will thus be well advised to integrate their state into the system of global economic interdependence. They seize this option not out of fear of otherwise suffering from negative sanctions imposed on them. States integrate into the web of global economic exchange and interdependence because of the advantages connected with that integration.

That does not imply that the present international order is all harmony. The inequality that persists spawns conflict. Some set the patterns others have to follow. Even if that following serves them well, those at the lower end of the pecking order cannot ignore their lesser status and the fact that not they, but others set the rules. Nor can poor countries ignore the fact that while beneficial to them too the international order established by the more powerful is also favoring those more powerful. That aggravates the resentment already caused by the vast gap in wealth that separates the poor and the rich of the world.

In the very long run, the mechanism of the economy as such might perhaps come to narrow that chasm in wealth. But this long run would

be very long indeed. In between, this wide gap in wealth will undermine
stability in the world and frustrate efforts to tackle problems common
to all inhabitants of the planet. That danger is evident today already.[4]
It will become worse with the poor of the world being increasingly
aware of their low status and of the abundance in other countries to
which they have no access. This is a challenge that economics as such
cannot tackle. It has to be addressed by politics.[5] Rich countries have
to assist poorer ones not just because of human solidarity. They have to
assist them also in view of their proper interest in global economic and
political stability.

For Progress in Welfare: Politics and Economics Have to Complement Another

As this example demonstrates, the economy alone cannot shape
world order. Politics has to intervene. We started this chapter in noting
that the interpretation of history as provided by Karl Marx seems rather
plausible, with the economy determining the world order. We now have
to qualify that view. Karl Marx did not perceive of politics as something
autonomous. He defined politics as the mere mirror image of an underlying economic situation. Politics would be the "superstructure," passively
reflecting this underlying economic reality. But national and international
politics are more than mere tools of the dominating economic interests;
and politics are also more than the mere rational pursuit of material well-
being. Therefore, it is not just the economy that impacts upon politics.
It is also the other way round. Politics and political developments on
one side, the economy and economic developments on the other side
mutually influence each other.[6]

Economic development for instance, is impeded by corruption. Rising wealth alone does not make it disappear. Politics have to intervene
and drive the fight against corruption in order to remove this obstacle
on the road to greater wealth. But at the same time, greater wealth offers
citizens a secured existence which makes it less risky for them to support the political fight against corruption. It lets them confront officials
who parasitically appropriate part of what properly should be their own
share of common wealth. Wealthy countries are less corrupt; and this is
so far both economic and political reason.

Table 10.1 Index of (Perceived) Corruption
The Ranking of Selected States

New Zealand	9.4	Kuwait	4.1
Sweden	9.2	Brazil	3.7
Canada	8.7	China	3.6
Germany	8.0	India	3.4
Austria	7.9	Mexico	3.3
UK	7.7	Jamaica	3.0
US	7.5	Algeria	2.8
Slovenia	6.6	Egypt	2.8
Cuba	5.5	Vietnam	2.7
Poland	5.0	Nigeria	2.5
Turkey	4.4	Russia	2.2
Italy	4.3	Venezuela	1.9

Source: Transparency International, CPI 2004.

The complementary and mutually supportive function of the economy and of politics becomes evident too, in the data on a more or less sound natural environment. We tend to assume that increased economic activity comes at some cost to the environment as we are tempted to believe that higher production and consumption will necessarily result in environmental degradation. That might be true for some environmental problems. But for others the connection is not that stringent. Emission of sulfur dioxide or the pollution of water, for example, does indeed increase as countries emerge from poverty. But from a certain point on—when per capita income reaches—about US$ 4,000—the damage to the environment is being undone. As the graph below demonstrates, the emission of sulfur dioxide is being reduced from that point on.[7]

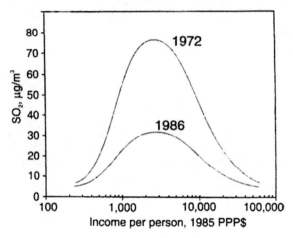

**Figure 10.3 The Connection between GDP Per Capita
and SO$_2$ Pollution in 47 Cities and 31 Countries
(Income in 1985 PPP US dollars)**

Source: World Bank 1992.

That abatement of emissions is not an automatic consequence of rising wealth. If politics would not force them to do otherwise, industries would continue to minimize the costs of production and would abstain from costly investments in air filters and wastewater treatment plants. These investments are forced upon them by politics. And politics is under pressure from citizens to clean up the environment as these citizens begin to care about damaging emissions once their most urgent needs, such as for food, cloth, and shelter have been met. This nexus between citizens and politics is the closer, the more democratic a political system.[8]

Markets rest upon social conventions. These conventions have to be backed by institutions with the capacity to establish formal rules and with the capacity to also enforce them. Markets therefore depend on politics. Politics and markets are interlinked and mutually dependent on each other, with democracy being the most effective link between these two spheres.

Democracy and markets also share the same fundamental mechanism. Both markets and democratic politics provide for permanent, peaceful change. Firms that are not competitive are being eliminated. Newer products substitute for older ones. Political incumbents lose support and are being replaced by an alternate set of political leaders;

the newer and more functional substitutes for the old and increasingly useless. Markets and democracy thus facilitate an evolutionary process[9] which permits the better to replace the good. Without the mechanism of markets and democracy, we would still live in a world of stagnation. We would remain stuck in pre-modern times with everlasting fights over the same spoils.

Wealth and markets, politics and democracy evolve together. As wealth has grown, so has the number of democracies.

Figure 10.4 Trends in Types of Government, 1946–2006

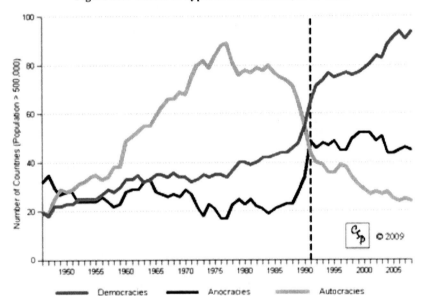

Source: Center for Systemic Peace.

Neither Markets nor Politics Are Clockwork Mechanisms

As Francis Fukuyama has claimed, democracy and markets will prevail over all challenges that may claim to organize politics and production in alternate ways. But his claim for history ending in universal democracy and universal, market-based wealth holds true, in the very, very long run only; that is if we look at that evolutionary process in the perspective of millennia.[10] In the meantime and in the short to medium run, that progress to universal democracy and wealth might be halted or reversed. Both markets and democracy are endangered by such reversals because they depend on producers and consumers, on citizens and politicians behaving rationally. Such rationality does not always prevail. Humans might be misled by theories or ideologies that pretend to be rational and founded in reality, but that are unsubstantiated in fact. Or humans might even abandon any pretext of rationality and yield to darker and dangerous instincts.

Francis Fukuyama himself has acknowledged as much. He qualified his optimistic outlook in juxtaposing an irrational motive to the motive of rational self-interest. Taking a cue from Greek philosophers, he termed that other motive *pride*. Other intellectuals have pointed to different urges that also work against the rational behavior such as it would be required for the orderly functioning of markets and democracy. Konrad Lorenz pointed to a genetically conditioned, irrepressible aggressive urge. Sigmund Freud diagnosed a kind of death wish opposed to the life sustaining drive of the *libido*. Most of the political disasters heaped upon the European continent since the beginning of the 19th century have been motivated by identity politics that ignore rational self-interest and instead enhance group identity and solidarity at the cost of de-humanizing outsiders.

Whenever rational interests clash with such darker forces, the latter are likely to prevail. How otherwise to explain the exuberance of crowds that welcomed the advent of suicidal World War I; or the enthusiasm of the US public for the unprovoked, utterly senseless war in Iraq? How otherwise to explain the bloody dismemberment of former Yugoslavia, or the persistence of the conflict between Palestinians and Israelis? Democracies tend to be peaceful. Markets enhance cooperation. But both are disturbed when the stronger forces prevail over the rational quest for tangible benefits.

Politics are about means and ends. They have to be guided by a view of the future one wishes to attain; and by views on the tools available to reach that goal. Politics thus should be rational. But that remains an abstract ideal. Politics never can be completely rational. Rationality would call for perfect knowledge and transparency of a kind that is not available, given the complexity of modern societies. In lack of such firm knowledge, we have to rely on mere hunches and assumptions. Ideologies also intrude. As they condition thoughts and actions, they do not bother with reality. They even might ignore it willfully.

Ideologies at Work

In the 1990s, one of the main challenges of politics had been to facilitate the transition of communist states to democracy and toward market-oriented economic activities. I had been involved in this task for seven years, first at the OECD Centre for Co-Operation with Economies in Transition in Paris; and later, as senior political counselor, at the London-based European Bank for Reconstruction and Development (EBRD).

Looking back at these two institutions, I have to conclude, with some bitterness and also with some personal guilt, that both of them had not always been up to that task. Advice given by the OECD and the EBRD often proved inappropriate. Why has this been so?

Societies, political and economic systems are conditioned historically and culturally.[11] They do not lend themselves to a quick transformation as suggested to them, or imposed upon them from the outside. The OECD and the EBRD tended to ignore that simple fact. Another reason for inappropriate advice was a hefty stock of smug self-confidence. No doubt dimmed the conviction of one's own system being the best and the notion that it could be exported to other countries; and applied in the turmoil of a complete change-over of political and economic systems.

Haughty smug, self-confidence and arrogance also clouded the view on the patient one intended to cure. Ideology precluded the recognition that, notwithstanding all its dysfunctionalities, the communist regimes had nonetheless been successful in some areas. A public health system and a sufficient educational system had been put in place. Housing had been provided for the masses that had switched from a rural into an urban existence. Industries had been created that worked in one way or another. They were served by a well-qualified workforce. This was a base one could build on. But "Western" ideology did not permit recognition of those achievements of communist rule. It dictated a complete, unconditional break with the past; a start from point zero.[12]

Simple ignorance aggravated the problem posed by intellectual/political arrogance. The challenge of transition from communism was unprecedented.[13] One had not given it much prior though, and thus relied on the illusion that what had worked in one's own country would work under different circumstances and in other countries too.

Were these mistakes just accidental? Or is there more that lurks behind them? The way an economy is structured is closely intertwined with the way privilege[14] is distributed in this economy. And that distribution of privilege, on its turn, is justified and legitimized by ideology. In devising programs and concepts for assistance in the transition from communism, substantial economic, political and ideological interests of the "West" were at stake. They had to be safeguarded. The programs by the OECD and the EBRD were thus of a nature to reaffirm the ideologies that supported the political/economic systems of those states which provided help to the formerly communist countries. Little attention was paid to the conditions of those at the receiving end of such advice.

One such interest of the dominant "Western" states is vested in the promotion of equity capital markets; and in the notion of them being of unique value at all phases of economic development. Recommendations offered by the OECD and the EBRD reflect this preference for a leading role of equity capital. Equity capital markets were preferred as tools for prompting a rapid transformation of state-owned industry into a privately owned one. Shares would be distributed in the population via vouchers and the magic of an economic turnaround would then come about automatically with a minimum of fuss. One would go to sleep in a centrally planned economy and would wake up in a market economy the other day. Yet contrary to such claims, "voucher-privatization" proved a failure. It did not establish responsible ownership in companies. It encouraged useless and damaging speculation.

Another recommendation—this time again from OECD—was equally reckless. It concerned the Soviet system of delivering social services. In communist times, these services were largely provided by state-owned firms. They ran health clinics, kindergartens, and nurseries. They provided for housing and for vacations, etc. The OECD suggested that such a mixing of social with economic functions should not endure. In abstract, that might have been a viable notion. In the meantime, though, the main question was the one as to the changeover from this Soviet system of rendering social services to an alternate system. Who if not firms would provide these services? How would these services be financed? The OECD did not answer such crucial questions. It provided nothing but the recommendation that Russian firms should unload themselves from such social obligations. They did and that contributed to the breakdown of Russian social and health services.[15]

A dogmatic insistence on the superiority of private enterprise in each and every instance also turned against the EBRD itself. The flagship publication of the bank is the annual "Transition Report." It reflects the prevailing ideological preference for the private over the state. The 1997 issue of the report was devoted to the privatization of banks and culminated in the conclusion that even in Russia and under all circumstances, privatized banks would do better than any bank still held by the state.[16] The EBRD itself had heavily invested in such a Russian private bank. As it turned out later and contrary to first appearances, this bank had largely functioned as a money-laundering engine for some newly rich tycoons. In the Russian crisis of 1997–1998 this bank failed and the EBRD had to register a loss so heavy that it wiped out nearly all the profits it had made in previous years. The sole major Russian bank to survive unscathed was the state-held savings bank ("Sberbank"). It is surprising to say the least, that the EBRD could flaunt its ideological preferences for private banking at a time when it itself had to suffer the very substantial negative consequences of this preference.

These examples taken from my experience demonstrate a failure of politics to rationally guide the economy. Some of such failures may be explained by intellectual laziness; by an inclination to stick to prevailing theories even when they have become outdated and should have been revised in view of new evidence. But that does not explain all of it. If we look at the examples I quoted, we will detect that the theories underlying these political recommendations do not err in a random way—erring in one direction and then in another one. They are tilted in one direction only. Theories on the economy and on politics tend to favor those in power and to sustain their hegemony. A change in such theories would undermine this hegemony by eroding its intellectual justifications.

What at first sight seems to be an intellectual question only reveals itself as a political stratagem to justify and maintain power and privilege.

The political task of complementing and guiding the process of economic evolution is therefore complicated by the lack of consensus on the nature of issues and by lack of consensus on the tools to apply. Conflicting interests frequently hide behind such intellectual controversies. It is not by accident that wealthy countries tend to portray the prevailing economic order as the best possible one and as the one to benefit all; whereas poorer countries, in their turn, perceive the prevailing order as unjust and disadvantageous to them.

But even if such ideological battles would not blur the vision, even if there were agreements on the nature of a problem and on the ways to tackle it, even then the tasks of global political action would be complicated by widely differing interests. Even if we assume that all countries would be carried forward by an economic upward trend,[17] they still would be at different levels of economic development;[18] and therefore in need of different policies. At an early stage of industrialization, for example, states tend to protect their nascent industries from overwhelming foreign competition. Once, however, they have advanced into the ranks of the wealthy countries, they switch preferences and become ardent promoters of free trade as such freedom of exchange now benefits their industries which have matured and have become fully competitive.

Different interests and different ideas on optimal, global politics persist also among countries that are on the same level of economic development. Both democracy and markets do not come in one brand only. Variations exist in the practice of democracy. Democracies may be "guided," "neocorporate," "presidential," "parliamentary," "liberal," or "illiberal." Market economies too do not simply come in one version only. There are "state-capitalist systems," "developmental economies," "social-market economies," economies with a small and with a big share of the GDP being administered by the state, unadulterated market economies, etc. Inevitably, there is competition and even conflict between these models.

Yet even when not distorted by ideologies, and even when not impaired by widely differing interests, the mechanisms of democracy and markets might fail for deficiencies that are inherent in those mechanisms themselves. Expectations in the economic markets and in the political market of democracy are being shaped by hunches on the actions and intentions of the other participants in these markets.[19] A political party might win at elections because it is expected to win. Prices for raw materials might rise solely for the reason that some expect them to rise and others learn about these expectations and thus purchase at prices higher than those justified by supply and demand.[20]

Melding Economic Globalization with Globalized Politics—the Hurdles

These arguments point to hurdles that have to be overcome in the task of matching the globalization of the economy with globalized politics. Let us sum them up:

a) With the onset of the Industrial Revolution in the early 19th century, the world economy has started to expand rapidly. Since then, growth has proceeded at an ever-faster pace. In human history there is no precedent for that development. It has transformed the world.

b) Consumption and production have become globalized. Goods produced in one part of the world may be consumed in other parts. Production too, has become global with transnational corporations spreading it over locations in different states.

c) This has undercut the goal of political and economic autonomy. States, firms, individuals are enmeshed in a web of interdependence that spreads across the globe.

d) Both the increase in production and that interdependence have made that not just advantages, but problems too, are now being shared throughout the world. The number of *common goods* has multiplied that have to be shielded by common efforts; and the number of *common bads* has grown, that have to be thwarted in joint action of all global actors.

e) The change in the nature of the world-economy has altered the very nature of relations between states. It has transformed the nature of power. It is no longer based on the capacity to force others to do something against their will. It is based on superiority in economic performance. In a system of open trade, such a superior performance by one participant is beneficial to (most) others. But that should not obfuscate the fact that a more or less superior performance determines the pecking order among states. States are not all of equal rank.

f)   Contrary to claims of traditional economics, the economy alone does not in itself produce optimal outcomes. It can do so only in conjunction with politics. As the economy has gone global, politics have to follow. Tip O'Neil, the former speaker of the US House of Representatives once claimed that *"all politics is local."* Some still is (and that is good so). But a growing number of issues and many of the truly important ones, have to be dealt with in cooperation between many states or even on a global level. In that sense *"all politics has become global."*

g)   Politics and the concepts that guide them, usually lag behind the actual issues they should address. As the wheels of the global economy turn ever faster, and as the volume of "common goods and common bads" is growing, politics have been slow in catching up.[21]

h)   Politics both on the national level and on an international/global level are not a self-regulating, clockwork mechanism in which the sum of many *rational choices* automatically produces optimal rules and decisions. Politics navigate in a complex[22] system. Politics have to deal with conflict, with opposing, mutually exclusive interests and values. Politics are not just about tangible, material interest. They also have to deal with, and have to respond to other human urges such as the yearning for a firm identity.[23] Politics, furthermore, are captive to ideologies that blur the distinction between the feasible and the utopian. Decisions have to be made in face of unknown data and on the face of unknown consequences. And politics are of course, also about power, about the capacity to have prevail one's own views and interests.

Just as in national politics, on a global level too, politics are not a science, but a profession and art, melding persuasion with threat, fighting, and compromise; empathy with the needs and views of others with a hard-nosed insistence on one's own position. National politics already are being shaped by a multitude of more or less visible actors. In global politics their number and variety is greater still.

International organizations are such actors. They have made for tangible progress in global governance. It would not have occurred without them.

Notes

1. From the mid-18th century on to the end of the 20th century, growth in the global population had outpaced growth in the global production. By now, this is no longer the case. We have entered a more benign phase of economic growth exceeding population growth.

2. It used to be that just a few very big firms from very rich countries had achieved such status as "transnationals." This is no longer the case. Many medium-sized firms have become transnational and so did quite a number of firms from still poorer countries.

3. Contrary to the teaching of American neoconservatives, communism was not "vanquished" by the power of the United States. It collapsed because it lost legitimacy and support in the population and even among political elites. Communism collapsed because it could not deliver the goods, "Western" economic and political systems could deliver.

4. It became obvious, for example, in the refusal of poorer states to accept a binding limitation for the emission of "greenhouse gases" that cause global warming, or in their refusal to yield positions to permit a successful conclusion of the Doha Round of free trade negotiations.

5. The imperative to help the poorer countries has been well recognized for decades. Indeed, assistance by the wealthier countries has increased over the years (while still being far below the official target set by international agreements). But experience with such assistance has also been sobering. It has mostly failed in being effective. That proves that processes like economic growth are difficult to impose from outside. They have to be rooted in the respective society itself. This observation does not invalidate the obligation to provide development assistance. But it calls for more serious evaluation of what works and what does not work.

6. Politics are also more than just some band aid applied to the body of the economy; they are more than mere "doctors at the sick-bed of capitalism" (Tarnover—German Social-Democrat)—with no other function than those of curing the passing illness of a basically sound "capitalist" system.

7. The curve depicted in this graph is called the "environmental Kuznets curve." The Russian economist Kuznets had established a similar connection between rising wealth and income inequality. Inequality grows in the first phases of economic growth; to decrease later as a certain level of average income had been reached.

8. The political system, on its turn, connects back to the economy; because there is a correlation between wealth and democracy. The wealthier a country, the greater the chances of its being governed democratically. Few of the very poor countries are democratic. All wealthy countries are. Greater wealth implies enhanced existential security, which, in its turn, permits greater plurality and tolerance. According to an index compiled by the Vienna Institute for Economic Comparison, these are the most tolerant states: Sweden, Netherlands, Iceland, Denmark, Canada, France, United States, Australia, Finland, New Zealand, and Luxembourg. And these are the least tolerant ones: Turkey, Bangladesh, Korea, Jordan, Algeria, Egypt, Armenia, Nigeria, Indonesia, Azerbaijan, and India.

9. In absence of continuous economic and political change, a feudal class would become established that would smother both democracies and markets, as proven, most recently, by the example of Nazi Germany and of the Soviet Union. Both regimes had their origin in idealistic, even eschatological movements. But they had no inbuilt mechanisms to permit change because they were conceived as being millennial. Both regimes were not challenged by the likelihood of ever-possible change; and both soon became corrupt and inefficient.

10.   This is an assumption that seems plausible. But it is not cogent if we consider the proposition in the timeframe of thousand years. Even within that relatively long timeframe, we have witnessed periods of long economic political and cultural decline, lasting for centuries. Most well known is the long decline that set in with the end of the Roman Empire. In Meso-America a century-long decline followed the demise of the Maya Empire.

11.   In the language of political science: they are "path-dependent."

12.   Tellingly caught in the phrase that one can "cross an abyss (of the transition from communism) in one single leap only" as would be impossible to cross it with two leaps.

13.   Though certain historic parallels were in place; especially in the post-1945 transition from state-controlled war economies to the economies adapted to the circumstances of long-lasting peace.

14.   In Marxist terms: "surplus value" is being distributed. It seems worth reflecting upon that Marxists (and pre-Marxists) had proposed that the value of product would be determined by the labor input required. Ricardo's theory of comparative advantage that successfully replaced this "labor value theory" presupposes the existence of still widely autonomous national economies with neither capital nor labor moving across frontiers; and with technology being a constant. Ricardo's theory does not fit with the present reality of economic globalization. Ricardo claimed that cloth would continue to be produced in Britain even if the cost of this production would be higher than the costs of production of cloth in Portugal. Under present conditions, the production of cloth would move to Portugal where production is cheaper. Britain would lose jobs in the manufacturing of cloth. That is a certain return to the Marxist notion of labor input and the input of other "facts of production" being the decisive factor in determining the value of product.

15.   Accompanied by a wholly unprecedented decline in average life expectancy.

16.   I argued—unsuccessfully—that I very much would prefer a still state-owned bank in Slovenia to a recently privatized Russian one.

17.   A heroic assumption, as some countries seem unable to participate in the global-ized economy. They decline instead of advancing; and are ultimately threatened by complete failure (that is breakdown of the state itself).

18.   Just as *within* states, there has been a growing diversity in wealth and economic "density," visible especially in bigger states like China and the United States.

19.   Something the successful financial trader and speculator George Soros has termed the "reflectivity" of markets.

20.   The effect of such decisions will be the more severe the less elastic supply and demand, and the more likely therefore big changes in prices caused by even rela-tively small, frequently speculative purchases or sales. This is the main reason for the price of crude oil having fluctuated so wildly, with dire consequences for all of the world economy. It seems obvious that a regulated price agreed upon between consumers and producers would better serve the interests of both sides.

21.   The last and most tragic proof: the world financial crisis. It has long been clear that the world economic institutions built after World War II like the World Bank, the International Monetary Fund, or the Economic and Social Council of the UN, are in dire need of reform and transformation. As hardly anything meaningful was done, these institutions had only a minor role in efforts to combat the worldwide, dramatic downturn of the economy.

22.   "Chaotic system": according to systems theory. Chaotic systems do not have one single "solution" but a multitude of them. They are shaped by many variables, and a small change in one of them might make for a completely different outcome. "Chaos-theory" is an apt metaphor for politics.

23.   Defining "in-groups" and "out-groups."

11

International Organizations: More Than Reflections of Narrow "National Interests" of Their Member States

Diplomatic work done within international organizations is called multilateral diplomacy. This field of diplomatic activity is expanding rapidly—not at least because of the growing number of these organizations. According to the Union of International Organizations, 7,080 of them existed in 2002. That big number is the more astounding, because international organizations are something quite new. The first modern one[1]—the Universal Postal Union—was created in 1863 only. Its foundation was necessary and inevitable. With world trade expanding and international mobility increasing, one simply could not have done without an institution to regulate and streamline trans-frontier postal exchange.

Since then, borders of states have been swamped by a flood of goods, services, persons, and information. The stark increase in global interdependence created by such vast trans-border flows finds correspondence in this equally stark rise in the number of international organizations. Just as in the mid-19th century one could not have done without the Universal Postal Union, one cannot do today without the many other international organizations that shield and regulate interdependence. It is difficult to imagine a wealthy and stable world to exist without a World Trade Organization, without a World Health Organization, without an UN High Commissioner for Refugees, without a World Intellectual Property Organization, etc.

These organizations are at the core of global governance. Their function is central. It therefore should be the primordial task of diplomacy to support them and facilitate their work.

Is this always the case? My own experience at the OECD, at the Council of Europe and at the European Bank for Reconstruction and Development makes me hesitate to answer in the affirmative. It makes me suspect that in its fixation on bilateral relations between states, traditional diplomacy sometimes tends not to promote, but to obstruct the mission of international organizations. This is not to imply that as a rule, overall and in sum, diplomats have impeded the progress in global governance made possible through these international bodies. Quite on the contrary, in the absence of diplomats, many of the decisive breakthroughs in global governance would not have come about. Diplomacy and diplomats were instrumental in making international organizations meet their goals.

It is clear, though, that a specific version of traditional diplomacy does not promote the role of international organizations. Such dysfunctional tendencies of traditional diplomacy are rooted in outdated ideas on the true nature of international organizations. According to these outdated notions, states would remain the only global actors. International organizations would be nothing more than their passive tools. All that international organizations could provide are air-conditioned or heated rooms, translation and secretarial services, and some rules to structure the clash or concurrence of the interests of their member states. Over and above that, and that is in essence, international organizations would have no function or nature of their own. The administrative bodies that keep those organizations running would also be nothing more than the humble servants of their member-state masters.

But anyone with a more detailed knowledge of those organizations, anyone who has worked with or in them, knows such views to be wrong. International organizations have a weight of their own. Their secretariats and their leaders make a difference. They matter.

The Mere Existence of International Organizations Is Proof of the Readiness of States to Recognize the Existence of a "Common Good"

International organizations embody the resolve for joint action. The Security Council of the United Nations embodies the resolve to avoid war. The World Trade Organization embodies the resolve to maintain world trade at a high volume. The World Health Organization embodies the accepted necessity to thwart global health threats, etc. International organizations are tangible proof of this political consensus and they guarantee it with varying degree of efficiency.[2] This implies a resolve to uphold common norms, and the resolve to sanction those who deviate from such norms; and to mete out such punishment even if doing so carries some costs for those who do the punishing.[3]

The Power to Move Things Forward and to Set an Agenda

Let us assume something that is quite common in international organizations. The rule-making body of such an organization—the "Board" or the "General Assembly"—passes some vaguely worded decision and charges the Secretariat with implementing it or with the elaboration of more specific proposals. The Secretariat is thus endowed with quite some room for discretion—with quite some say over actual policies. Behind the scenes, some member countries will maneuver to influence the decision-making of the Secretariat. But in that, they only can go so far. The persons charged with that task are international civil servants. As such they are largely shielded from pressure exercised by member-countries.[4]

As a Rule, the Staff of the Secretariats Will Be Able to Muster More, and More Relevant Knowledge on Issues Up for Decision

The staff in international organizations will have dealt with a certain issue for a long time. It will have acquired expert knowledge. As a rule, this knowledge will be more detailed than the one available to those diplomats who are formally charged with supervising and directing them. In the course of their career, diplomats wander from one country and from one job to another. On many technical issues they therefore gain limited knowledge only. The staff of international organizations can also tap into information available worldwide, whilst diplomats will mostly rely on information provided to them by their head offices. Such information given to diplomats by their home offices is likely to be less broad and precise, and also more partisan than the information available to the staff of international organizations.

The Person Heading the Administration of an International Organization Matters

Nations differ in their appreciation of resourceful persons as the heads of international organizations. More than bigger states, smaller ones depend on close, firm, and predictable international cooperation. Smaller states therefore prefer strong personalities as heads of international organizations; whilst bigger, more powerful countries often tend in the other direction and prefer them to be meek.[5] Frequently, these more powerful states have prevailed. When not, impressive secretaries-general have left a deep imprint, as did Dag Hammarskjöld and Kofi Annan at the United Nations, or Jacques Delors at the European Union.[6] In nominal and merely legal terms, these three persons would have been nothing more than the servants of their member-state masters. In practice, they have opened new fields of cooperation and activity and have achieved what no single member state could have achieved either by acting alone or by using international organizations as its tool. Jacques Delors merged the economies of European states into a single, integrated internal market. Dag Hammarskjöld pioneered the UN peacekeeping operations. Kofi Annan moved the United Nations back to the center in the worldwide fight against poverty.

A Staff Increasingly Independent from Their Original Home State

On appointments to the staff of international organizations, member states on the one side, and the directors and other administrators of such organizations on the other side are still engaged in a war over turf. Both fight for the final influence over such appointments. This fight is the fiercer; the more senior the position in question, the greater the political implications of the decisions in which the staff member will be involved.[7]

Most of the tasks of international organizations are complex and technical. Trust in the expertise of staff members is thus their most valuable asset. As they have to safeguard this asset, the process of selecting staff has become more targeted and refined. Staff members now understand that they owe their position to their professional record; to recommendations of peers engaged in the same field; to the list of their publications; to the result of intensive background checks; and less to pressure exerted by diplomats of their home country, eager to see their nationals in positions of influence at international organizations.[8]

Diplomats representing their state are losing ground in the turf-war over the staffing of international organizations. Increasingly, therefore, the allegiance of the staff in secretariats will be to persons and institutions that are not those of their own home country. Next to contacts to their colleagues in the same organization, their main professional contacts will be with those persons all over the world who are engaged in the same field as they are. Increasingly staff members of international organizations will define their identity less through their nationality, and more by their work at this international organization. They will assert this identity through ties in the worldwide peer group of experts dealing with the technical problem they also deal with, just as diplomats assert their identity in moving in the peer group of their diplomatic colleagues.

Staff in Secretariats Is Not Distracted by Side Issues

Sitting in the back rows assigned to the retinue of the foreign ministers who act as members of the board supervising the work of the Council of Europe, I knew what to expect after a statement of the foreign minister of Cyprus: namely a lengthy statement by his Turkish colleague with repeated assurances that what we had heard had actually not been said. For him, the Republic of Cyprus did not exist. These rhetoric games of the Turkish foreign minister did not resolve the problem of Cyprus. But they took 10 minutes of the precious time ministers had for their discussion. In a similar vein, proceedings on even urgent issues have been burdened in international organizations by Arabs who made them hostage to their grievances over Israel. Discussions on international trade were often complicated by positions taken for reasons of mere national prestige or for shallow politicking. International civil servants wish to conclude negotiations with results acceptable to all. Diplomats, on the contrary, often ride their national hobby horses thereby slowing or otherwise impeding this effort.

To conclude: international organizations solve a *collective action problem* that would arise if each of their members would just pursue its immediate and narrow self-interest even if such a course of action would be detrimental to the common interest of all member states.[9] International organizations embody consensus on global common goods that have to be safeguarded, and they have the administrative capacity and an information advantage that they can put at the service of such a consensus. International organizations therefore do not just represent the *smallest common denominator* of their member states. In solving collective action problems of their members, they have become the *optimal common denominator.*

Yet we have to ask whether global governance by common institutions has not moved a step beyond that already. We have to ask whether an international public sector has emerged, that escapes the veto-power of national politics; and which already has transmuted—in a *de facto* manner—into a *supra-national authority.*

This question has two aspects: the aspect of a demand side, and the aspect of a supply side. Looking at the demand side we would have to wonder, whether we can witness the emergence of a *global* "polity"—that is an assembly of politically motivated persons from different states—that calls for, and supports this international public sector. On the supply we have to scrutinize institutions already present in such realm no longer under the complete control of nation states.

Let us deal with this second aspect first.

Notes

1. The Commission administrating the navigation on the Rhine is older still; but its mission and reach is more limited of course.
2. ...or to take the terms used to describe the function of the European Commissions: secretariats act as the "guardian of the (a) treaty."
3. As proven by experiments, in "behavioral economics." Participants in such experiment punish those participants who act unfairly. They do so even when that implies that they forego some economic benefit.
4. A recent example: a high-ranking UN staff member of British nationality had criticized the former US ambassador to the United Nations, John Bolton, for his undermining of the United Nations. This is remarkable, as the United Kingdom is the closest European political ally of the United States. The actions of this international civil servant thus prove that he and his peers may very well disregard sacred policies even of states they originate from.
5. The then-secretary-general of the United Nations, Boutros Boutros-Ghali, was too independent and self-assured for the taste of the United States. Secretary of State Madeleine Albright (the US "foreign minister") wished him to be "more of a secretary and less of a general." See also the example, quoted earlier of the US support for a weak candidate for the post of an OECD secretary-general.
6. This however cannot longer be seen as a mere and classical international organization. The European Union is something specific; midway between such an international organization and a federal state.
7. This has not prevented the diplomatic representatives at these institutions from trying to intervene even on appointments to minor positions—such as to the corps of tour guides in the United Nations building in New York (Moynihan, p. 1980).
8. This does not apply to top positions in some international organizations (such as, for example, "deputy secretaries general," or "vice-presidents"). They still are selected in a process of diplomatic horse-trading, with the nationality of the candidate being the decisive factor.
9. And as we have argued in the discussion on the "prisoner's dilemma," the pursuit of a narrow self-interest will be detrimental even to the long-term interest of the country that takes such a narrow view of its own interests.

12

Moving beyond "Optimal Games": The International Public Sector

What is meant by the term "public sector"? Within a state, it is defined as the realm encompassing all those goods and services that are not produced in the private sector. Such public goods and services are numerous: internal security, rule of law, basic education, public health and sanitation, insurance against indigence in old age, public transport; and so on.

One of the defining political battles of the last century was over the borderline between the public and the private sector. Should health insurance or old age insurance be in the public or in the private sphere? Should urban transportation and should other communal services be public or private?

In different states, different answers were found to that question. The trend toward the relative growth of the public sector is obvious though. In general, the wealthier, the more "modern" a state, the greater the size of its public sector.[1] This results from the greater complexity of modern society, which makes for an increase in those tasks that best can be dealt with through common efforts. Private criminal justice, private environmental agencies, or private banking supervision would make little sense.[2]

What holds true for the community of interdependent citizens living within a state that holds true too for the interdependent states of the world. They also are faced with a growing number of tasks that best can be executed by common efforts. Not just the national public sector is expanding. Inevitably, the same holds true too, for the global public sector.

Many of the tasks in this global public sector are being addressed by traditional international organizations. These deal with collective action problems that arise from the dichotomy between the legal independence of states and of their actual interdependence. International organizations put global governance as exercised by independent states on its optimal level. But they still leave it there on this level defined by the cooperation of states.

We have to ask though, whether there is a level of global governance in a realm beyond and above states.

The *Universally Acknowledged Rules of International Law* seem to be in this higher domain. States are bound by these rules even if they have not agreed to them.[3] They observe these rules even when doing so runs counter to their interest. But further investigating this issue on the relation between international law and global politics would lead us too far into a different field. So we leave it, at this instance, with noting that states are constrained by parts of international law to which they have not expressly agreed.

But next to the example set by the Universally Accepted Rules of International Law there are other examples to demonstrate the existence of a global governance no longer under the full control of states:

- States are bound by rules to which they have not formally agreed.
- States have to follow directives of organizations they do not participate in.
- States execute directives of international institutions instead of these international institutions executing their directives.

Transnational corporations and the globalized financial markets are the most prominent among the institutions that can impose themselves on states. They merit special attention and we therefore will deal with them in a separate chapter. Let us first look at other cases of states not being fully in charge of global governance.

States Are Bound by Rules to Which They Have Not Formally Agreed

International Organizations are active in the international public sphere and there provide public goods and public services to the community of states (but now increasingly also directly to the citizens of these states). The formal charter of most international organizations stipulates that all major decisions be taken by unanimous vote. All member states would have to agree. In practice though, most of these international organizations have sidestepped that requirement. Actually, most of their decisions are based on *consensus*.

Consensus does not equal *unanimity*. Unanimity implies that everyone agrees expressly. Consensus implies that nobody disagrees expressly.[4] The two are not the same. For various and sound reasons, a state might not wish to obstruct a decision all other members of an international organization have arrived at. But this state might still think it unwise to expressly endorse such a decision. When the chairperson of the meeting concludes with the remark "I believe that we now have arrived at a consensus" on this or that issue, the representative of the state that still holds reservations simply stays mum. He may issue a brief statement afterwards, explaining why he could not completely share the view of others; or why his country would implement that decision in a peculiar way.

Notwithstanding such *a posteriori* explanations, the statement of the chair on a consensus having been found will take the place of a formal vote. Generally, it will also bind the country that had uttered some reservations in its *a posteriori* declaration. That implies that states can be bound by international decisions they have not expressly agreed to—and that even in cases where the formal charter of an international organization would have excluded that eventuality by requiring unanimity for binding decisions.

At some instances, though, things have evolved even further into the direction of a *consensus minus one*. It widens the possibility of imposing the will of the majority on the one dissenting member state. That principle of "consensus minus one" permits arriving at a politically binding consensus, even though one party had not simply stayed mum, but had expressly objected to a course taken by the rest of the member countries. The most notable example for that is provided by the Organization for Security and Cooperation in Europe—OSCE, which, in 1992, decided that in case of a state's "clear, gross and uncorrected violation of OSCE commitments," a decision may be taken and become binding without the consent of that single state that objects to this decision.

The method of deciding by consensus is even used in those international organizations that would have the option of deciding by a majority vote.[5] The power of even strong international organizations is limited still. They have limited means to actually execute their decisions. They have limited capacity only to force a state into doing things it does not like to do. So there is a premium on getting this state to accept a solution most other partners in the negotiations aim at. That is why the *process* of arriving at a consensus is as important as the final outcome of this process. The goal of getting everyone to agree on a course of action or on a wording of a legal instrument implies lengthy and difficult negotiations.

The Facilitator

The success of such negotiations very much depends on the person who acts as the "facilitator." The facilitator tries to bridge a gap. On one hand are those issues that emerge as a consequence of the growing interdependence of states and that need to be addressed and resolved. On the other side of the gap is the uneven will and the uneven actual capacity of states to contribute to the solution sought.

This gap cannot be bridged by someone trying to impose his preferences by outwitting others; by hiding important information; by distorting facts; by dividing a group into antagonistic camps; or even by threats. The bridging must be done by a facilitator. This person must be seen as being an honest broker motivated not by self-interest but by the aim of arriving at results acceptable to all. He or she has to become trusted in that capacity. A good facilitator should never show signs of impatience. He or she should have an open mind and be able to listen and seriously consider all ideas and proposals. The facilitator should refrain from hiding differences, but should accept them and have them discussed openly, portraying them as helpful rather than as damaging.

Many persons can be successful as facilitators. Yet when highly political issues of global governance are at stake, we will find that a disproportionally large share of them are diplomats. This is something we should retain for the final judgment on the role of diplomats in global governance.

Decision-making by consensus already implies a still minor step in the direction of diminishing the dominance of states in global affairs, as a state can be bound by such consensus even against its original preferences.

That step becomes wider and politically more significant where: *Some international organizations have been endowed by their funding documents with the power to rule against member states.*

The most prominent example is the United Nations. Its central and politically most relevant organ is the Security Council. It decides with a qualified majority of its 15 members, with each of the five permanent members[6] having a veto power and thus being in a position to block a decision they do not like. The remaining 187 member countries of the United Nations are not so privileged. They have to abide by the decisions of the United Nations Security Council even if they object to them. The Security Council deals with threats to peace and security and its decisions might result in measures as consequential as embargos on trade or even on calls for armed intervention. National sovereignty thus becomes curtailed by such decisions, which is a definite break[7] with past traditions of international relations.

International trade is certainly a central element of the present global regime. It is central too, to interests of each of the world's states. In view of this centrality, world trade is subject to a host of rules and is being under the oversight of powerful international organizations; the mightiest being the World Trade Organization (WTO). In case the WTO has to decide on a trade conflict that had sprung up between two or more of its member states, it may impose its findings on the parties of such a conflict. These have to accept the WTO ruling even though doing so is not always in their interest.

The United Nations and the World Trade Organization are core institutions of the present regime of global governance. Member states have to accept their rulings even if they object to them; just as they have foregone the option of *not* being part of such organizations. Today, a state does not have the option of *not* being a member of the United Nations.[8] A bigger and modern state does *not* have the option not to accede to the World Trade Organization. In fact thus, states have to accept that their independence has been reined in by such international organizations.

Yet developments have gone even beyond that and have reached a point *where states become obliged to execute decisions of international bodies of which they are not a part.*

According to the abstract notions of international law, all states would be equal. All of them would be clad in the same armor of sovereignty and be endowed with the same right and capacity to rule exclusively in their "internal affairs"; each of them being endowed too, with the same right to participate in international decision-making. The actual practice is widely different though, as states have to abide by decisions taken by a group of states they are not members in. Such decisions by others might not bind them in a strictly legal sense. But in practice they have little choice but to follow on a path trodden by others, and mightier ones.

Fitting example are decisions taken by the so-called G-20. Twenty countries, prominent in the world economy, are members of this group. In early April 2009, they met to set a common course in reaction to the world financial crisis. By the time this book will be published, the actual effects of their decision will be known. Doubtlessly, much hinges on that actual outcome. The liquidity of banks will have to be restored. Demand for goods and services will have to be boosted by coordinated fiscal and monetary policies. Financial institutions and instruments will have to come under better and tighter control. And world trade has to be kept free of protectionist measures that otherwise might threaten to end in a replay of the 1930s, when growing restrictions to international trade caused its decline and thus aggravated the economic crisis and accelerated the march toward conflict and war.

We now count 195 states in the world. Therefore, the G-20 represents no more than 10 percent of this worldwide community of states. But not only will the remaining 90 percent of states be affected by the decisions of the G-20 summit. They will also have no choice but to accept for themselves the tasks and rules this 10 percent of states agree upon.

With members as diverse as India and the United States, the G-20 can nonetheless be seen as being somehow representative of the wide diversity of all the states of the world. This is not the case for other restricted groups whose decisions have worldwide impact nonetheless. One example for such a group is the Australia Group.[9] It was founded in 1989 with the purpose of having potential provider countries control and restrict the export of chemicals that could be used in the production of chemical or biological weapons. At present, 41 countries adhere to this group. That implies that about 140 countries are not members though the decisions of the 41 member countries of the "Australia Group" will affect them. They will not be able to import certain materials. They have no vote in the definition of such material whose export is controlled and restricted.

"Groupology"

G-77:   Founded in 1964 as a loose federation of developing countries to represent their interests.

G-33:   Founded in 2006, it is a bargaining coalition of developing countries for negotiations in the World Trade Organization.

G-20:   This is a group—originally of ministers of finance and central bank governors—of the most important wealthy countries and the most important "emerging" countries.

> It first met in 1999. By now some of the meetings are also among heads of state and government.
>
> G-8:   Is a forum for eight economically and politically powerful states. The group started out in 1975 as the G-6 with Germany, the United States, Japan, the United Kingdom, France, and Italy as members. With the entry of Canada in 1978 it expanded to G-7, and with the inclusion of Russia in 1998 it became the present G-8. The original agenda of financial and monetary problems has expanded significantly to also include issues of arms control, environmental protection, terrorism, etc. This cooperation is sustained by continuous contact between relevant government members and higher civil servants. At present, the G-8 is overshadowed by the G-20.

But with this we still are within the realm of states: one state deciding on what another has to do or not to do; with the other state being excluded from such decisions. But there are instances when states become bound by decisions not taken by other states; or by a group of states they are not member in.

States May Become Bound by Decisions Taken by Entities That Do Not Represent States

Many culprits are now blamed for having caused the onset of the world financial crisis. Among them are the chairman of the US Federal Reserve with his loose money policy; rapacious investment bankers peddling "poisonous," high-risk financial papers; insouciant home-buyers who overestimated their capacity to service their mortgages and so on.

One of such suspects is the so-called BASLE II agreement concluded under the auspices of—the Basle-based Bank for International Settlements (BIS). The BASLE II agreement set new minimum standards for the equity capital of banks that would have to underlay their assets (i.e., credits and similar instruments banks have provided). This change of standards caused quite some turmoil. One may doubt, nonetheless, whether it really did contribute in any significant manner to the outbreak or the worldwide crisis. Clearly though, this agreement had far-reaching consequences for states and for their citizens. State laws and regulations had to be adjusted.

Who then stood behind this important new agreement? It was concocted not by states, but by central banks. The BIS is not an organization of states but an instrument (and a clearinghouse) of the world's central banks, all of whom pride themselves on being independent from government. States had to execute and bear the consequences of a policy not they had defined, but that had been set by a body in which they had no say.

The BIS has come into limelight as a consequence of the turmoil in worldwide money and capital markets; and as instigator of the controversial BASLE II, agreement. Yet there are other organizations too that are not the usual international organizations, as their members are not states. Nonetheless they agree upon and promote rules states will have to follow. These organizations are as independent of states as is the BIS.

One of them is the International Electro-Technical Commission (IEC).[10] This is the central organization for establishing norms and standards for all forms of electric and electronic use and equipment. The width of these tasks is documented by the IEC—working through 93 technical commissions and 80 sub-commissions, as well as through no less than 700 working groups.

One may fairly say that life as we know it today would not exist in absence of such an organization. We are surrounded by, and dependent on things electric. These would not function, were there no worldwide agreement on common norms and standards. One should suppose that a task as essential as this is as much part of governmental responsibility as the maintenance of internal security and the provision of education. It is not. States are not members of the IEC. Members are the national committees that differ in their composition. Civil servants from the national administrations are present in some of them.[11] Others are dominated by representatives from industry.

The standards and norms established by the IEC have to be enforced. The enforcement of these norms and standards is the task of national governments. Just as in the case of the standards for banks set by the Bank for International Settlements, in this case too, governments have to enforce rules they had no voice in shaping.

Global compatibility of electrical equipment is a *global public good*. It is an essential one. Imagine the havoc that would result from eight different norms for alternate current existing side by side. Or of 20 different kind of UBS plugs that connect computers with peripheral equipment; or the waste of energy that would be caused by each state having distinct norms for the transmission of high-voltage electricity. That would preclude the creation of transnational electrical grids, which are essential for the steady and economic supply of electrical energy.

These examples underline the relevance of the international public sector. This sector produces services no single government can provide alone; and it provides services private enterprise cannot provide either, as long as it acts on the impulse of strict and immediate maximization of profit. Much of the work in this realm is done through traditional international organizations. Their decisions are still largely shaped by their member states. But in this chapter, we have observed a gradual shift away from the absolute dominance of states. Some decisions in traditional international organizations are no longer under the exclusive and total control of its member states. Some of these organizations pass decisions that are binding, in a *de facto* manner, even on states that are not their members. Finally, we have found that there are some very important organizations in which states are not members that nonetheless pass weighty decisions. Such decisions may have to be executed by states, even though they had no voice in shaping them.

Clearly, we have to reassess the view of the world being shaped by international relations. The relations that shape the world today are no longer under the exclusive control of "nations." That holds true even for norms that ultimately have to be enforced through tools available to states only.

One type of new actors entering the global playing field are international organizations not of governments but of private citizens. They act on the global scene without the intermediation of governments.

Notes

1.   The trend had already been recognized by the late 19th-century German economist Adolph Wagner (hence the term "Wagner's law"—see the later chapter on the enduring significance of the states).

2.   The "Coase Theorem" would maintain otherwise. If markets were perfect, everything could be in the private sector. That argument abstracts from two essential human conditions. First, knowledge is never complete and the "transaction cost" are therefore high. Second, human beings are "social animals." They are not exclusively motivated by the prospect of "maximizing personal utility." Group behavior largely determines individual behavior.

3.   The United States seems ambivalent as to the binding power of international law. If my perception is correct, then a majority of US legal scholars would assess as binding only those international rules that had expressly been endorsed by US lawmakers.

4. As defined in the Rules of Procedure of the OSCE (Organization for Security and Cooperation in Europe): "consensus shall be understood to mean the absence of any objection expressed by a participating state to the adoption of the decision in question.... Any texts which have been adopted by a decision making body by consensus shall have a politically binding character for all the participating states...."

5. Such as the international financial institutions (IFIs). Votes there are weighted according to the economic power of each member state—an example of economic power reigning supreme. But these IFIs also have quite some power to support their decisions with "sticks and carrots." Unanimity is therefore less essential in their work.

6. China, France, Russia, the United Kingdom, and the United States.

7. The significance of this break becomes evident in the fact that neutral Switzerland, while host to numerous UN organizations, became full UN member only in 2002. Switzerland's long hesitation in applying for UN membership is explained by its taking seriously the constraints imposed by its permanent neutrality. This neutrality would oblige it to desist from participating in armed interventions or embargos while the UN Security Council could very well oblige any and all of the UN member states to do so, even if a member state would have preferred not to get involved in a conflict by pointing, for example, to its status as a permanently neutral state.

8. In recent history, accession to the United Nations has implied the recognition of a state as a state. In terms of international law, it has constituted a state as a state.

9. Restricted groups with a similar purpose: The "Wassenaar Arrangement," the "Missile Technology Control Regime," or the "Nuclear Suppliers Group."

10. Another and probably better know example of such a semi-private organization with a global normative function is ICANN—the International Corporation for Assigned Names and Numbers. It is a private non-profit organization under US law and with seat in the United States. Nonetheless, it functions as a kind of global Internet government.

11. The United States, for example, is represented by the American National Standards Institute.

13

Non-Governmental Organizations, Nations without a Territory, and the Fractured Global "Polity"

"I have been elected by Swedish voters a few weeks ago—but who has elected you?"
—Sweden's minister for development assistance in a discussion with
international non-governmental organizations at a World Bank meeting

In 1995, negotiations started at the OECD on a "Multilateral Agreement on Investment—MAI." Over the preceding decades, trans-border investment had expanded rapidly. Such investments touch the interest of both the country that does the investment and of the country that receives the investment. Hundreds of bilateral agreements had been signed so as to provide a legal frame for settling possible conflicts between these two sides. Evidently, having a maze of such treaties is not a very efficient way to address the issue. Both the countries making foreign investments and the countries receiving them would be better served by one common multilateral treaty all sides could agree upon.

It was for this purpose that, within OECD, negotiations began in 1995. The negotiators came from the administrations of OECD member states. Most of them were higher civil servants from either the ministries of finance or the ministries of the economy. This then was a group of insiders, inevitably focused on the narrow field they were specialized in. Other parts of the national administrations were not involved. Neither was the public as these negotiations were in secret. One should also add that the project had been strongly pushed by the United States with the aim of securing for their investors protection from all sorts of inconvenience and harm that might burden them in the country they had invested in.

Negotiations proceeded at their normal pace though resistance to the project began to gather when the first draft for such an investment treaty was leaked to the public in 1997. This resistance was organized by international non-governmental organizations (INGOs) such as the Friends of the Earth, or the Public Citizen's Global Earth Watch. They objected to the far-reaching protection foreign investors would be granted. According to the draft for the treaty, even the creation of a special court would have been allowed, sidestepping the courts of both the investing and of the recipient country.

The capacity of the recipient country to enforce stringent environmental and labor standards could have been curtailed. The precedent of an US-Canadian treaty provided substance to such fears. A ruling based on that treaty had foreclosed for Canada the possibility to impose new, stricter environmental regulations on a firm in Canada that had been created by US investment prior to the passage of these new, stricter environmental rules. A court interpreted these new Canadian rules as some sort of a "creeping expropriation of US investors" and thus contrary to the US-Canadian treaty on investment.

The campaign of various international non-governmental organizations against the draft of the Multilateral Agreement on Investment was successful. In 1998, first France and then other states withdrew from the negotiations. They collapsed.[1]

A report to the French National Assembly had recommended to the government this step of abandoning the negotiations. The report had been drafted by Catherine Lalumiere.[2] It contains the following lines:

> For the first time, one is seeing the emergence of a global civil society represented by NGOs which are often based in several states and communicate beyond their frontiers. This evolution is doubtless irreversible. On one hand, organizations representing civil society have become aware of the consequences of international economic negotiations. They are determined to leave their mark on them.
>
> Furthermore, the development of the Internet has shaken up the environment of the negotiations. It allows the instant diffusion of the texts under discussion, whose confidentiality becomes more and more theoretical. It permits, beyond national boundaries, the sharing of knowledge and expertise. On a subject which is highly technical, the representatives of civil society seemed to us perfectly well informed and their criticisms well-argued on a legal level.[3]

This assessment of INGOs done by Catherine Lalumiere highlights a remarkable development. By 1945, one counted just 1,000 INGOs. From then on their number rose exponentially. By the year 2007, 60,000 INGOs existed according to the Union of International Associations. At the same time, cooperation of these INGOs with the official, state-based "international organizations" has become broader and more intense. Many INGOs have obtained *consultative status* with the United Nations and with its Specialized Agencies. In 1946 only 41 INGOs had a consultative status with the UN Economic and Social Council (ECOSOC). By 2003, this number had risen to 3,550. The greater number of INGOs and their more prominent presence would lead us to assume that we have entered a new phase in global affairs, with INGOs establishing themselves in a field that previously was controlled by governments exclusively.

The causes for this development seem obvious. The jet plane has eased international travel. Costs for the transmission of information via fiber optic cables or satellites have dropped significantly. English has been widely accepted as the language of international communication. Literacy has increased worldwide. The Internet has become the base for cyber-communities that link persons with same interests and views wherever they live.

The growth in the number of INGOs and their greater prominence is also due to the fact that issues addressed by INGOs have become more numerous and more pressing. These are issues that call for a coordinated, common response not just of states, but also call for the direct involvement of citizens from all over the world. As we had remarked before, the global commons that have to be preserved have expanded; as have the global bads that need to be curtailed. Frequently, public authorities had yet to be alerted to the urgency of such tasks and INGOs were successful in doing that: they had been instrumental in arranging for a debt relief of poor countries; as they had been instrumental in the work for a treaty that banned certain types of land-mines; or in the Montreal Protocol that lead to a reduction of emissions that destroy the ozone layer of the earth; or in the greater urgency now accorded to the fight against corruption.

All this might tempt us into losing a sense of proportion and to describe as unprecedented the function INGOs have gained in global governance. It is not. The impact the massive and worldwide antislavery movement had in the 19th century is hard to ignore; as is the worldwide 19th century movement for female suffrage. Both of these movements had been effective in reaching their goals.

Yes—by now, the number of INGOs has grown greatly. But that has not been paralleled by a growth in the overall membership of all INGOs taken together. Some of the pre-World War II INGOs had an impressively large membership. Thomas Richard Davies (2008) claims that earlier INGO campaigns—such as the one for disarmament in the 1920s—could mobilize a greater number of persons than even the most powerful movements that arose in the time after World War II.

INGOS are not only handicapped by their overall membership not having expanded with their greater numbers. They are handicapped also by the fact that their membership is not representative of the world population as a whole. It is even not representative of all layers of society within a single state. INGOs have their social base mostly in the upper ranks of wealthy societies. They exude an aura that ranges from duty-bound, aristocratic "noblesse oblige" or benevolent paternalism, to a missionary zeal to convert uninformed outsiders to the true religion.[4]

Their relatively narrow social base handicaps INGOs. The influence of each of them might also be reduced because the number of INGOs is now much greater than it had been in the past. This plurality implies a certain splintering of political energy. That is aggravated by the great variance among them. They diverge from another due to different membership, different aims and the different ways of operating.

One thus should beware of subsuming all of INGOs in just one group, so as if all were similar.

- *CONGOs* are government-operated INGOs. They may have been set up either to hide the governmental character of their activities and/or so as to attract outside funding.
- *DONGOs* are INGOs organized by one or several countries that provide development assistance.
- *QUANGOs* are quasi-autonomous, non-governmental organizations. We already had mentioned one such organization in the previous chapter, namely the International Electro-Technical Commission. States are not members of such organizations, but they may be represented in them by persons or institutions that are non-governmental. While fulfilling governmental functions, QUANGOs are nonetheless independent from governments in their decision-making.

Most prominent among the QUANGOs is the International Committee of the Red Cross (ICRC). It has gained the status of a veritable subject of international law, being able to act on the same legal level as states. The ICRC might even be seen as some sort of nascent supra-national entity with an authority not just comparable to the one of states, but with authority *over* states.

ENGOs are environmental INGOs such as Greenpeace, Global 2000, or the World Wildlife Fund.

Helsinki Watch Committees were established with the aim to monitor the implementation of the human rights provisions of the 1975 Helsinki Accords.[5]

Transparency International, founded by a retired World Bank staff member, has put the spotlight on the bane of corruption. Transparency International produces a much-respected international index that ranks states according to the relative lack, or the relative prevalence of corruption.

Amnesty International has made widely visible violations of human rights and has effectively mobilized against such abuse. Its country reports provide detailed accounts on the state of human rights in nearly all states of the world. These reports carry greater credibility and weight than pronouncements even of the UN Human Rights Council.

There are INGOs that are *relief-oriented,* such as Médecins sans Frontières, or that are *development-oriented* such as the INGOs that support micro-finance schemes in poor countries.

The World Bank divides between INGOs that are *operational* (mainly in the field of development assistance); and those that act as *advocacy groups* (Save the Rain Forest).

While some of the INGOs are very critical of governments and even confrontational, others thrive through cooperation with governments. Some are even financed by governments—at least in parts. Médecins sans Frontières obtains nearly half of its income from government sources. The (Christian) faith-based organization "One World Vision" got 55 percent of the finances for its development assistance programs from US government.

Such use of INGOs by governments might become problematic when the work so subsidized by a government is highly political. A case in point is the US support for Ukrainian NGOs in the run up to the so-called Orange Revolution of 2004, which brought about a "pro-Western" change of government. It is alleged that the United States transferred to politically active Ukrainian INGOs no less than US$ 200 million[6] to support their campaign for political change. That is no paltry sum. Yet this investment of the United States in INGO proxies might prove counterproductive in the long run. Instead of providing a firmer base to the new government, the assistance from abroad might have tainted this Ukraine government with the suspicion of representing foreign interests and not the "authentic" Ukraine. The support of the US government might also damage the reputation of several INGO that were active in this campaign as it casts doubt on their independence and objectivity.

Overall, such drawbacks resulting from cooperation between governments and INGOs are, however, more than balanced by advantages that generally accrue to both sides. Governments may benefit from those advantages that are associated with outsourcing in general. Outsourcing of governmental functions to private organizations often permits greater flexibility in the use of money. It tends to reduce some costs of operation. Outsourcing can also result in a certain "de-politization" of activities. They are no longer seen as reflecting governmental policy and purposes. That is significant especially in the realm of official development assistance. Official development assistance provided by one government to a government in a less developed country is inevitably linked to politics. Political considerations, such as strategic military ones, enter the decisions as to who gets what and at which conditions.

Assistance channeled through INGOs, on the other hand, may escape those constraints and can prioritize the actual development impact of projects instead. It is thus more likely that such projects will not just be of a nature to please the president of the recipient country or its military, but that they will benefit its population. Development assistance administered by INGOs may, in fact, simply bypass governments in recipient countries. Not a few of these governments are inefficient and corrupt. Even if they are not, they tend to favor "top-down" economic and social development, whereas most experts consider development to be a "bottom-up" process, contingent on the "empowerment" of smaller communities. INGOs find it easier than official governmental institutions to promote such a "bottom-up" development process.

Why then are INGOs able to influence politics? What is their base of power? To answer that, let us first ask for the political base of an entity with a longer history. What is the political base of states? States rest on the political base of a consensus of their subjects/citizens. These have either elected their representatives and governors; or they at least tolerate them by failing to overthrow them. States thus rest on a "polity"; they rest on a political community. This community is recognized as such by those who are part of it, and it is recognized as a distinct community by outsiders.[7] This polity has emerged due to past history; due to a comparatively intense internal economic interchange; due to a dense web of intrastate communication of all sorts; and due to shared values and tasks. It is the base in a polity that makes states legitimate.

But what makes INGOs legitimate? True—easier communication has now facilitated the trans-frontier bonding of individuals who fight for the same cause. That makes for a sense of commonality just as a sense of commonality unites the citizens of a state. Those who participate in such a global web organized by an INGO can also provide it with material resources. Unlike governments, INGOs cannot impose taxes. But like governments they can raise money for their purposes. They have no army or police. Nonetheless they do have means to impress on others their views and interests.

Humans now find it easier to organize politically also on a global level. We therefore witness the emergence of a global polity that stands next to the polity of citizens contained within the bounds of states. Events organized by INGOs at the fringes of big international conferences are proof for that. Delegates to these INGO meetings frequently outnumber the number of delegates that represent their respective states at such meetings. Nor are the two types of meetings simply in parallel, without any exchange taking place between them. At the World Bank/IMF annual meetings, a full day is usually given to encounters and discussions between the two sides. In the time between such major conferences, INGOs are routinely consulted by international organizations. They have provided substantial input, for example, in the articulation of criteria for sustainable development that projects of major international development banks have to meet.

Yet with all these activities and with all of their resources, INGOs still represent a part of the political spectrum only. They fight for values and interests that are specific to some groups and not to others. States however, have to deal with many such groups in their internal politics. Trade unions press for higher wages. Industrialists exert pressure in the other direction. Environmental groups seek to preserve the purity of environment whereas farmers want to exploit the land. Utility companies want to build nuclear power plants; while citizens object in those communities where such nuclear power plants should be located; and so on. It is the duty of governments to reconcile these conflicting views. Governments must also take account of the views and wishes of the vast majority of citizens who are not represented by any of those groups. Periodic elections test the efficacy of governments in doing this job of consensus building and of reconciling conflicting views and interests. Elections also test whether governments have been effective in representing all of the polity of their state.

A world state or world government does not exist so as to do that job on a global level. No worldwide institutions and organizations are in place that could reconcile all conflicting views and interests that clamor to have a voice in global governance. There is no world government because the global polity, such as is exists, is fractured and diverse.

The preamble of the Charter of the United Nations—written by an American poet—wants us to see it otherwise: "We—the peoples of the United Nations...." The preamble thus wants to convey the notion of a single global polity that would transcend and obliterate national boundaries. Against that claim we have to hold the reality of a world in which the rich are separated from the poor by a chasm as wide as never before in human history; the reality of a world in which identity politics and narrow nationalism are virulent still. Who when asked for his identity will respond by saying: "I am a citizen of the world?"[8]

And yet: are we not witness, at the same time, of a worldwide consensus emerging in answer to the most urgent problems that afflict people of the world regardless of the state and the regime under which they live? And does that consensus not find expression in some of those big political projects that have been pushed by INGOs worldwide?

Development assistance: governments in wealthy countries no longer have the discretion to either provide it or not to provide it. A global polity leaves them no choice but to share resources with the poorest of the world.

Preserving the global commons—environmental protection: Interests diverge widely in this realm, as is evident in the battle over the implementation and extension of the "Kyoto Protocol" to limit the emission of greenhouse gases. But in principle and here too, governments no longer have the option to simply absent themselves from such global efforts.[9]

Disarmament, and particularly disarmament in weapons of mass destruction: There is pressure on governments to proceed in this direction. They might manage to ignore that pressure and continue to develop and produce nuclear arms. They might successfully secure internal political support for their ambition by stocking national fears and flattering national vanities. But in the long run, they have to pay lip service at least to this common goal of banning weapons of mass destruction.

Most basic, though, is the fact that *the option of simply refusing all cooperation is foreclosed.* States can no longer withdraw into the cocoon of national self-sufficiency. That option has failed when tried by rich states—such as the United States under the administration of George W. Bush, as it has failed when employed by weak states, such as North Korea.

This then is the core issue in global governance: how to reconcile, on a global level, the conflicting claims of nations and INGOs and how to do that in absence of an all-powerful, worldwide governing institution; how to do this in absence of a single strong and coherent global "polity"; and how to translate into action that nascent sense of a global commonality that emerges on some of the most pressing global problems?

In all of these reflections on a global polity and on the nature and impact of INGOs, we have, till now, studiously ignored one unpleasant fact. We have made it appear that non-governmental groups that impact on global governance would all be motivated by some altruistic motives so as to improve the lot of mankind. But there are plenty of internationally active non-governmental organizations that respond to different motives.

Take religions and their splinter groups. They work for salvation and for the afterlife. To various extents, they might also be involved on this side of eternity. They might devote considerable energy to help fellow humans. But even for those global religious groups that do a lot of charitable work, this is but adjunct to their main mission, which is a religious, non-material one. So it is problematic to consider them in the same group as INGOs that concentrate on this world and not on the afterlife.

Nonetheless, we would unduly deplete the ranks of constructive INGOs if we ignored religious organizations such as the Catholic Relief Service, CARITAS, or the Quakers with their deep commitment to humanitarian causes. But religions and their global activities are very diverse. The role of some can become divisive. Should one respectfully recognize as global players small religious sects such as the Scientologists,[10] or the radical Catholic organization Opus Dei? It is difficult not to take account of the substantial and often international charitable activities of Muslims. But should that imply that we also recognize as international partners the Muslim Brotherhood, which undermines governments with its claim for a world order not based on states but on faith? And if we recognize and duly cooperate with the Muslim Brothers, should we also deal in the same manner with its even more radical offspring, such as Hamas?

Evidently, there are a number of globally active international organizations that are more or less indifferent to worldly affairs. But over and above that, there are quite a number of international organizations motivated by overtly pernicious goals. Among them, international criminal cartels such as the Colombian drug cartels or the Mafia are the most notorious.

The groups of pirates on the coast of Somalia[11] are international in their activities. They are financed by some sort of venture capitalists in Arab countries. Their targets are international—of course—and their activities impact on international trade and on global security. Are these groups part of global governance or do they pose just one of the many problems global governance should tackle?

While the answer for the pirates is obvious, it is less obvious for some of the terrorist groups that pursue political goals. Hamas, which rules in Gaza, and Hezbollah, which rules parts of Lebanon, have been defined as terrorist groups. But no lasting solutions to problems in Palestine and in the Lebanon could be found without them being involved. We are constantly admonished not to recognize terrorist groups, and not to negotiate with them. But that will not make them go away. As most of them cannot be eliminated by the military or the police, one will have to deal with them in other ways. In that sense, they are INGOs just as much as "CARE" or "Greenpeace."

Nations without a state are a special kind of INGO. If we were to define a nation exclusively by the language used by its members we would arrive at a very large number of such nations. About 6,000 different languages are being spoken worldwide. The United Nations, though, only count 192 member states. That would make for 5,808 nations without state. Fortunately, we are far removed from that. We only consider as "nations without a state" those that have gained a high degree of global/international presence and still lack a proper state. The Palestinians are the best known among this group; as were the Zionists before the international recognition of the State of Israel in 1947. The Sahraouis (inhabitants of former Spanish Morocco) gained solid international support for their project of national independence (from Morocco) but moved ever further from realizing that dream due to the lack of serious international pressure on the Morocco government. The Tamil secessionists in the north of Sri Lanka (formerly Ceylon) found wide support among the Tamil diaspora. They were certainly among the international players till the Sri Lankan army crushed their military arm in 2009.

Not just the Tamil diaspora had gained global relevance. So has the diaspora of several states that also had sent large waves of emigrants abroad. Such a diaspora might enter the international scene in accordance with the government of their original home country. But it may also do that with an agenda of its own. Irish-Americans gave money and political support to the terrorist IRA that fought for the annexation by Ireland of the northern part of Ireland (which is under the rule of the United Kingdom). Croatians expatriates in Canada supported Croat nationalists in their struggle for independence from Yugoslavia and in the subsequent war against Serbia; just as the worldwide Armenian diaspora supported

Armenia in its war against Azerbaijan; and just as the AIPAC—American Israeli Political Action Committee—tends to support the most unyielding parts of the political spectrum in Israel. One can thus conclude that such diasporas are potent global actors; and that, more often than not, they are more nationalist and radical than those of their former co-nationals still living in their home country.

Discussions on the role of INGOs remain mostly mute on those more problematic INGOs, ignoring both their very real impact on global affairs; as well as the need to take account of them and involve them in a political process.

As we have noted, INGOs with their impact on international relations and global governance are not completely recent. On some issues, like slavery and female emancipation, they had an important say in the 19th century already. What is new, though, is the great diversity of INGOs and the great diversity of subjects they care about and address. New are also the methods of mobilization and communication used by them.

But the main difference to the past lies in the way INGOs have by now become involved in global governance. No longer are they mere, one-issue lobby groups that act on and through governments. They have become independent global actors with immediate and direct impact on global governance. They are directly involved in establishing its agenda; with setting the rules; and with enforcing them. We will analyze this their new function in one of the latter chapters of this book.

Notes

1. Some maintained that this was due to a "Dracula effect." Just as Count Dracula could survive in the dark of the night only, and would to die if hit by daylight; so this treaty too, could survive only in the closed atmosphere of secret negotiations, and withered when made public.
2. Prior to that, she had been a very successful secretary-general of the Council of Europe.
3. Quoted after Wikipedia, "Multilateral Agreement on Investment."
4. In my career, I had to deal with some Austrian non-governmental organizations involved in development assistance. They had been effective politically. Their moral fervor and engagement had put the question of help to the poorer countries on the political agenda and it kept it there. They had managed to pressure a laggard administration into greater efforts in this field. They stood behind many of the more successful aid projects.

    But, on occasion, their fervor and engagement made me suspect that it had its origin in a certain dissatisfaction with, and even estrangement from, their own societies. Some of their projects made me wonder whether they were not motivated by a desire to realize in poorer countries the dream of a simpler, more authentic life, not shaped by the race for competitive consumption and shaped by the pressure for a maximum of money income; so as if these NGOs were seeking the vicarious satisfaction of overcoming in poorer countries the economic and social order that had proven so very resilient at home. Not surprisingly, such dreams were destined to be disappointed.

We should take such dreams as what they are. They might be impractical and unrealistic. But they are not irrelevant. We should not judge them on their operational value but see them as part of a necessary utopian enterprise. Political entrepreneurs who articulate and propagate such visions have been essential in moving history forward. By reaching for the unrealistic and impractical, they have created room for stepwise progress. A vision of utopia is necessary so as to keep politics open and fluid and to prevent a sclerotization of politics and of society.

5.   In then still communist Czechoslovakia, this was the function of Charta 77—a grouping of political dissidents. In 1989, Charta 77 had a prominent role in the transition from communist to democratic rule.

6.   According to the *New York Times*.

7.   See also Karl Marx's notion of a "Klasse an sich" and "Klasse für sich."

8.   After more than 50 years of European integration, even Europeans will answer the same question not by saying: "I am European." They will answer instead by affirming their identity as French, Austrians, Slovenes, etc.

9.   Not whales, but whale hunting nations are destined to decline in numbers.

10. ....which Europeans regard with deep skepticism, fearing "Scientology" to seek a totalitarian hold over its adherents.

11. More precisely: the breakaway "Puntland" part of former Somalia.

14

Public Opinion and Foreign Policy Elites

"Governments were meant to deal with governments, not with private individuals or opinions of foreign society."
—*The Education of Henry Adams, 1995*

At the dawn of modern diplomacy, in the 17th century, it was clear who the sovereigns were whom diplomats had to serve. It was the rulers—the princes. Their subjects had no voice in affairs of state and certainly no voice in the dealings with other princes.

Yet by the end of the 18th century, these subjects had begun to revolt. They did so first in France and in the United States and then, over the next 200 years, in much of the remaining Americas and Europe. The absolute rulers were first reigned in and then replaced by democracies.

Citizens came to claim the role as the true sovereigns. Those who governed would be there to execute their will. Constitutions expressly assign to the citizens that role as sovereigns with parliaments there to represent them and with governments, on their turn, being subservient to parliaments. At least in a formal-legal sense and according to the text of constitutions, that holds true also for dealings between states. In this field too, citizens would ultimately be in charge.

These abstract rules of constitutions might please crowds and flatter their self-esteem, making them feel to be the true masters in a realm that, earlier on, had been the preserve of a narrow elite. Such sentiments find their correspondence in laws that ascribe to elected parliamentarians a say not just in internal policy, but also in external affairs. In order for international treaties to become effective, for example, most constitutions demand them to be approved by parliament. Qualified majorities are required for a formal declaration of war.[1] Foreign policy is also tied to parliamentary approval in less direct ways. In parliamentary democracies, foreign ministers are responsible to parliaments and could be dismissed by a vote of non-confidence in case a majority of deputies should become displeased with their performance. Parliaments also have to approve expenditures associated with activities carried out by these ministers. If they want to use it, this power over purse strings is a potent one.[2]

But even with these powers, parliaments have not become the institutions with the greatest say in shaping international relations. In the realm of internal politics, the reign of the parliaments might be tighter. But they have lesser influence on issues of foreign relations and of global governance. Here, the ministers in charge of these issues, as well as their diplomats will act with greater independence.

This greater independence from the parliaments is inevitable and necessary, given the nature of diplomacy. Diplomats deal with persons and institutions that are beyond the reach of purely national politics. Voters in state A cannot determine the position of those negotiating for state B. They have a say on what happens within the borders of their state; but only rarely will they be able to directly influence events and polices in other states. They are even unable to tightly control the diplomats negotiating on behalf of their own state. The result of negotiations between state A and state B will be shaped by mutual compromise. The outcome will not be determined exclusively by just one of the two states. Furthermore, the diplomats involved in such negotiations need a certain leeway. If they are to succeed, they cannot follow a strict script handed to them before by parliament.

But parliament's power is also limited in a more fundamental way. The outside world now penetrates deeply into a realm that formerly was the exclusive fief of internal politics. National politics has to accept that the number of issues is growing which are not under its sole grasp and influence. National politics would, of course, prefer to have a say on whatever impacts on the life of citizens. But in this it will be frustrated by the ever-stronger impact of things that swap across borders.

Yet if we stay within this narrower realm in which nations may continue to shape international/global affairs, we still have to consider whether it would be wise to grant the public a stronger say. How directly can and should parliaments, how directly should the public be involved in such decisions on international/global issues?

Ever since democracies came to exist, the battle over this question has moved to and fro. At the end of the 18th century, the framers of the US constitution reacted against what they perceived to be the egocentric policies of European princes, indifferent toward the wishes and the well-being of common people and involving their countries in endless wars. As the "framers" of the US constitution saw it, a commonwealth where citizens would have greater say in external relations, would be more peaceful and would better serve the interests of all. Over the next century, the notion persisted in the American public that the US political system would be superior to, and thus would prevail over, the decadent European one, because the American political system was more open, and American citizens had a more direct control not just over internal affairs, but over external relations[3] too.

Indeed, World War I seemed to justify US reservations toward this European system, where external politics were conducted among elites and in secret. The US public could point to generals and diplomats in Europe who had secretly longed for, and schemed for, that war. Treaties negotiated by diplomats behind closed doors had made for a mechanism that, in the end, had made this war occur as if by necessity. They had left in the dark the public who then had to pay a high price for the arrogance and insolence of their ambassadors and generals. At first sight, this would seem to validate the notion that it is prudent to involve the public in diplomacy. This public would prefer peace and compromise and therefore would effectively neutralize the military and the diplomats who had been lusting for confrontation.

But the story of the virtue of masses and of the irresponsibility of elites is not that straightforward. All over Europe not just the elites, but the "masses" too, had greeted the outbreak of the Great War with jubilation. That mood had not changed even after the war had continued for three years and as millions of soldiers had already been shredded in the mud of the trenches.

In the United States of the 19th century too, we lack consistent prove for the peace enhancing effect of public participation in international relations. The senseless 1812 war against the United Kingdom was very popular, as were the wars against Mexico and Spain.

Immediately after the World War I, the *anti-elitists* had the upper hand. Diplomacy had to be in public view. International covenants should be "open and openly arrived at." The peace treaties of 1919 were negotiated that way. Citizens in the countries of the victorious Allies were well satisfied with these new arrangements. In politics driven by public opinion in the victorious countries, responsibility for the war was assigned to the losers—the Central Powers—exclusively. Very much to the delight of the population in victorious Allied countries, the losers were saddled with the penalty of heavy political and financial burdens.

Secret diplomacy had discredited itself as it had facilitated the outbreak of the war. But the consequences of this new and more public form of conducting international relations were not that gratifying either. The harsh treatment meted out to the losers of the war helped to prepare the ground for the next world war. One can rightly wonder if events in the 20th century would have taken another course, would the negotiations for a "Post World War One Order" have been conducted not in the glare of the public, but by diplomats and in secret.

Traditional diplomacy has internalized the rule not to hit an opponent that has been beaten to the ground already. At the dawn of the 19th century, one had not inflicted such humiliation on France when the Congress of Vienna prepared for a new European order after victory over Napoleon. That wisdom paid off in the form of long enduring peace in the first half of the 19th century. Hundred years later, in the peace negotiations after World War I, pressure from the public made it impossible to follow the same sound policy of not overly exploiting the victory over an opponent.

With serious difficulties and conflicts building up in the 1920s and the 1930s, the notion of diplomacy being conducted in the public lost much of its attraction again. So did associated notions and institutions such as the League of Nations, established to make wars impossible. They slid into oblivion. The consecutive years were again dominated by the advocates of diplomatic discretion and secrecy. Hans Morgenthau and his *Politics Among Nations* became the intellectual point of reference with his legitimization of traditional and discrete diplomacy. The newly created United Nations paid lip service only to the ideal of the public, of the "people" being in control. In fact, the United Nations Charter charged a directorate of five major powers (the permanent members of the Security Council) with guarding the "Post World War Two" order. This was almost a return to a set up established 150 years earlier at the Congress of Vienna by the creation of a *concert of nations*, with five major powers safeguarding stability. Traditional diplomacy saw itself rehabilitated and upheld in its claims for being shielded from public opinion.

Today, the issue is not as to whether we should accept the claims made for the superiority of secret, big power diplomacy. It is obvious, that it has become impossible to conduct diplomacy and shape international relations in secret and behind the back of the public. Governments are forced to accept the public as an important actor in international relations.

Democratic governments try to sway public opinion to support their policies. In doing that, they use various means—from plump propaganda to subtle, behind-the-scenes influence on opinion makers. The public, on the other hand, has frequently become mobilized on international/global issues. At some instances, it has pressured governments into a drastic reversal of policies. But on other occasions, the public has failed in such attempts as it could not effect such a turnaround of official foreign and security policies.

The US public was successful, for example, in forcing the US government to withdraw its military from Vietnam and to concede victory to the Communists. Without such pressure from the public, the US political establishment would not have been ready to accept a humiliating failure. A repeat of that occurred 30 years later with the US public raising the pressure for an early disengagement from the quagmire the United States itself had created in Iraq.

But at other instances, the pressure of public opinion was not that successful because the sentiments were not as strong and as widely shared as they were in the rejection of the engagement in Vietnam and in Iraq. The European movement for unilateral nuclear disarmament could not force the United Kingdom or France into destroying their—sizeable—nuclear arsenals. In the United States, a broad mobilization of the public could not oblige government to take more effective steps so as to halt human slaughter in the Darfur province of Sudan. Therefore, the record is mixed on the public actually affecting security- and foreign policies.

But the same holds true also for efforts made in the other direction by governments with the intent of swaying public opinion in favor of its policies. Frequently, such efforts by governments were in vain as they could not alter public opinion. And it is not clear at all whether it would have been better if governments would have succeeded in bringing the public on their side. Again the case of Iraq is instructive. In a wave of shrill nationalism, the US public went along with government for a while without casting doubt even on the most blatant incongruities served up by US spin doctors—such as the claim that the war was necessary so as to eliminate weapons of mass destruction hidden in Iraq. As France opposed the war, France and the French were vilified. In the cafeteria of the US Congress, "french fries" were renamed "freedom fries." But in the end, such propaganda and such manipulations were too much at odds with facts. They could not prevent the turn of public opinion against a continuation of the war.

All this raises the question as to whether in foreign affairs—in the long run and on the average—the public is wiser than the elites; or whether it is the other way round. As we have seen, the answer provided by history is a mixed one. So let us search for an answer from political science. At periodic intervals, the Chicago Council on Global Affairs does opinion polls on international issues. Many such polls are taken in other countries too, but the Chicago one is unique inasmuch as it differentiates between the opinion of US foreign policy elites and the opinion held by the rest of the US population.

These polls show that on economic issues, the public is less internationalist than the elites. It is more inclined to shield the US market from foreign competition and less enamored, in general, with the globalization of the economy. But otherwise the US public is more internationalist than the elites. It provides stronger support for the United Nations, and stronger support too, for international development assistance to the poorer countries. Most significant, though, is the divergence with elite opinion on questions of war and peace. In the general public, there is a strong aversion against the use of the military in foreign relations. To quote from the sum-up on the Chicago poll done in 2008:

"Americans support a number of changes in foreign policy including talking to enemies, making a deal with Iran, setting a timetable to withdraw forces from Iraq, using force against terrorist groups operating in Pakistan, participating in a new climate change treaty, and generally pursuing a more multilateral approach to U.S. foreign policy."

This finding dovetails with one that has been tested repeatedly and that is now accepted as established truth. In democracies, where elites depend on the public, wars are rare. Democracies do not wage war against each other. Qualifiers had to be added to this finding, such as the qualifier that the finding holds true for established democracies only and not for young ones; or that the peacefulness is more the result of wealth that is typical for the vast majority of democracies. Nonetheless the conclusion remains valid: wars have become less likely where citizens have a greater say in foreign policy.

The public as such is also less likely than elites to be swayed by lobbies that have a heightened interest in this or that issue. Unlike "AIPAC—the American Israeli Political Action Committee," the US public does not call for a bombing of Iran; and unlike the lobby of rich Cuban exiles in Florida, it does not wish for a continuation of an aggressively hostile policy toward the communist regime in Cuba. In a similar vein and on another continent, it is doubtful whether in France the public would have truly supported the decision of government to officially recognize as genocide the slaughter of Armenians at the hand of Turks that occurred in the early days of the Turkish Republic. This decision by France had been urged by the Armenian diaspora in France, but it has damaged relations with Turkey. We conclude therefore that the public as such is generally in support of continuity and moderation; and more so than diverse elites and lobbies that attempt to influence foreign policy.

Nonetheless, elitists still maintain their claim for an exclusive say over foreign and security policy by pronouncing the public not fit to be heard and included in decision-making. The public would be ill informed about international affairs, and therefore would lack a basis for sound judgment. That is certainly true. Polls reveal astounding gaps in even basic information on international matters. But that applies equally to most issues of internal politics. Polls establish the same amount of knowledge or ignorance on both internal and external affairs; and the same amount of interest or lack of interest. The public is not less interested in international affairs than it is interested in purely national politics. Nonetheless, few politicians would dare to exempt the public from any say on internal policies just because it lacks precise knowledge on issues up for decision.

There will always exist a gap between the perceptions, opinions, and preferences of the public, and the actual policies and actions of governments. But in international/global affairs this gap is wider than the gap that exists when issues of internal politics are at stake. Yet this is due not to an indolence of the public that would be diffident to everything beyond the narrow borders of the state. This gap between public perceptions, opinions, and preferences on one side, and actual politics on the other side is due to the very nature of international politics.

As we had noted on the outset, it is in the nature of external affairs that they adapt less easily to national political preferences than do internal matters. That is bad news and would oblige politicians to convey back to their voters the impression of being pretty powerless in attempts to influence events that occur outside the borders of their country. There are few things politicians loath more than having to concede to a lack of influence. So they hide this impotence behind empty posturing: "Iran will not be allowed to have nuclear weapons" so as if that really could be prevented by means actually available to the United States; or—for the case of Austria—"we will stand in the way of more nuclear power plants coming on line in Europe"—so as if that could be prevented by an Austrian veto over the decisions of other European countries. In a similar vein, politicians are disinclined to clearly inform their public about the concessions they were forced to make in international settings.[4] Austrian members of government, for example, often hide from their voters unpopular decisions they had agreed to in the Councils of the European Union.

The distance between public opinion and the international reality is thus made wider not due to failures of this public, but by the failure of politicians who do not do what is demanded of them: to explain their decision at international venues and to convey back to voters the motives and pressures that had made them decide this way and not the other one. That widening of the gap is detrimental to effort to establish a popular basis for global governance. It is detrimental too, to national politicians who will see their repute and credibility undermined in the long run.

Yet this transmission belt from the public *via their governments* to the international realm is still the most important one by far. It is the one that has to carry the greatest load of transactions. It is not at least because of failures in this most relevant of all such "transmission belts" that other such mechanisms of transmission have gained in relevance.

As it stands now, there are three ways the public and the public's opinion can impact on international relations:

1) Via the governments that are in office; thanks to the decisions made by voters in elections.

2) Via their representatives in parliaments.

3) And directly, by bypassing both governments and parliaments— with an impact immediately on other international actors. This may be done either by individuals acting alone; or with greater effect, by formal or informal, transnational groups that have been established to influence international politics.

We have already discussed the impact of international non-governmental organizations on global governance. So let us then, in the following chapter, deal with the influence parliaments have on foreign affairs—either via their own governments; or directly by becoming themselves actors on the global scene.

Notes

1. An oddity, since the times are long past when wars started with a formal declaration of war.

2. Lately, parliaments and parliamentarians have also entered the international scene in a more direct way. On occasions, they have become independent international actors themselves and we shall have a look at this remarkable development in the next chapter.

3. In parts at least, that sentiment of an inherent superiority is present still in today's United States.

4. The most prominent example: the failure of the J. F. Kennedy administration to inform the public of the fact, that the end of the "Cuban Missile Crisis" had also been brought about by the US concession to withdraw US medium-range nuclear missiles from Turkey. Instead, the end of the crisis was presented to the US public as a unilateral US victory, feeding a misguided sense of the US being almighty and able to face down any opponent.

15

Parliamentary Representation beyond the Borders

"I had been member of the budget committee both in the French Assemblé and in the European Parliament (i.e., the parliamentary body of the European Union). In the French Assemblé, I found it to be impossible to move a single franc from one budget position to another one. The Assemblé could not alter the budget submitted by government. In the European Parliament, I succeeded in moving literally millions of Euros from one budget position to another one."
　　　　　　　　　—*The French minister of European affairs, Alain Lamassoure, to the Austrian ambassador in 1996*

Parliaments were conceived to function as the sturdy bridge between citizens on one side, and on the other side the governments which actually administer a country. According to constitutional blueprints, parliaments should exercise that function also in the realm of the external relations of a country. Here too, parliaments should represent citizens and translate their wishes into instructions to the administration.

In theory, parliaments would therefore stand at the top in the hierarchy of state institutions. They would stand for the collective of citizens that became the new sovereign by replacing kings and princes. In practice though, the political role of most parliaments is limited to the function of a thermometer that registers public opinion in periodic elections. According to fictions of constitutional law, governments would be at the whim and mercy of parliaments. In practice it is the other way round. Parliaments are dominated by the executive branch.

This is so in most of Europe. It is different in the United States. Due to its history and due to the peculiarity its political institutions, the Congress (the Senate and the House of Representatives) provides a formidable counterweight to the American president and to his administration. That is true also in the field of foreign relations. The Senate Foreign Relations Committee and the House Committee on

Foreign Affairs have an important say in US foreign policy. They can block projects of the US administration and impose their own version of policies instead. They can do that even on issues that are essential in the whole system of global governance. The US Senate, for example, refused to ratify the Comprehensive Test Ban Treaty banning the testing of all nuclear warheads.[1] This treaty is a key part in international efforts to stop the proliferation of nuclear weapons. Its non-ratification by the US Senate has therefore handicapped efforts to establish an effective and worldwide barrier against the further spread of nuclear weapons. As the example demonstrates, foreign diplomats are well advised to get to know and stay in contact with US congressmen and senators who are members of these two committees that are so decisive in shaping the international relations of the United States.

Yet in nearly all other democracies, parliaments carry lesser political weight. That was true, in particular, for any weight they could bring to bear on the shaping of international relations and on global governance. While generally low, this actual foreign policy role of parliaments varied from country to country; it varied over times, and it varied with the issues that were at stake.

Up to quite recently, that made for a rather lukewarm interest of the Austrian parliament in foreign affairs. By the end of 1950s, all immediate, major, and still-open foreign policy issues of Austria had been settled. Full independence was regained in 1955. Relations with Germany and Italy had been normalized; and permanent neutrality had provided the country with a comfortable and secure position given the rigid stability of the East-West arrangements on the European continent.

That did not imply a wholly passive foreign policy role. Quite the contrary—that stability provided a secure base for the ambitious foreign policy forays of Austrian chancellor Bruno Kreisky; with his attempts to move things along in East-West relations;[2] with his search for new and common ground in the relations between wealthy and poor countries;[3] and with efforts to provide an impetus for a settlement of the conflict between Israelis and Palestinians.[4] The Austrian public and the Austrian parliament watched these forays of the chancellor with a mixture of pride and bewilderment. But in all of that, they definitely did not see a role for themselves.

In the years following, the Austrian parliament only entered the scene if and after the public had become emotionally engaged in an issue at stake in foreign relations: when, for example, Austrians were taken hostage in a foreign country; or when tabloids fanned fears about nuclear power stations in neighboring states; or when media and politicians played on century-old prejudices such as the traditionally tense relations between Austrians and Czechs. The emotionality of such debates stood in no proportion to their relevance in the wider field of global governance; and in no relation to the true foreign policy interests of Austria.

By now, external conditions have changed that before had permitted such smug introversion to persist. The demise of the Soviet empire, the rise of East Asia, the waning influence of the United States, the integration of Europe, and last not least the accelerating globalization have put an end to that old and stable world order. They have initiated a period of rapid transformation with unforeseen events, new chances, new risks, and repeated crises. The public has become acutely aware of the growing impact events in foreign countries have on their lives. This greater sensibility and realism of the public resonates in the corridors of parliaments. Unlike in the past, the engagement with foreign policy issues has acquired an aura of heightened political relevance.

As one of the consequences, parliaments and parliamentarians have begun to act in this field all by themselves and independent from foreign ministries and diplomats. Increasingly, parliamentarians have sought to influence events by becoming directly active in international/global affairs. Institutional arrangements are in place that facilitate their transcending the merely national level of politics.

The Inter-Parliamentary Union (IPU) provides such a forum for the international activities of parliamentarians. It is quite old, having been founded in 1889 already. If there were such a thing, the IPU would constitute the worldwide trade union of members of parliaments. The IPU thus deals with the working conditions of parliamentarians mainly and not very much with the foreign policy issues these parliamentarians have to address. Accordingly, the IPU is of limited political relevance.

Other more consequential venues for parliamentarians have come to exist much later. Immediately after World War II, the most prominent addition was the Parliamentary Assembly of the Council of Europe. It wields substantial political influence. Since then and especially over the last decades, the number of other venues and organizations has grown, that facilitate the direct involvement of parliamentarians in international affairs.

The arrangements vary:

a) according to the degree of independence from their government parliamentarians enjoy in these venues;

b) according to the higher or lower impact that work in those bodies will have on actual policies.

The following graph portrays these two dimensions:

Figure 15.1 Parliamentarians as Direct Actors in International Relations

Parliamentarians as direct actors in international relations

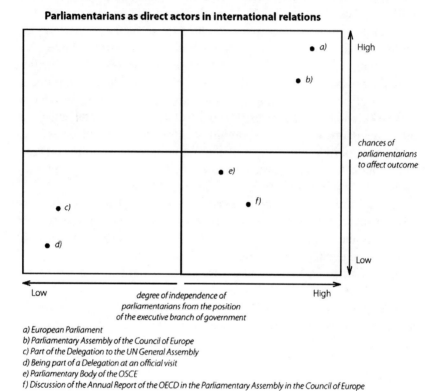

a) European Parliament
b) Parliamentary Assembly of the Council of Europe
c) Part of the Delegation to the UN General Assembly
d) Being part of a Delegation at an official visit
e) Parliamentary Body of the OSCE
f) Discussion of the Annual Report of the OECD in the Parliamentary Assembly in the Council of Europe

Figure 15.1 demonstrates that the historic development has been from the lower left corner to the upper right one. It went from a low independence and a low practical relevance, parliamentarians had in international affairs, to greater independence and greater practical relevance. The process seems to be driven by two motives. First by the motive of parliamentarians to actually do what they are elected for—namely to deal with issues that voters feel to be important, even if such issues originate from beyond the borders and/or can be solved in an international context only.

International institutions, on their turn, might wish for an added political legitimacy that the visible involvement of elected officials can provide to their work; narrowing what is described as the *democratic deficit* of such international bodies with their frequently weak links to national electorates.

Yet these are long-term, drawn-out processes and at the moment we are still faced with a wide array of arrangements that facilitate the participation of parliamentarians in international affairs.

1) *They become members of the national delegation at official visits to other states; or they become members of delegations dispatched to meetings of international organizations*:

Some states and Austria too, have made it routine to include parliamentarians in delegations sent to the annual meetings of the United Nations General Assembly in New York. These parliamentarians do not participate in the roll calls taken in the various committees of the General Assembly. That task is left to diplomats. But they do sit in these meetings; and they do have their voice in the morning briefings at the Austrian Delegation. The parliamentarians are chosen not just from the ranks of the governing parties. The parties of the opposition too, are given the chance to send deputies to attend the UN General Assembly.[5]

The participation at the General Assembly provides members of parliament with a unique opportunity to gain first-hand knowledge of the many fields of global governance the United Nations is involved in. It provides them with access too, to otherwise not accessible sources of information.

In a similar vein, parliamentarians have been included in delegations on occasion of official visits to other states. Whether that happened was dependent on the importance to Austria of the country visited; the relevance of issues that were raised during that visit; and last not least on the interest, track record and standing of the members of Parliament asked to join the delegation. Parliamentarians from border districts have thus, for example, become members of the Austrian delegation on visits to a country on the other side of the border.

2) *Special committees or assemblies for parliamentarians have been added on to international organizations.*

Over the last half of the century this has become routine. Hardly any of the major and politically relevant international organizations now lacks such a special forum for deputies from national parliaments; a prominent example being the OSCE—the Organization for Security and Cooperation in Europe.[6] But even some minor, sub-regional bodies (such as the Central European Initiative—CEI) have established such a forum for parliamentarians. These parliamentary bodies are mostly consultative. Unlike the Boards or the Assemblies of international organizations, they cannot issue binding decisions. Still, they do carry political weight, not least because more than diplomats, parliamentarians feel free to speak their mind and to call a spade a spade.

Some international organizations use existing international parliamentary bodies to gain for themselves such added political legitimacy and political echo. The Parliamentary Assembly of the Council of Europe (CoE) fulfills that task for two international organizations I worked for; namely for the Organization for Economic Co-Operation and Development (OECD); and for the European Bank for Reconstruction and Development (EBRD).

For the latter, the involvement of the Parliamentary Assembly of the CoE was not that deep. It boiled down to a daylong visit of a small parliamentary delegation to EBRD headquarters in London, with the first half of the day spent in discussions with the president and with the vice presidents of the Bank; while in the second half of the day parliamentarians were free to seek information from other top officers of the Bank.

As behooves in view of the wide scope of its work, the OECD came in for closer scrutiny. Before appearing there in person, the secretary-general of the OECD had already provided the Parliamentary Assembly of the Council of Europe with a written report on the activities of his organization. He dwelt on its main points in a speech before the Assembly and then had to stand through an extended period of frequently critical questioning. The gain was, I believe, on both sides, with parliamentarians being informed on salient economic and social developments; and with the OECD secretary-general becoming aware of political imperatives his organization should heed in its work.

3)   In purely legal terms, the Parliamentary Assembly of the Council of Europe would have consultative functions[7] only. But in reality it is more powerful. In its composition, it mirrors the political composition in member states' parliaments.[8] This makes for a rather direct linkage to the political reality back home. Members of the Council of Europe's Parliamentary Assembly do not lack self-confidence and they are eager to strike out on their own. The Assembly and not the Council of Ministers had thus

been instrumental in some of the more relevant initiatives of the Council of Europe. The most noteworthy among them was the establishment of an effective, supra-national mechanism for the protection of human rights. The Assembly also took a leading role in the suspension of the membership of European states that had reverted from democratic to authoritarian rule—something the Board, staffed by diplomats, would have been loath to do.

4) The European Parliament of the European Union with its directly elected deputies is a fully fledged parliament already with true powers to decide and direct.

The European Union is, of course, no longer a simple international organization but an institution half way between such an organization and a federal state. It is noteworthy that the consolidation and strengthening of the Union had been accompanied—and advanced—by the constant rise of the power and prestige of its parliament. It was not always that high. For quite some time, elected politicians regarded a function there as a second choice and would have preferred a seat in their national parliaments. No longer is this the case. The realization that members of the European parliament may wield substantial influence was instrumental in this reversal of preferences.

As mentioned, the Parliament of the European Union is not typical for other parliamentary bodies attached to international organizations. These are less powerful. Nonetheless the Union is often seen as a model that other international organizations would like to emulate. This will not be easy and that would take some time. But is it unlikely in the long run? The present position and influence that the European Parliament has gained could mark a target other parliamentary bodies attached to international organizations might move closer to in the long run. One day, in the still distant future, parliamentarians may have found that they may address problems on an international level more effectively than they can do when working in the settings of purely national parliamentary assemblies.

Such stronger international engagement might help parliaments to escape from under the dominance of governments and might help them to regain at least some of the status and power constitutions had formally assigned to them. Going international, they could shed the factual restrictions imposed on them in most parliamentary democracies. They might escape into an international realm of greater freedom from the executive branch of government; and could then reimport this greater freedom back into their native political system.[9]

Practice in the Parliamentary Assembly of the Council of Europe provides an example for such a "feedback loop." Governments may largely control these deputies in their own, national parliament. But governments have lesser control once these deputies sit in the Parliamentary Assembly in Strasbourg. There, they do not always vote in conformity with their own government's policies.[10] Frequently, they tend to vote in line with the votes of politically like-minded deputies from other countries.[11] Back in their home country, it will not be easy for them to dissociate themselves from their vote in Strasbourg, even if that vote did not fit with their governments' policies.

How has that growing international role of parliaments affected diplomacy and what, at present, is the administrative interface between these two spheres of traditional diplomacy on one hand and of parliamentary diplomacy on the other?

a)   On the most basic level, diplomats help parliaments in a practical way. They arrange for international meetings, facilitate travel, prepare the way for parliamentary fact-finding missions, clear questions of protocol and access (for example, in intended visits to prisons) etc. Some of that work might be shared with the nascent foreign offices parliaments have established themselves. But as these offices do not have the same broad international presence as ministries of foreign affairs, the latter will become involved more often than not.

b)   Diplomats provide help in smoothing relations between parliaments and the ministries and ministers of foreign affairs. It is common for high-ranking diplomats to appear in hearings before the foreign affairs committees or to supply these committees with written information. If the president of the parliament or if a delegation of parliamentarians set out on official visits, they are, as a rule, provided by the diplomatic service with information on the situation in the country they are about to visit; and on issues that are likely to be raised once they are there.

c)   Diplomats also become involved in the substance of the international activities of parliaments. They do not just deal with the administrative tasks that surround these activities; and they do not just act as representatives of the minister and of their bureaucracy in providing information to parliaments. They become expert-servants to the parliamentarians and help them in formulating and implementing *their* version of foreign policy. Diplomats may be seconded to the parliament for special tasks; or they might be seconded to participate in specific missions (as for example in fact-finding in troubled regions). They might be seconded as foreign policy experts to the caucus of a party represented in parliament, etc.

d) Increasingly, parliamentarians have an input into the web of global governance. Parliaments are thus one of the many new actors which, next to states, shape global governance. The warps and woofs of an input provided by them, as by so many other new global agents, still have to be configured into one coherent fabric. That fabric has to be constantly adjusted to changed circumstances and requirements. Diplomats are not the only one at work in this process of consolidation and adjustment. But they are crucial facilitators.

How does all of that impact on traditional diplomacy? At first sight, the gain of terrain made by parliaments seems to narrow the turf of diplomacy. One would tend to assume that, as parliaments obtain greater say in international affairs this would automatically diminish the role of diplomacy. But such a judgment would be based on a zero-sum view of the issue with the gain of one side bringing automatically a loss to the other side.

Two facts militate against such a zero-sum view.

- First, the whole field is expanding, and with it the tasks incumbent on each of the two sides.
- Second, each of the two sides uses different tools and is bound by different rules and traditions. Each side is imbedded in different national and international networks.

This is why the two sides are not involved in senseless, zero-sum battles over turf. They are mutually complementary.

One important caveat has to be added, however. Much of the base that provides political legitimacy to the international activities of parliamentarians is still the political base in their home state. As most other decisions in global governance, such decisions by parliamentarians too, must still gain their political legitimization within the narrow confines of single states mainly.

That limitation notwithstanding, parliaments are now one of the new players on the international field. Next to them there are other and equally significant ones. But before we deal with them, let us first look at how states may try to directly influence the public in other countries, bypassing the official channels of traditional diplomatic communication.

Notes

1. Existing treaties already forbid all but the underground testing of smaller nuclear weapons.
2. Together with Finland, Austria had been instrumental in starting the so-called "Helsinki Process" that established the Conference on Security and Cooperation in Europe (CSCE), later transformed into the OSCE.
3. Culminating in the—unfortunately not very successful—North/South Cancun summit conference.
4. Kreisky was the first "Western" statesman to plead for a "two-state solution," that is for a separate Palestinian state.
5. Inevitably, some of the parliamentarians so selected do not involve themselves too deeply in these official duties and regard the sojourn in New York more as an opportunity for sightseeing, museum hopping, and shopping. But they are the exception. Most of the delegates act more duty-bound.
6. The OSCE was instrumental—together with its predecessor, the CSCE—in bringing about an end of the Cold War; and it is now is essential in efforts to stem a new deterioration in relations between USA/Europe on one side, and Russia on the other; and in efforts to stem the erosion of democracy in Eastern Europe.
7. If one disregards certain rights, such as the right of the Parliamentary Assembly to elect the judges to the important European Court on Human Rights.
8. Delegates are selected according to the relative strength of parties represented in national parliaments.
9. It was precisely for this reason that a "Transatlantic Legislative Dialogue" between US and European parliamentarians was created, as a part of the formalized structure of negotiations between the European Union and the United States.
10. The degree of independence of parliamentarians from official governmental policy also depends on the nature of the international organization they are active in. If that organization has as members countries that are very much alike, and that thus share many problems, it will be easier for parliamentarians to shift alliance from their government to a transnational group of like-minded deputies. That is not the case if the member countries starkly differ from another—as they do in the United Nations. Parliamentarians from Syria and from Israel, for example will not easily find common ground under a transnational political alliance including both of these countries.
11. Organized into transnational political caucuses, such as the caucus for European Social Democrats, or European Christian Democrats.

16

Public Diplomacy

"Oh," said the queen when the ambassador presented to her the press counselor as "my counselor for public diplomacy." "Oh," she said with a wry smile, "has it come to that? Has diplomacy gone public now?"

The ambassador smiled back at the queen and did not reply. Would he have been less inhibited by etiquette, he could have asked the queen whether the concept of public diplomacy was really that foreign to her, given the kind of activities the queen herself engaged in during official visits to foreign countries: going to orphanages, cutting ribbons, promoting British exports; or addressing local parliaments in public session under the glare of television cameras.

Obviously, the wry tease by the British queen was not based on her being unaware of the purpose of such activities when she was abroad on a state visit. The remarks of the queen do, however, reflect her conviction that such activities are not part of true diplomacy. True diplomacy would be discrete. It would not be conducted in the open. It would be the task of seasoned professionals, shielded from the pressure of volatile, ever shifting public opinion.

Yet even in the past, diplomacy had never been completely isolated from the public. Even in the past, diplomatic envoys had not just dealt with the sovereign they had been dispatched to. They also tried to relate to the public and to impress on it their own relevance and that of their country.[1]

Ambassadors representing the Ottoman Sultan at the imperial court in Vienna, well-aware of the part music played in Viennese life, kept a Turkish orchestra that entertained the Viennese with public performances. Their impact is still audible in the "Turkish" pieces composed by Mozart and Schubert. Western representatives in early-modern Tokugawa Japan also used music and ostentation to gain status with the public.

Usually restricted in their movements to the small trading enclave of Nagasaki, they were permitted a once-a-year visit to the faraway capital Edo (now Tokyo). They made the most of this annual pilgrimage, using it to show off with the wealth of their attire and with marching bands.

Some such earlier versions of public diplomacy were already more political in nature. In the early 19th century, the British population had become rather negative toward the Habsburg Empire and toward Habsburg rulers. The negative opinion was fanned by the British press.[2] The Austrian chancellor, Prince Metternich, therefore instructed his envoy to the United Kingdom to bribe editors of leading newspapers so as to entice them into a more friendly journalistic treatment of the Austrian Empire.

Such precedents do not establish an unbroken continuity of public diplomacy because democratization and globalization have given it a wholly new dimension. The foreign relations of a state are no longer shaped by a lonely prince-sovereign, surrounded by his most intimate counselors. They are no longer shaped exclusively either by an all-powerful executive branch of government and by its small camarilla of foreign policy mandarins, well-isolated from political pressure groups, from public opinion, and from interference by elected representatives sitting in parliament.

Globalization has changed the game too. Today, information ignores state boundaries and cultural divides. It is produced and consumed worldwide. Its political impact is also worldwide. Attempts to provide information, to correct information, or to give information a political spin thus have to ignore state boundaries too.

Politicians and their diplomats, for example, would be amiss in their duty, if they did not react to a grievous factual error in an article on their country published in a respected major magazine, such as *The Economist*. The rejoinder might be written by their ambassador in London. More likely, it would be written by someone else. The fact that the paper that published the article was printed in London, and the fact that the reply had come from a faraway country is not relevant. In that sense, geography has become irrelevant. Content and credibility are relevant. We can be certain that the author of the rejoinder to the article in *The Economist* will not have transmitted this rejoinder via diplomatic channels. He will not have used the country's embassy and the British Foreign and Commonwealth Office to forward it to the magazine. Most of other types of *public diplomacy* also bypass these official channels and ignore the claim of foreign offices to monopolize politically relevant exchanges between their country and another one.

Much in international relations, much in global governance is public by now. This is because:

-   information which is the base of politics has become both public and global.
-   a growing number of states are democracies. Their politics are thus influenced by opinions of the voting public.
-   actors other than governments now participate in global governance. Their involvement and the dealings with them should be transparent.

These changes have transformed any public diplomacy as it might have existed before. In its former version, public diplomacy still avoided overly overt "interference in the internal affairs of another state," proscribed by the traditional diplomatic code of conduct.

Whatever the rules of abstract international law and whatever the traditional codes of diplomatic conduct such interference in internal affairs has become widely tolerated by now. Forty years ago it was less tolerated still. When on an official visit to France forty years ago, Bruno Kreisky, the Austrian chancellor, had contacts not just with the government. He also called upon the then-leader of the opposition, Francois Mitterrand. The political adversaries of Mitterrand were the official hosts of Bruno Kreisky and they were not amused. Basing their negative reaction on the claim that Kreisky would have illicitly interfered in internal affairs, they summoned the Austrian ambassador to the French Foreign Office for a dressing down.

Today, a repetition of such a negative reaction would seem quaint. In Europe at least, this kind of interference has become routine. Political parties campaigning for elections think nothing of inviting to their electoral rallies politicians from fellow parties in other countries,[3] even if the political party which issued such an invitation is in opposition and even if the person so invited is therefore assisting efforts directed against the incumbent government.

Public diplomacy is a very broad concept. In its widest meaning, all diplomacy would be public that is in the open and not behind closed doors and in secret. An alternate definition would assign a more restricted meaning to the term. In the following we will use this more narrow definition: we will use the term "public diplomacy" for that part of diplomatic activity that is not secret, that is not conducted via the traditional and exclusive channels of official communication; and that aims to convey to the public, to opinion leaders or to specific groups information and views that reflect the interest of the diplomat's home country.

It is only in theory and according to outdated protocol, that ministries of foreign affairs still maintain a monopoly as the recipients of interventions from foreign politicians and diplomats. In fact though, foreign ministries have long since ceased to be the exclusive channel for such communications and transactions. By now, interventions from outsiders in one country's politics routinely reach beyond counterparts in ministries of foreign affairs. They might target just a few, select key persons and opinion makers. Or interventions might extend further to a broader public so as to sway that public on a certain issue at stake in relations between two countries.

Public diplomacy might aim at nothing more specific than embellishing the image of a country. States might be tempted into efforts to alter misleading, dysfunctional, and frequently negative stereotypes attached to them. Such stereotypes are grating. Small wonder that counties wish them to vanish.

- Americans would be resourceful and practical, yet motivated by economic/material considerations mainly.
- Germans would be efficient, humorless, and inextricably linked to their Nazi past.
- French would be haughty and given to the abstract. Eating well and having leisure would be their top priorities.
- Italians would be great lovers and singers, but they would not be great warriors.
- Swedes would all be blond and welfare state addicts.
- Dutch would wear wooden clogs.
- Indians would all be poor.
- Austrians would be easygoing slobs, great in skiing and in nothing else; and so on.

These images are misleading:

- The French outperform the Americans in (per hour) productivity and hold the world record in the consumption of tranquilizers—a fact that shows them as nervous and anything else than loose and easygoing.
- Sweden is not dragged down by an allegedly demotivating and wealth-destroying welfare system. Statistical indicators,

such as per capita computer density show it to be efficient and modern.

- Americans are less pragmatic than commonly assumed. More than nationals of many other states, Americans are motivated by non-material goals. They pursue them even at great costs.

Worldwide cooperation would be facilitated were such stereotypes discarded. But bringing about such a change is not easy. Humans stick to simplifications and stereotypes because in their absence they would drown in the task of continuously updating their world-view by integrating into it the relevant data they would have to sieve daily from an ocean of freely available information.

Public diplomacy should therefore not attempt the impossible and enter into costly and untargeted public relations campaigns just for the sake of altering a deeply entrenched, stereotypical image of a country. Such stereotypical images can only be dislodged if the pressure to do so becomes really strong and if the change of a traditional image has thus become inevitable. Americans might still believe the Chinese to be economically backward and mired in poverty, if they did not have to deal with a flood of Chinese imports, many of them of a high-tech nature. Americans might have tended to see the Soviet/communist system as inherently primitive and technologically laggard, until forced into dropping such prejudice when the Soviet Union beat the Americans in the race to launch the first earth-orbiting satellite.[4] Germans and Austrians might have smugly believed in having a superior educational system as long as that assumption had not been proven unfounded by comparative international studies.

If undertaken at all, attempts to correct the image of a nation have to connect to such moments of fluidity when in view of newly emerging facts, traditional, stereotypical views of a nation have to be revised. Even then, such campaigns to alter an image should focus not on the image as such. Such campaigns should instead connect to concrete political issues. The goal of addressing such specific issues must be shared in the country the campaign is targeting. The realization of pursuing identical goals facilitates a change of images two countries hold of each other. One cannot bang one's way into the hearts and minds of other nations. One has to use the openings provided by common goals. According to Trauttmansdorff, an Austrian ambassador, "Diplomacy is the art of walking through open doors; it is not the art of breaking down closed doors."

How Not to Do It: Part One

Karen Hughes had been appointed undersecretary for public diplomacy by President George W. Bush, eager to burnish in foreign countries the badly tarnished image of the United States. During President's Bush first term in office, Karen Hughes had served him as an influential counselor on internal politics. During the president's second term and in her new function, Karen Hughes was dispatched to foreign countries, there to sway public opinion in favor of the United States. In Arab countries, in particular, the image of the United States had become very negative. Karen Hughes thus concentrated much of her efforts on Arab countries. These efforts were in vain. They even proved counterproductive as they worsened an already bad image of the United States. Why?

a)   The negative image mainly resulted from what Arabs perceived as wrong US Middle-East[5] policies, favoring the Israelis and biased against the Arabs. Any public relations exercise therefore was bound to be in vain as long as it was not accompanied by changed US Middle-East policies.

b)   Though she tried, Karen Hughes did not succeed in linking her message to Arab concerns. In Cairo, for example, she addressed women's groups attempting first to establish commonality ("I, as a wife and mother…"). That was not credible, with Cairo women seeing her—and rightfully so—not as one of their own, but seeing her as the US undersecretary for public diplomacy. Karen Hughes should have stuck to that role that she could not escape anyhow.

c)   She was preaching top-down, lecturing the audience on the superiority of democracy and she did that in a country ruled autocratically by a president supported by the United States. The missionary zeal of pointing to US-style democracy as the only true way and the willful obliviousness of circumstances that kept democracy out of reach must have made her listeners chafe.

How Not to Do It: Part Two

The "Campaign" to Repair the International Image of the Late Austrian President Kurt Waldheim

Kurt Waldheim, a two-term secretary-general of the United Nations, was elected in 1986 to the largely ceremonial, but nonetheless politically important office of president of Austria. Material surfaced in the last phase of the electoral campaign that proved Waldheim to have been part of the German Wehrmacht intelligence team on the Balkans. Waldheim had hidden (or not acknowledged) that part of his past, prompting his opponents to use that fact against him; and prompting a hostile reaction in the United States. Waldheim turned these attacks to his electoral advantage, claiming that during these times on the Balkans and in the German Wehrmacht he would have "just done his duty." That claim gained him the sympathy of thousands of Austrian voters who had also been drafted into the Wehrmacht and who felt threatened by a stigmatization of that service. They shielded themselves from self-doubt by also hiding behind the notion of having done nothing "but their duty."

The United States reacted to Waldheim's election by banning him from entering US territory (on which he had lived for so many years). Other nations also showed him the cold shoulder and he was shunned internationally. Drawing an honorable conclusion, he decided not to run for a second term as Austrian presidents usually do.

Whatever the formal legal basis for the US decision, it was testimony to irritating double standards. Waldheim could have been charged with obfuscating or lying, but not with war crimes. The Japanese emperor, who very well could be blamed for such crimes, was not banned from US territory, but was welcomed on official visits. Neither did the United States sanction German politicians who had been members of the Nazi party—something that Waldheim never had been.[6]

Feeling treated unfairly, Austria decided on a countercampaign to repair its image and the image of its president. That campaign was an utter failure. It did not cause anyone to reconsider prior positions. It just served to harden them. Why?

1) The lack of credibility: Waldheim had lost it by never becoming clear about his past. He never provided convincing
   explanations for not having been open about it right away.
   Whatever he did and said, opponents felt that he should
   not be trusted.

2) The lack of empathy for, and understanding of the motives
   of his critics: Few wounds are still more open and bleeding
   than those caused by the annihilation of the East/Central
   European Jewish population—an annihilation Waldheim
   must have witnessed when serving with the German
   military intelligence in the Balkans.[7] Waldheim and those
   employed to improve his image simply did not show, or
   failed to express what should have been expressed in view
   of this lapse into inhumane barbarity. Waldheim himself,
   always driven by burning ambition and imbued with self-
   righteousness, was oblivious to the moral implications of
   the questions he had raised by his pronouncements.

3) A failure to perceive the centrality of the issue he had
   put before the public with his claim of "having done his
   duty." The issue is central to the Austrian political identity.
   It is central to the identity of Western nations that had
   vanquished Hitler. And it is central to the post-world war
   global order.

Austria had defined itself, and had based its post war existence,
on the claim of having been the first victim of Nazi Germany.
In the time of the World War II, it would not have been part of
Nazi Germany or allied with Nazi Germany. It would have been
occupied, with the German Wehrmacht being a hostile foreign
force. Waldheim's dictum of "just having done his duty in the
Wehrmacht" ran counter to this claim and myth, as one cannot
define in honorable terms of "doing one's duty" a service that had
been defined as having been forced and involuntary according to
the then-prevailing official Austrian doctrine.

If this did stir discussion in Austria itself, it was bound to
prompt a violently hostile reaction in other Western countries.
Still today, they continue to largely define themselves through
their role in the war against Hitler's Germany. In fact, the whole

postwar world order can be seen as an institutionalized reaction against Nazi Germany. The admission of allegiance with Nazi Germany implicit in the notion of "having done one's duty" ran counter to that international consensus and put Waldheim on the wrong side of the fence.

4) Waldheim's countercampaign also suffered from its technical ineptitude. It could not heave on board impressive, morally respected Americans or West Europeans. It never succeeded in forcing opponents into a serious public discussion. It never managed to erase Waldheim's stigma as obfuscating and not worthy of trust.

Lessons from These Two Failures of "Public Diplomacy"

Both Karen Hughes and Kurt Waldheim tried to deal with, and turn around, negative public perception. Both failed. Both tried to "sell" their version of things. But both did not really address what motivated opposition and hostility toward them. They failed to engage a hostile audience because they lacked empathy and understanding. They overplayed their own importance and did not budge from their own worldview, being incapable of seeing things also from the perspective of those they tried to convince.

The reader might have wondered all along why we deal with such questions under the heading of public *diplomacy.* Why use the word "diplomacy" for activities which seem to be just efforts of public relations?

Some knowledge of the technicalities of public relations might indeed come useful in campaigns like the ones pursued by Hughes and Waldheim. But to be successful, these campaigns should have been more *diplomatic.* They lacked this ingredient. They lacked what diplomats should and could add as part of their professional skills. This is the capacity to listen; the readiness to see the world also through the eyes of others; the facility of using the views and interest of these others so as to promote one's own aims.

Many of the routine activities of diplomats are not even aimed at transforming a traditional and often erroneous image of a country. Many are of a more general nature still, intended to generate in their host country diffuse good will both for themselves and for their home state.[8] Diplomats host social events. They participate in charities. They chum up to high-profile public figures so as to be seen with them. They participate in public discussions, attend funerals and weddings, and give non-controversial interviews in public media. They always dress correctly and suppress all signs of misgiving or rancor. They are fluent in the art of flattering small talk and they shun topics that might entail controversy.

All that is probably useful in establishing and supporting social networks diplomats have to rely upon in their host countries. In that limited way, such activities are not completely void of purpose. But what they cannot do is to alter even by a jota the image of a country that is being held by the general public of the host country.[9] Nonetheless, many diplomats devote themselves to these activities with relish and abandon. One cannot avoid the impression that these activities are frequently self-serving; that they are there for their own sake without having, or seeking justification in a political goal. Those wheels turn in the void. They create the impression of purpose where no purpose exists. One even may surmise that diplomats seek refuge in such activities as their professional life is steadily being drained of substantial political content.[10]

Such general and aimless goodwill activities cannot really be considered to be public diplomacy. As we have seen, public diplomacy has to be defined in more narrow terms. Yet even if more narrowly defined, that task will still call for resources and skills. Not all diplomatic services and all diplomats are in a position to provide them. One of their handicaps is the language diplomats are accustomed to use. Over long stretches, diplomats move in the peer group of other diplomats. Doing so, they have evolved their own coded language. This sort of coded language does have its use when directed at fellow diplomats; just as similar coded languages are useful in the communication between members of other specialized professions. But such a language is not readily understood by the general public. It impedes communication between diplomats and non-diplomats.

The Norwegian political scientist I. Neumann provides an example for difficulties that ensue when diplomats stick to their own rules of communication even when the audience so addressed is not the community of other diplomats but an interested outside group or the public in general.

As a part of an experiment to "imbed" observing political scientist into the machinery of diplomacy, Neumann had been assigned to the

Norwegian ministry of foreign affairs.[11] In an article for a journal of political science he describes the drafting of a speech for the Norwegian minister of foreign affairs.[12] He was given the chance to provide such a first draft. This draft was based on what he saw as the concerns of the public the speech was addressed to. Neumann's draft was rejected in horror. It was replaced by a compilation of contributions made by each of the sections of the Norwegian Ministry of Foreign Affairs. Such an approach might have its use if the speech would have been directed at diplomats and foreign policy specialists in other countries as it would have acquainted them with the position of Norway on issues at the top of the international political agenda at the moment. But these specialists were not the audience to listen to that speech. The audience was the informed Norwegian public. This public was interested in questions of more immediate concern to Norwegians. It could fairly expect these questions to be explained in a common language and not in a language used in the corridors of the United Nations. The speech, as it then had been written in the usual way by Norwegian diplomats, did not serve its intended purpose of making the public understand the contribution of foreign policy in promoting the immediate interests of the Norwegian public.

Neumann's story holds a more general lesson. Politicians know how to address an audience and how to use its interests and emotions. Writers of editorials know how to deliver an opinion in a way that is enlightening to readers of newspapers. Many diplomats lack that know-how.

As part of that know-how, they should be aware that it is frequently wise not to be the one to deliver a message; but to have that done by a highly regarded person of another nationality, preferably from their host country. This employ of third persons is preferable, because as civil servants of their states, diplomats are rightly perceived as tools of these states and as such are seen obliged to tread the official line. That attaches to their enunciations the suspicion of being nothing but propaganda.

This suspicion is the first thing diplomats have to dispel when communicating themselves with the public in the country they are posted in. The best way to do that is by starting not with one's own views and wishes; but with those known to be held by the audience. Problems and differences have to be faced squarely. Ignoring these will raise doubts on the relevance of the whole exercise. It is highly counterproductive to deny or belittle known facts; to avoid core questions; or to play for effect and emotions so as to detract attention from serious issues.

One has to start out by acknowledging reality, even where such reality is onerous and not flattering to the diplomat's home country. I once sat at a dinner next to an ambassador from Sudan. He earnestly maintained that no cruelties would occur in the Darfur region of Sudan; and that if they occurred, they would do so not as the result of his government's actions. Such crude attempts to distort or deny reality will inevitably damage the standing and repute of a diplomat. They will also damage the reputation of the country he or she represents.

Efforts of public diplomacy have to be consistent, long-lasting, and narrowly targeted. An ambassador engaged in public diplomacy should not be permitted to ride his personal hobby horse, with his successor from the same country being permitted to ride another one. Continuity is required and for it to persist, the public diplomacy of that country has to serve a clear, concrete, and pre-defined purpose. Such precisely defined public diplomacy should be an integral part of a country's larger, long-term strategy. It should be part of a national plan on where a country wants to position itself and where it wants to go. The tools and channels of communication used in public diplomacy have to be built and maintained in a steady, long-term fashion. Trust of leading media, for example, has to be established and carefully nurtured over generations of succeeding ambassadors. Obviously, the diplomatic services of a few countries only will meet these criteria.

Diplomats must know their place. They must be aware of what they can do, and aware of what they cannot or should not attempt. A diplomat active in bilateral relations can and should have contacts to those persons who may influence decisions that are relevant to the diplomat's home country. He or she should know the views and interest of these persons and be respectful of them. Diplomats should be capable of also thinking with the head of these contact persons of their host country and they should be ready to put that knowledge and expertise at the service of their home state. This is their core competence and their specific function in the web of worldwide information and communication.

And they should be conscious of the narrow limits to their capacity to deliver information and opinions. For whatever is done in the field of public diplomacy—either by diplomats or by other persons—all such efforts have to be done in recognition of the fact that the information, the images, the sentiments thus promoted are just a minor—a miniscule part of the information that is publically available from other sources. That leaves only tiny niche for public diplomacy. Therefore, the content of a message has to be concise and specific. The audience to be reached has to be targeted precisely. The media used to deliver the message must be carefully chosen. And the message so transmitted must have a well-defined political purpose.

How It Might Be Done: Gaining Support for a Project of the European Union

During the time that Austria held the presidency of the European Union in 2006, its embassy in Washington had organized a conference on the feasibility of transforming the United Nations Environmental Program—UNEP into a full-fledged UN Specialized Agency. This was done upon the prompting and with the support of the European Commission. EU member states were interested in such a transformation because it would provide a stronger administrative underpinning to UN environmental activities. Such a reform had, however, been blocked by the United States, opposed as they then were to any strengthening of international organizations. Many US experts—and experts especially in the field of environmental law and regulation—did not share this negative attitude of their government.

In order to sustain that opposition to the official US position and so as to keep alive the option of an eventual change of US policy, the Austrian Embassy organized a conference on that issue. It was co-hosted by the prestigious Georgetown University Law School, which later also published the proceeding in one of its magazines, specialized on questions of international environmental law.[13] The European Commission was grateful and the event can be seen as having had the intended effect. Why?

a) It provided support for a constituency that already existed, and it strengthened this constituency by arming it with good arguments and the intellectual backing from speakers drawn not just from US environmental groups and academia, but also from the business community and from the International Financial Institutions based in Washington.

b) Hosting and co-sponsoring the conference, Georgetown University made evident that this was not just a European political project, but that the issue merited serious consideration also in view of US interests. Georgetown University further provided the weight of prestige and intellectual credibility to an event that it would not have gained would it have been organized by foreign diplomats only.

c)   The issue was narrow and well defined. But while being such a narrowly defined project, it still fitted into the wider efforts of both the European Union and of Austria; with the Union trying to engage the United States on a broad range of regulatory questions and at the same time defining itself as a constructive global partner of the United States. The project also fitted with the Austrian ambition to retain and strengthen its reputation as promoter of international law and as supporter of the United Nations.

d)   The ensuing publication put the proceedings on the Google-Wikipedia radar-screen, so to say. Information produced at the event was therefore not lost for the future.

Enter the Electronic Age

Yet in probing into the use and function of public diplomacy, we will have to expand the frame of reference. We have not done so in the examples just quoted. Up to this point, we have dealt with public diplomacy in its traditional institutional setting of a diplomat from country A being sent to another country B, trying to influence the public in this his host country, attempting to sway it in favor of his own state. This traditional setting is contingent on the acceptance of state borders as defining the reach and style of public diplomacy. But these borders have become irrelevant in many instances. We may, for example, no longer assume an exclusive national nature of every *polity*—that is of every group of politically active persons which may influence political decisions. Next to national polities, others have sprung up that ignore borders and that impact on world governance directly and not via state representatives.

Wishing to influence outcomes, diplomacy should not remain bunkered down in the ivory tower of autonomously produced and autonomously consumed information. It has to become involved with all those that are active in articulating views on global affairs. The constituency that has to be reached by such efforts is global. Someone tasked with shaping the politics toward Lebanon for example, would have to stay in contact not just to opinion leaders, researchers, and analysts in Beirut, but he will have to deal with all those in the wide world who are involved in a high-level discussion on Lebanese politics.

National politics wishing to be part of global politics will therefore have to gain access to, and will have to address these new, worldwide audiences. Diplomats seeking to preserve a role in global governance will have to deal with these global polities. In order to do so, diplomacy has to adapt its tools. Those proven adequate in traditional bilateral settings may no longer suffice in dealings with a new, *delocalized global polity*.

In particular, public diplomacy will have to make full use of the tools and the opportunities provided by the media created by the "electronic revolution." Modern public diplomacy will, for instance, have to duly acknowledge the central function of databanks and search engines. Its messages have to be of a sort as to connect to these databanks and search engines. This modern version of public diplomacy will also have to adjust to the individualization and fracturing of a formerly coherent public realm of political information, with distinct groups each living in their proper sphere of information with no overarching sphere joining, these many distinct entities under the roof of one commonly shared universe of political information. Modern public diplomacy should therefore be prepared to address each of these specific sub-groups and to do so in a way and with content that seizes the attention of the audience targeted.

If one aims at a proactive foreign policy, it will not suffice for ministries of foreign affairs to simply have websites, as all of them now do. It will not suffice to use these modern media simply as new and supplementary carriers for the distribution of information. The electronic communication should invite participation. It should be interactive.[14] If one aims at a reform of a specific part international humanitarian law, for example, one should be ready for a two-way Internet dialogue with humanitarian groups and individuals all over the world who are interested in this very subject.

Diplomats and their political masters should have a close look on how politicians had used the Internet and other electronic media in recent electoral campaigns. They should have a look too, at some path-breaking innovations made by the US Department of State in the field of this new "electronic public diplomacy." Two high-ranking US diplomats have been charged with watching over this field and with tilling it.[15] They use "Twitter" to interact with an expanding audience in order to keep this audience involved in the most recent US foreign policy issues and moves. This their audience now numbers half a million and with that it has become the third largest Twitter audience of anyone working for the US government (after the audience of President Obama and the audience of Senator McCain).[16]

In these musings over "public diplomacy" we have dwelt on efforts to affect the opinion of the public, or the views of opinion leaders in foreign countries. This, after all, is the assignment implicit in the very notion of public diplomacy. But we should not completely ignore another dimension. Efforts are also needed as regards the information the public in one's own country has on questions of international/global issues. The main task of this internal public diplomacy is the one of "laying the cards on the table." If the foreign policy of a democratic state is to remain effective and rational, citizens must come to share not just its goals. They must also come to understand the immutable givens and constraints a country is confronted with when pursuing these goals in an international/global setting. These "cards have to be laid on the table" and that is a task incumbent on elected politicians mainly. Its success depends on their skills in connecting with public opinion and on their ability to get the media to carry their message. But according to my experience, in a limited way, next to politicians, higher-ranking diplomats from the ministries of foreign affairs[17] (or the State Department) could also become involved. They carry some credibility with the public as they are seen as neutral experts not suspected of being subservient to this or that narrow purpose of internal politics.

International Cultural, Scientific, and Educational Exchanges

A broad field of activities exists which is commonly also subsumed under the notion of "public diplomacy." These are the officially sponsored and/or officially administered programs of educational, cultural, and scientific exchange. Such activities have expanded vastly over the last decades. The question is as to whether these programs could or should be considered an integral part of foreign policy, as tightly linked to concrete and immediate foreign policy goals as other forms of public diplomacy.

The answer to that question is not that clear. A cultural exchange program, for example, must make sense not just in terms of foreign policy; it also must make sense on its own, in its cultural terms. It thus is a hybrid program—a program with two masters. One master pursues a foreign policy goal and the other one a cultural, goal. The two masters might not always agree among themselves.

By its very nature, art is often unsettling and divisive. Sometimes it is also explicitly critical of the country it comes from. Diplomats with the immediate interests of their country at heart and mindful of the reactions in their host countries might thus be excused feeling queasy about welcoming and supporting some cultural exchange programs. I remember, for example, an Austrian ambassador in a European country who protested over the instructions to have performed a play by a renowned Austrian writer, outrageously critical of his country, which the playwright pictured as proto-fascist and as the meanest and most despicable political creation on earth. If judged from the perspective of pure art, the ambassador was wrong, of course. The play has high literary merits. It should thus be shown. But the ambassador has a point when fearing that the public of his host country might misunderstand the piece as a balanced and objective information on Austria—something it definitely was not.

Similar conflicts might emerge in the realm of scientific exchange. Such exchanges might very much benefit the country that is on the receiving end. But they might, at the same time, facilitate theft of intellectual property—or worse—the acquisition military know-how.

In such conflicts, one is usually well served to take the long-term and optimistic perspective. In the long run, such exchange programs usually served both of their "masters," with positive consequences both in the realm of political relations as well as with positive consequences in the scientific, cultural, or educational realm.

I myself, and many young Austrians of my age group, had benefitted from the US Fulbright student exchange program. I had profited enormously, and so had—to all evidence—the other Austrian exchange students. Most of them had ended up in prominent positions and thus able to leave their mark on events in Austria. Nearly all of them also seem to have been "branded" in a particular way by their sojourn in the United States. I feel that they have become more open, more communicative and more enterprising than those young Austrians who were not so privileged by a stay in the United States.[18]

If seen from the perspective of overall US foreign policy, the very ambitious and large-scale Fulbright student exchange was just part of Cold-War efforts to firmly tie Austria to the "Western" part of the European continent. The United States funded literary magazines, radio stations, theaters, and newspapers. It did so in a very intelligent way, always granting to the recipients of such largesse vast freedom in the exercise of their discretion and judgment. It sealed such support not with the Star-Spangled Banner, but with the red-white-red colors of the Austrian flag. The best-liked radio station was financed by the Americans. It was not named "Radio America" but "Radio Red-White-Red". Its reporting was considered more objective than the reporting of the official, state-owned radio station. In hindsight, it is obvious that these US programs did indeed serve their intended political purpose of firmly tying Austria to the "West." But it is evident too, that they had contributed also to the cultural, scientific, and educational revival and opening up of postwar Austria.

But nonetheless—such programs are investments in a distant future, with positive pay-offs likely but not assured. Furthermore, such pay-off will frequently accrue more to the side of art, of science, of education, and culture. Only rarely will the returns be in form of immediate foreign policy advantages. This is inevitable. In order to function, a science-exchange program, for example, must make sense, in first instance, in terms of science. A cultural exchange program must make sense, in first instance, in cultural terms. Only when it does, might it also bring some long-term foreign policy advantages.

In view of the technical and not overtly political nature of such programs, they are frequently used as door openers especially in instances where relations between states are anemic or even hostile. Even in the midst of the Cold War, scientific and cultural exchange programs between the United States and the Soviet Union continued. They provided a foothold for an eventual expansion of relations. In a similar vein, there were talks as such a scientific exchange program between the United States and actively hostile Iran bent on confrontation.

The not overtly political nature of such programs also defines the role diplomats assume in the articulation and implementation of such programs. They might have a role in initiating them and they might have some supportive function in their running. But the substance of such programs will be handled by cultural, scientific, educational experts.

Notes

1.   At an exhibition at the Vienna "Kunsthistorisches Museum," a 17th-century painting pictured the arrival of the new French ambassador at the city gates. It depicted no less than five ornate, fully gilded coaches each drawn by three pairs of horses.

2. It still is. Not just the notorious British "yellow press," but even allegedly respectable papers like the *London Times* wallow in a hostile attitude towards Germany and Austria.
3. This has to be done prudently. Some such invitations might still be of a nature as to cause a hostile reaction in the native electorate, with the emotions of hurt nationalism more than compensating for any electoral advantage the invitation of the "foreigner" might have provided. A Swedish prime minister might be welcome as a speaker at an electoral rally in Poland. A Russian premier probably wouldn't.
4. The result was the so-called "Sputnik crisis." It triggered greater US efforts in the field of education and research.
5. The politically correct term for the region: West Asia.
6. All states are equal; but big states are more equal than smaller ones.
7. Especially the extermination of the millennial Jewish community in Thessaloniki/ Greece.
8. *Faites aimer la France*—"Make them love France"—was the broad and diffuse instruction provided in the early 19th century by the French foreign minister Talleyrand to his diplomats. Diplomats all over the world seem to have heeded that advice ever since. They see their task as generating general goodwill for their home state.
9. The many social and public relations activities of the French embassy in Washington did not shield the French from being called "cheese-eating surrender-monkeys" when they wisely failed to support President George W. Bush in his—at the outset very popular—war against Iraq.
10. See for example the contribution of a German ambassador to a conference on the future of diplomacy held at the Austrian Diplomatic Academy in the year 2000 (Paschke 2000) who maintained that "public diplomacy" would have become the primordial task of German diplomats posted in other EU member countries.
11. Which seems to have had second thoughts, as the experiment has now been terminated.
12. Neumann I, 2007, A Speech that the Ministry Might stand For—Or Why Diplomats Never Produce Anything New, in *International Political Sociology*, 2007/1, pp. 183-200.
13. The report was also made available online.
14. One does not have to go to the extremes of the Swedish embassy in Washington of having an avatar of the ambassadors available for chats in "Second Life."
15. *New York Times*, July 17, 2010.
16. The two diplomats also apply these their technical skills to foreign policy areas that are not strictly "public diplomacy"—such as the implementation of what US Secretary of State Hillary Clinton had defined as a new human right: namely the "right to connect" to the Internet; or the right of setting up interactive websites in response to large-scale disasters.
17. Higher Austrian diplomats were, for example, mobilized to provide information to the Austrian public in the run up to the referendum on the country's membership to the European Union.
18. One has to accept too that even such long-term positive pay-off is not always assured. The Egyptian intellectual Sayyid Outb, later to become the founder of the extremist Islamic and radically anti Western "Muslim Brotherhood," had been converted to this negative attitude during a two-year sojourn in the United States, studying at prominent US universities such as Stanford. The "close encounter" with a foreign culture thus might also be experienced as something unsettling and threatening, triggering a hostile reaction.

17

Delocalization

"We found out about the Bush doctrine by downloading it from the White House website, one French diplomat noted."
—Quoted in *"Re-Shaping World Order,"*
Foreign Affairs *88/2*

The parameters of traditional diplomacy were defined by geography. A diplomat gathered information in one geographic place—namely the host country—that would not have been available in another place—namely the home country of the diplomat. He represented the specific culture of his home country that had no parallel in the culture of his host country. Friends and enemies were states with distinct frontiers and with a precisely defined location on the globe.

The world has since disappeared where everything relevant could be assigned Latitudes and Longitudes. Most obviously, this is the case with information. It is gathered, evaluated, and consumed in a web of worldwide communication. Some specialist on Yemen teaching at a major US university is likely to have more data on Yemen available and superior tools for evaluating them than 95 percent of all foreign ambassadors stationed in Sana, the capital of Yemen. Even someone not so specialized on the intricacies of Yemenite politics will do a decent job in gathering and evaluating political information on Yemen, provided that he (or she) has a knack for using the Internet and global data banks, has some political sensitivities and an open, critical mind; with knowledge of the Arab language being an added advantage.

Who Stores More Information: Databanks or Embassies?

I worked at the OECD between 1993 and 1996. These were the times before Google and Wikipedia. But databanks already existed that stored vast quantities of political and economic information. Accessing these databanks was costly. I could overcome that hurdle because the OECD paid for my use of one of the most comprehensive of such databanks. I recommended to my former colleagues in the Austrian Ministry of Foreign Affairs to also pay for access to that databank—to no avail. Bureaucracies are conservative and they are conservative especially in the allocation of money. They tend to continue to pay for what they used to pay for; and they shy from spending money on things that are new and that did not have any claim on the budget before. So my former colleagues in the Austrian diplomatic service could not do what I could do. I could mine political and economic data on specific countries. In my case, these were countries that used to be communist and that then had entered a more or less successful process of "transition" toward market economy and democracy.

At that time, a friend of mine was the Austrian ambassador in Moscow. As no funds were available for setting up embassies in all those new states that had come into existence after the dissolution of the former Soviet Union, the Austrian Moscow embassy was also made to represent Austria in all of these new states. That is how my friend came to represent Austria in Kyrgyzstan. I do not know how often he actually had been in Bishkek, the capital of Kyrgyzstan. Given his limited budget for travels, that cannot have been more than once a year. But I—on my computer and via the data bank—had been there every other week. I read the pronouncements of the Kyrgyz president as they were translated into English by a BBC Service. I read the country reports of international organizations like the IMF and the World Bank. I read the assessments of the human rights record in documents of the US State Department and of Amnesty International. I had access to pronouncements of the opposition; and learned how experts at various think tanks saw the country.

So I invited my friend, the Austrian ambassador to Kyrgyzstan to a wager on who would know more about the country's situation and politics. We never compared notes. But I am certain to have won. I could use tools that were not available to my colleague in Moscow. His closer geographic proximity to Kyrgyzstan—and his official position as ambassador to that country—provided him with no comparative advantage in gathering information.

In some cases, an ambassador who is actually residing in a country and who is well-acquainted with its ways and with its leaders might still have an edge in gathering and evaluating some bits of information, as he can judge such information in the light of the whole political and cultural atmosphere of his host country. But this advantage is limited. Politicians using reports by diplomats should be aware of that. They should accept diplomatic reports just as one, and certainly not as the most important source of information.[1] These other and more relevant pieces of information do not originate in just one well-defined geographic place. They come from around the globe.

What holds true for information as used in foreign policy decisions is equally valid for most other types of information. There is hardly any major breakthrough in science that would not be based on information that is shared across the globe. This makes is difficult to assign to one specific person in one specific location the merit of having been the sole originator of such a scientific breakthrough. By now, the majority of articles in science journals are also signed by more than a single author. Frequently, these authors are not nationals of one and the same country.[2] In geographic terms—where then does the crucial knowledge reside that had resulted in a scientific achievement; on which latitude and longitude?

Accumulated knowledge and information is the crucial input into the development of national economies and of the economy worldwide. The contribution of *traditional factors of production—labor and capital*—is insignificant in comparison.[3] Among those traditional factors of production, labor is mostly immobile. The overwhelming majority of workers seek employment in or near the place they live in. Capital is highly mobile but its contribution to lasting economic success is a minor one. The more strategic factors of production—knowledge and information—do not lend themselves to a ready geographic identification. Which geographic location to ascribe to modern business practices; or to the standardization of products and processes?

Production itself has become delocalized.[4] After consumption has gone global, production has followed.[5] How to establish the true geographic identity of an enterprise with a French chief executive officer; with engineers from India and Germany; that uses raw materials from Australia and Africa; whose shares are listed on the New York Stock exchange; a good part of which are held by an Arab Sovereign Development Fund; and that is incorporated in the Canton of Zug in Switzerland?

The question as to localization and geographic identity gains its full political significance if we address it to information that is imbedded in culture. Culture is information that functions as a kind of non-biological genetic code. Like the biological genetic code, it determines behavior and—again like the biological code—it is but slow to change and does so but under the pressure of a competitive struggle for survival.[6] It is difficult to overestimate the economic and political relevance of culture. More than anything else, it determines the chances of success in using existing knowledge and information for economic development; for modernizations; and for the establishment and consolidation of democracy.

What has changed is not the political and economic relevance of culture. It remains highly important. What has changed is the coincidence of a certain culture with a certain, clearly delineated geographic location. Hundreds or even thirty years ago, there were few in Europe that identified themselves as fundamentalist Muslims. These were assigned a geographic location much further to the East. By now they have become firmly imbedded in many more Western geographic locations.

Two City Blocks Apart: High-Income Britain and Poor Pakistan

The European Bank for Reconstruction and Development (EBRD) I was working for in London between 1997 and 2000 is located on a newly developed and very expensive stretch of real estate at Bishopsgate along the busy Liverpool street railway station. This is at the extreme eastern end of the London City, which functions as the financial hub for much of the world. Walking two city blocks further to the east from Bishopsgate, one comes upon Bricklane. No marble or high rises there, but soot stained town houses built in the early 19th century. Most signs on shops are not in English, but in some foreign language and in foreign letters.

A few shops sell garments for the pilgrimage to Mecca. Others offer food unknown to the average Brit. Two hundred yards away from the centers high finance is a world that has little in common with British tradition and culture.

The Economist explored this world in some detail. It found it to be part of a seamless web connecting communities and families in Pakistan to those who lived there. In Bricklane, weddings are arranged with suitable spouses hauled to London from Pakistan. There is a constant to and fro between these two locations, facilitated by cheap air travel and by the British passports of the Pakistan community living in Bricklane. Cultural patterns such as they shape family and communal life remain solidly those of Pakistan. That holds true even for the second and third generation of immigrants. Those along the Bricklane in Eastern London live there in a purely geographic sense only. Their true home and source of identity is many thousands of kilometers further to the east in Pakistan. This sense of a Pakistan identity is strong as it has the power to shape lifestyles and the general outlook on the world.

On the other hand, such substance and power might be lacking in places that have a clear geographic identity but not a true cultural one. A former collaborator of mine—open-minded, curious, alert, and easygoing—had been appointed ambassador to the Philippines. Once there, he enjoyed the usual privileges of ambassadorial life, but nonetheless returned to Austria sadly disappointed. He was not sure of really having been at a distinct place. He felt having been posted in a copy of some American suburb. In more or less perfect English, the elites he met talked of the latest Hollywood movies they had seen and of their past or future shopping trips across the Pacific.

My former colleague had been posted to Manila. But "there was no there there." His embassy was in a spot clearly defined by latitude and longitude. But these coordinates proved irrelevant. In a cultural sense and with a function of establishing identity, Manila did not exist. My colleague had searched in vain for a truly and authentic Philippine culture that would give a voice to the uniqueness of Philippine historic experience. He was looking in vain for an articulation of specific Philippine interests in global affairs. All he found was avoid.

The coexistence at close proximity of cultures that are distinct or even incompatible is nothing unprecedented. In fact, such multiculturalism had been the norm in many places. It existed, for example, in the Ottoman and in the Austro-Hungarian Empire. The small towns, the "Stetls" of Galicia at the easternmost part of Austria-Hungary, were populated by ethnic Germans and Austrians, by Jews (who spoke their Yiddish version of German), by Ruthenes (close to the Ukrainians), and by Poles. Each of these groups stuck to its own community and form of life.

Large-scale migration, such as the one that brought Pakistanis to East-London is not unprecedented either. In the United States and in some of the bigger and wealthier countries of Europe such as France, the share of the foreign born population was as big at the turn from the 19th to the 20th century as it is today. Most of the major US cities then had their "Little Italy," or their "Chinatown."

But two things have changed since which do not allow us to take such a past as a precedent for today Modernity brings about, and calls for a widening of contacts between all groups of a population. In the past, the interface between distinct groups, such as those that lived in the "Stetls" of Galicia, was restricted because of the limited function one group had for the other one. Contacts were restricted to trading in this or that; or to providing this or that service. Otherwise these groups could remain isolated from another. In today's world, such relative isolation seriously impairs the economic and social prospects of that specific group. It becomes detrimental too, to the rest of society. Modernity would necessitate participation of all across a vast array of activities—political, cultural, and economic.

By now, however, strong forces work against an early and easy integration of immigrants into their country of residence. It is easier for today's migrants to remain in their former home country mentally, culturally, and—for periods—even physically. Holidays are spent back "in the old country." One returns there for festive occasions. The benefits of old-age insurance can be transferred to this country too, as it is there where one hopes to retire in the house built by arduous savings. In their country of work and residence, the old culture and language are kept alive not just by social networks but also by the television programs that can be received over satellite.[7]

We are, in fact, now faced with a wholly new phenomenon: that of the transnational family. Members of one and the same family—and even of a nuclear family—no longer need to share the same geographic location. Those new transnationals exist both at the top and at the bottom of the social ladder. At the bottom are migrant families from poorer countries whose members are dispersed between their old and their new home. At the top are the high-flyers who spend much of their time at airports and in hotels; or the long-distance commuters who fly home a thousand miles or so for the weekend;[8] or whose upwardly mobile children study abroad and there also gain their first work experience.

One and the same geographic place, such as a big city, can thus be home for distinct populations that have little in common save this accident of being on the same place as defined by latitude and longitude. Each of these groups may lead a live that is akin to a life lived in a completely different part of the earth. When I was posted in New York between 1978 and 1983, the South Bronx was a burned down and looted wasteland from which the state had withdrawn.[9] Life expectancy and infant mortality figures were similar to those in very poor countries. The South Bronx was then where I imagine Somalia being today. Yet in geographic terms it is located just across the Harlem River, a mile away from the super-wealthy Upper East Side of Manhattan.

On the other hand, places akin to wealthy Manhattan do exist in other parts of the world in sections of other big cities. They exist in sections of Mumbai or of Sao Paulo. Those are not cheap, superficial copies of the original. The tempo and the whole flavor of life is authentically "Manhattan." Such wealthy sections in cities around the world are powerhouses that drive economies. They are nodes in the global network of interchange and communication. Though surrounded by poor regions, these dense agglomerations of wealth and information have gained global status and power.

That leads back to the question as to whom and what a diplomat represents. Diplomats used to represent states with a mostly homogenous population. They used to watch over the interests of an economy that still was autonomous to a large extent. Diplomats stood for, and represented a culture that saw itself as unique and distinct from others.[10]

But in today's world, does a British ambassador also represent Bricklane? Does he represent a transnational enterprise that happens to be incorporated in one of the British Channel Islands for reasons of convenience? The ambassador might be tempted to suppress such troubling questions and seek refuge instead in the notion that civil servants, such as diplomats, do not represent and serve a specific culture, and not a distinct economic interest. They represent and serve a legal/political order.

That order does not discriminate between fundamentalist Muslims or devout adherent to the Anglican Church. It treats the same all citizens, and all firms that are incorporated on its territory.

This is indeed a very enlightened, a very liberal, and liberalizing concept. It permits to bridge the divide between a growing inner diversity of states on one hand, and the need on the other hand for a strong state to perform all those added functions modernity had heaped on it.

Nonetheless we cannot be oblivious of the practical implications of such growing inner diversity of states as it also impacts on the day to day work of diplomats; and as it affects their identity and self-image. A UK ambassador might rightly have qualms to represent tax fugitives that have escaped to the Channel Islands. Neither will he identify easily with fundamentalist Muslims who hold a British passport, but who reject democracy and who despise the British crown.

Diplomats used to represent distinct places on the globe that had an equally distinct political, cultural, and economic identity. This point of reference, central to their activity has become blurred. States still matter in global affairs. Diplomats are their tools still. But is has become more difficult to answer the question as to the cultural and economic nature of that state. Mere geography, the mere inside and outside of borders offers little help in the answer to this question.

It always has been the prime task of a state to shield residents from threats, whether they might emanate from their own territory or from the outside. This still is the primordial function of states. If they fail in it, they are bound to fail in everything else. In addition, modern states are supposed not just to thwart threats to their residents. Increasingly, they have been charged with suppressing harmful risks. Threats are used by persons or states to bend other states or persons to their will. No such intent is behind risks. They just exist. Risks and threats have two things in common, though. The growing complexity of modern societies exposes them to greater risks and it also makes them vulnerable to new forms of threats. Second, the sources of most of these threats and risks are not easy to pin down to one single and distinct geographic location.

This is obvious for threats to modern societies posed by al-Qaida—the terrorist group that plotted the destruction of the New York World Trade Center. Where is it located? Which place to bomb in retaliation? Afghanistan? Pakistan? Yemen? Somalia? Or perhaps the United Kingdom as, according to US intelligence services, it is from this country that Islamic fundamentalists are most likely to stage their next assault upon the United States.

Unfortunately, the risk of a serious worldwide economic crisis has materialized. But where did it originate? Whom to hold accountable? US consumers for overspending and undersaving? Rapacious hedge funds selling strange derivatives? The naives who bought these financial products? Or the Chinese who continued to pump money into the United States in order to keep their currency under-valued and their exports high? Or is the culprit the International Monetary Fund for failing to keep the world monetary system on an even keel?

Pandemics are nothing new.[11] Yet the vastly increased international mobility of persons has now made it more difficult to restrict counter-measures to a distinct geographic zone.

The gap is still widening between this new *reality of delocalization* and the way we think about[12] international/global relations, about security policies[13] and about the tasks of diplomacy. Vast sums are being spent still on the capacity to wage wars against other states or for deterring them by military might from entering a war on their turn. But how to deter an adversary if his location is not known? How to deal with risks that are not imbedded in a distinct geographic place? Whom to address for a remedy? Which telephone number to call?

These questions might invite us into a sort of agnosticisms: We do not know! We cannot act! Yet such escapism is ill founded. Because in an evolutionary, stumbling manner, we are already on the way to find responses. Were it otherwise, the social and political order we depend on would already have collapsed under its own complexity.

Notes

1. As I mentioned, I had been assistant to Bruno Kreisky—the Austrian head of government—for five years in the early 1970s. Kreisky had a reputation as eminent statesman, deeply engaged in foreign affairs. He gathered his information from high-quality international newspapers, and by being on the phone for a good part of the day, contacting a wide array of friends and acquaintances in other countries. He also read some reports from embassies—but only a few and mainly those from Austrian diplomats he knew and trusted. Such diplomatic reports were certainly not a major part of his "information diet."

2. That is true even for articles in political science and for the so-called science of international relations.

3. The accumulation of information and knowledge is called learning. But learning itself can be learned. Each country that has mastered the transition to a phase of fast economic growth has learned from the success and from the errors of predecessors. As a consequence, the process of the economic catching-up has become ever-more rapid.

4. The Marxist model has already taken account of the globalization of consumption; but still is wedded to the assumption that the crucial parts of production would

remain in a few well-defined "capitalist" centers. The neo-Marxist "Dependenzia" theory still clings to that assumption, concluding that "accumulation" could occur but in these few "centers," whilst the periphery would be sucked dry.

5. Toyota claims that the cars assembled in its US factories contain more parts produced in the United States than the cars assembled by General Motors. Is Toyota/US a Japanese firm or an American one? The SAAB convertible is a Swedish car! The Chrysler Voyager is an American car! Right? That is not so clear as both of these models are being produced in Styria—Austria. Are they Austrian cars for that? That is an open question.

6. These cultural norms that are transmitted from one generation to the next have been termed "memes." Memes are not the exclusive property of *Homo sapiens*. Primates and a few other animals like dolphins and some species of birds, also pass on to the next generation patterns of behavior that are not conditioned genetically, but that are product of a specific culture.

7. All over Europe one may spot immigrant quarters by the many satellite dishes that stick out of windows and balconies.

8. Nearly all the married Austrians, who work for the European Union in Brussels, have their spouses back in Austria. When I traveled through the Baltics in the mid- and late 1990s, just one of the married ambassadors had a spouse in residence. All others saw their families in trips back home over weekends. Affordable air transportation is one of the causes of this development. One other factor is the emancipation of women, many of whom will now have their own job and career and will be loath to quit them so as to accompany their husband to a strange location with few job opportunities.

9. Conditions in the South Bronx have improved since—not least thanks to the activities of ex-President Carter (whose merits and achievements have been sadly ignored by the US public as they were eclipsed by the boisterous vapidity of the succeeding actor-president). Carter had committed political suicide by reminding Americans of the limits to US power and lifestyle.

10. The notion of a unique and largely autonomous "national culture" has always been an artifact. This artifact was created by states seeking to strengthen their legitimacy by posing as guardians of a distinct, deeply imbedded, and immutable national culture. There never was such a thing. More often than not, it evolves not just from one unique "national wellspring," but from the collision of many cultures.

11. The plague—the Black Death—ravaged all of Europe in the 14th century with long-lasting negative consequences. It put an end to the relatively prosperous era of the High Middle Ages. In the years following World War I, the "Asian Flu" caused more deaths than the preceding slaughter on the battlefields. States are rightly concerned about a possible repeat of such disasters.

12. Articulated, so as to make its absurdity obvious, by the claim of US neoconservatives that it is states that stand behind terrorists. So that it would suffice to silence that state sponsor of terrorism in order to silence terrorism itself. With no evidence to back up their claim, they chose Iraq to prove their case. Terrorists are grateful.

13. The failure to adjust security policies to a new age is proven—in a spectacular and wasteful way—by the Austrian decision to purchase a few outrageously expensive supersonic fighter aircraft. The decision was made at a time when the threat of a war, in which such fighters could be used, had vanished in Europe. The budget of the Austrian defense forces being meager, the purchase of supersonic aircraft was detrimental to the basic capabilities of the army, which was constrained in its role of international peacekeeping.

18

The Quasi-Governmental Function of Transnational Corporations and of Financial Institutions

"In all my writings I have been friend of commerce, because I have been friend to its effects. It is a pacific system operating to coordinate mankind by rendering nations as well as individuals useful to each other. If commerce were permitted to act as the universal it is capable, it would extirpate the system of war."

—Thomas Paine, 1791

States and Enterprise at the Service of Growth

I once had been invited to a luncheon given by the secretary-general of OECD for a visiting head of government. The discussion over luncheon was on what OECD should recommend to its members as primary goal of policy. Both the visiting head of government and the secretary-general of OECD agreed that nothing should have higher priority than the goal of continuing and accelerating the rise in the productivity of their economies.

Sitting at the lower end of the table, I did not dare to inject myself into the discussion, though I felt the urge to do so. Wasn't it strange, I thought, that member countries of the OECD—all of them among the wealthiest in the world—should set themselves no other or higher goal that that of pushing for a faster increase in their wealth. Being rich already, these states would be well placed to address other human needs and desires instead of concentrating exclusively on a competitive race to consume and produce more. Shouldn't it be more important to them to keep the ecology in balance so as not to leave to posterity a wrecked and exhausted planet? Or shouldn't the establishment of a comprehensive system of health care; or of a broad and effective educational system merit priority over the goal to increase the sheer volume of goods and services?

I kept these questions to myself but continued to mull them. The longer I thought about it, the more I came to appreciate an inner logic behind the consensus on the priority of raising the productivity of the economy and of accelerating and welcoming a competitive race in wealth even between countries that were fairly wealthy already. Perhaps, I came to think, the head of government at the luncheon table knew that countries had no choice but to stay in that race. Aren't we caught in this treadmill of a never-ending economic competition? Can't we help trying to run faster and faster? And shouldn't we learn to appreciate that all other ways of organizing our collective life have proven to bring worse results?

Twenty years later the world economic crisis of 2008 seemed to support the point the head of government had made at the OECD luncheon table. With this crisis, world economic growth turned into decline. Consumers ceased to consume as would have been their duty. Investors ceased to invest as they should have. Misery resulted. The unemployed not only lost their jobs and income, but with them also their main basis of identity and their anchor in the web of social relations. Heightened economic insecurity translated into fear and aggression. Radical political right-wing movements, unknown since the fascist Thirties, gained strength in Europe.

These then are the tangible consequence of a halt in the race to outperform others in productivity. But for other reasons too, this race could not be stopped. It reflects the very nature of modern economy. Modern economies are based on a steady flow of new investment. They need the invention and sale of an endless succession of always new products. Modern economies wouldn't function without one business competing against another one and without entrepreneurs and their workers being in service of this competition.

The never-ending competitive economic race also has another essential function. It makes for permanent ups and downs. It makes for ever-recurring revolutions that destroy one enterprise or eliminate one product and substitute a new enterprise or new product. Not only economic but social relations too, are constantly being upset by these gales of creative destruction.[1] In absence of these gales, societies would quickly become refeudalized. They would become stratified into self-perpetuating classes, castes, and guilds. Not only wealth would suffer, but freedom too. The status of a person and his income would no longer be determined by what that person does. Just as in by-gone times, it would be determined by what that person is; by the social class, the caste or guild he or she belongs to. In absence of such a permanent reshuffling of social positions brought about by the economic race, societies would stagnate and ossify.

But even while thus accepting as inevitable the constant pressure to continue the competitive economic race, we still might wonder whether this pressure couldn't be mitigated somewhat. We might surmise that the wealth of already rich countries would permit them to do so. We might assume the race to become less intense as wealth grows.

It is true that greater wealth does permit states and persons to purchase things that are not narrowly economic. Growing wealth correlates with higher life expectancy. It correlates with longer and better education. It correlates with more intense and effective measures to protect the environment.[2] But greater wealth does not bring about a lessening of the competitive economic pressure that weighs on individual and states. It seems to heighten it.[3]

In the wealthy member countries of OECD, the political impulse to improve social services and to redistribute income is less acute today than it had been 50 years ago. Differences in wealth that once would have been considered obscene, have now become acceptable as they are alleged to result from a better or worse performance in the service of the economy. Ostentatious consumption is no longer frowned upon but celebrated. Senselessly costly handbags and outrageously expensive cars are being shown off to an appreciating audience as badges of social distinction. Up to the 1970s, part of the rising productivity in the economy had not been translated into higher wages and profits, but into more leisure time; into longer vacations; into a shorter workweek. Since then, this development has ceased. In the United States it even has become reversed.[4] The goal of maximal economic output has become supreme.

This intensification of the race of economic competition between individuals and between states cannot be explained by the inherent logic of the economy alone. Something else is at work. Humans are "social animals"—or to put it into zoological terms—they are one in the species of herd animals. As with most herd animals with humans too, there is a constant competition for rank. With animals, rank is established by fighting. Over long periods of their history, it was the same with humans. By now though, and in a setting of acute mutual interdependence, such bloody fights have become overly costly and dysfunctional. The irrepressible competition for rank is now being carried out via the economy.

This holds true both for individuals and states. The economy is no longer just the basis for existence and the prerequisite for the meeting of individual and collective human needs. Economic success has become a goal in itself. It establishes the rank of individuals and states.

Markets provide the legitimization of this order. According to the theory on the working of markets, rewards meted out by them would be nothing but just compensation for services an individual would have rendered to other individuals. The same would hold true for states. Their greater or lesser wealth would be justified and legitimized by the quantity and quality of goods and services they could provide to the community of other states. All would participate in this system to their own best benefit, consuming the things they like best and can best afford, producing those goods and service they are best apt to produce. In that sense, the system would be one based on free choice and consensus. No coercion would be needed. Small and big would deal with another on an equal footing.

Obviously, that this is not so. Wealth and poverty cannot be ascribed to the choice and aptitudes of individuals—and of individual states—only. The system as such makes for an uneven distribution of rewards. Free choice is a myth as it is severely restrained by the *path dependency* of economic development and by the basically social/collective nature of all economic activity. Neither are markets self-regulating and in no need of the state.

Contrary to the claims of free market ideology, we therefore do not live in the best of all possible worlds. But it is true, nonetheless, that this new economic world order is superior by far to the one it replaced. It is superior to a world order established by the use of military power. It is preferable by far to live with the terror of the competitive, never-ending economic race, than to live with the terror of continuous warfare and slaughter. In that sense, we can appreciate the US revolutionary Thomas Paine whom we had quoted above. He witnessed the onset of the end of this old era of warfare and seized the first glimmers of hope for a new era dominated by economic relations between individuals and states. He justly preferred the latter.

Nonetheless one has to mobilize for this never-ending competition just as one had to mobilize for the never-ending wars before. Poor countries have to start economic growth. So-called "emerging states" have to accelerate it. Countries rich already have to strive to stay on top. States and enterprise are partners in these efforts. One cannot do without the other. The relation between states and enterprise is not antagonistic[5] but symbiotic.

Transnational Corporations—Partners of States; or Their Masters?

In view of this symbiotic relationship, states do their best to make their enterprises succeed.[6] They do so by a variety of measures. They lower corporate taxes. They provide infrastructure. They support research and development. They educate and train the workforce. They assist in exports. They subsidize credit, etc. All these measures are to the benefit of enterprise. One is therefore led to surmise that enterprise would be in the driver's seat, with states and politics heeding its demands and taking its orders. But even if this were not the case, we still would have to revise the image of all-powerful politics and of enterprise being their meek, passive, and subservient object. Enterprise has gained a more prominent role.

This role is strongest where enterprise is no longer attached to one location exclusively, but has become active in different parts of the world. Many firms have done so. Rapid economic growth has resulted in a widening of markets. A good number of corporations followed this expansion of markets and have turned into transnational corporations (TNCs). By now, many of them have become global.

Transnationals are not unprecedented. German banking houses acted as transnationals in the late Middle Ages, financing wars and maritime traffic. Later, in the 18th century, vast joint stock companies such as the British East India Company and the Dutch East India Company assumed quasi-governmental functions in oversea territories they acquired. In the following phase of industrialization, transnationals became prominent through their clout in mass production. They were big and attached to the state of their origin mainly. By now though, a growing number of small companies have become transnational too. A good number of these transnationals—be they big or small—are no longer headquartered in one of the big and wealthy countries, but in still poorer ones.

Both the radical political Left and the radical, nationalistic political Right tend to picture transnationals as ruthless exploiters of the work-force, as destroyer of the environment, and as subversive of the existing political order. They might have merited such chastise in the past. Some of today's transnationals might merit it still. But on the average, the impact of transnationals on the local economy is not that negative. They pay higher wages than local firms. They tend to respect the tenets of corporate social responsibility. They are likely to be more aware of ecological constraints on their activities,[7] and are less likely to offer bribes to public officials.

Those concerns notwithstanding, transnationals still pursue their prime goal of maximizing profits and they will seek to have their host states accommodate this prime interest. They have a good chance of finding willing ears because not just they themselves are interested in their superior performance. Their host states share that goal. At some instances though, the interests of states and of transnationals do not converge. Notoriously, this is the case with their taxation. Transnationals want to lower it. States wish to maximize via taxation their stake in the economic success of a transnational enterprise. Similar conflicts emerge over regulations that states prefer to be tight and detailed while enterprise prefers them to be loose.

In such conflicts, transnational corporations tend to have the better cards. If opportunities at some other location are brighter, they will move there. States will be loath to see them leave and will try to entice them into staying by yielding to their demands. They will, for example, stand ready to lower already low corporate taxes; or to exempt transnationals from burdensome rules protecting the environment. Transnationals have therefore become not just partners of states. In that partnership they often tend to be the more powerful.

The one-sidedness of this relationship has resulted in a competition among states to entice transnationals with the most favorable conditions. Governments compete with each other in providing generous concessions to transnationals in order to have them invest in their state. Most well-functioning countries have established special offices, charged to lure incoming foreign direct investment (FDI). Kings, queens, other heads of state, prime ministers, and minister of finance and ministers of the economy make the round among corporations that are expected to build new production facilities abroad. Substantial sums are being spent on public relations and on advertising the alleged advantages of making a foreign direct investment in a specific country.[8]

States do this not just for prestige, but also for good reason. Those investments by transnationals may reach sizable proportions. They can add a few percentage points to the investments rate[9] of a country. Also, the facilities established through foreign direct investment usually achieve a higher than average productivity with a good chance that this superior productivity might percolate through the rest of the economy.

**Figure 18.1 FDI Inflows—Global and by Groups of Economies
(In millions of US Dollars)**

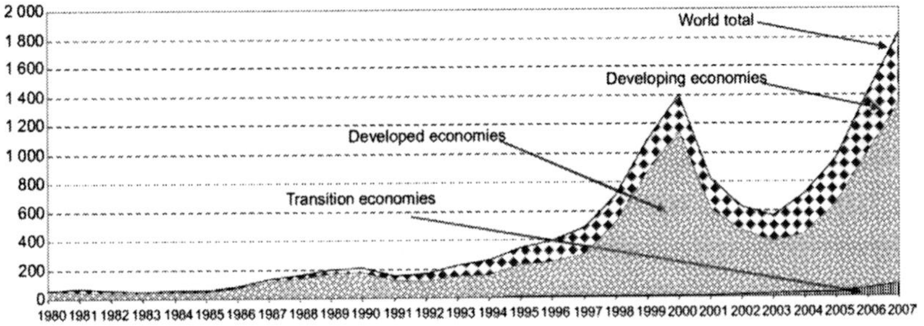

Source: **UNCTAD**.

For all these reasons, transnationals are showered with attention.

What Comes First? Washington or Bill Gates?

When the president of the People's Republic of China came for an official visit to the United States in spring of 2006, he did not go directly to the capital, Washington DC, as protocol would have prescribed. He first stopped in the State of Washington on the US West Coast in order to meet Bill Gates, the legendary founder of Microsoft and by now one of the world's wealthiest person and one of the world's most prominent philanthropists.

On the next day, the Chinese president continued his sojourn in the State of Washington with a visit to Boeing—one of the two transnational firms that compete in the world market for large aircraft.

Notwithstanding the official character of his visit, the Chinese president came to Washington, DC only on the third day of his visit. For him, meeting with transnational corporations was obviously as important as the meetings with officials in the US capital.

From my experience, I can recount a similar example as the Austrian head of government came for an official visit to the Netherlands. Unlike the Chinese president, he followed prescribed protocol by duly making his official calls in the first part of that visit. But that part of the visit to the Netherlands was the less important one. More relevant to him and to his country was the subsequent visit to the headquarters of Philips—a huge transnational firm with factories in Austria. Some of them were threatened by being closed. Many jobs stood in danger of being lost. Talks with top managers of Philips therefore were crucial to the Austrian chancellor and Philips received him with all due honors, flying him in via corporate helicopter and spreading a red carpet on the tarmac.

Yet in global governance, transnationals are by now more than mere objects of that kind of attention and courtship. They have become prominent actors themselves. In that capacity they will primarily promote their own interest. They will do so by lobbying governments either alone or as groups of industries. Such lobbying is carried out not just on a national but also on an international level. Lobbyists for industries do not just intervene with lawmakers and administrators in capitals like Washington or Paris. They promote their cause also with international organizations and at international conferences. States and international organizations can ill afford to ignore them.

Political activities of transnationals extend beyond such lobbying. They do more than wring concessions from states. They have become *quasi-governmental* as they have a say in defining the agenda for global governance; as they participate in global rule making; and as they have a function too, in enforcing such rules.

Three facts mainly seem to have brought about this change in the function of transnationals.

1) The web of expertise and know-how strung between transnationals will often find no counterpart in public administrations. When, for example, states set on the task to establish benchmarks for the production of renewable energy, they will have to know the parameters of what is technically feasible, at what cost, and at what date. The most recent and most relevant version of this know-how is not accessible to them without help from experts. Most of them will be employed by corporations active in the field of renewable energy.

2) States and transnational corporations share the goal of rapid economic development. This transforms transnationals into partners of government. Consequently, states will have to listen to these partners.

3) Corporations embody a kind of political consensus. A politician is elected because voters like the things the politician represents and promises. In a similar vein, corporations exist and reap profit because customers buy their products and thus "vote" for them with their purse.[10] A government might be opposed to its citizens owning cars. But if not physically banned from doing so, these citizens will purchase cars anyway. This "vote" for car ownership has political implications that cannot be ignored by politicians.

Financial Markets

Relations between transnationals, governments, and global governance become more complex and more fraught with consequence, where these transnationals are financial institutions. They become even more relevant for global governance when financial institutions merge their actions into the fully globalized financial market.

Financial markets sit at the top of the economic hierarchy. They sit where *surplus value* (the Marxist term is still fitting) is produced, where profits and savings are stored and distributed. They are, so to speak, the "heart" in the economic bloodstream. Yet—so as to stay with this metaphor—while the human heart is rigidly programmed; this is not the case with financial institutions and financial markets. Theirs is a wide scope of discretion which detaches finance from the real economy. This detachment results in destabilizing fluctuations. As a result, prices for financial products as essential as the prices for savings, credits, or for foreign currencies vary widely from one month to the next.

The danger inherent in this volatility in financial markets is heightened by these financial markets being upstream over other economic activities. An enterprise needing money for investment, or a minister of finance wishing to float a bond issue for his country, must line up at financial institutions and are at their mercy. The whole economy as such finds itself in a likely position. Financial institutions might be tempted to funnel savings not into productive investment but into "bubbles" (such as the American and Irish real estate bubbles). Following their own whim and herd instincts, financial institutions and financial markets might downgrade the credit of one state or upgrade the credit rating of another state. Such actions may result from the inner machinations of the financial markets themselves, while lacking any solid basis in the real economy. Such unfounded moves nonetheless impact on this real economy. They also impact on politics.

Detached from "Fundamentals": Prices as Basic as Those for Foreign Currencies

Over the last 15 years, the data on the real economy would have called for a steady devaluation of the US dollar, given the growing deficit in the US current account. The United States imported and consumed more than it produced and exported. This gap widened steadily. Financial markets ignored that fundamental fact. They could afford to, because they and not the real economy set the exchange rate for the US dollar and kept that exchange rate high. Financial markets thus created the "bubble" of an over-valued US dollar. And—for some time at least—that pseudo-reality of that bubble may prevail even in face of a situation in which the data for the real economy would call for a devaluation of the US currency.

There was no basis in reality too, when in early 2009, Austrian governmental bonds were suddenly downgraded by 100 base points. The Austrian current account was, and continues to be positive. Wage-piece costs were in steady decline. The downgrading was therefore not prompted by data from the real economy of Austria. It was caused by the opaque internal mechanism of financial markets. The self-appointed "masters of the universe" sitting at their desks in investment houses did not bother with the petty details of what was real in the economy. They followed the herd. Yet their actions created problems for Austrian taxpayers and for the Austrian economy that were real indeed. Their decisions resulted in a higher interest burden on Austrian public debt and in higher costs of credit to Austrian firms. Would that have been done by a foreign government, one would have termed it a hostile act.

Financial markets thus wield considerable power and influence on global governance with states being at their mercy.[11]

The Joint Venture—Cooperation between Transnational Corporation and States

The imbalance between the power of financial markets and the power of governments might become extreme. Yet even such stark imbalances do not preclude the two sides cooperating in global governance. In providing development assistance, for example, several projects might need "mixed financing." They might need financing both by state grants and by interest bearing credits offered by banks. The two sides might cooperate in combating fraud and they will have to cooperate in the general frame of overall economic and monetary policy. Some banks even became prominent in the promotion of corporate social responsibility with the aim to assure the ecologically and social compatibility of commercial ventures[12] they finance.

Not just financial firms, but firms in other sectors of the economy too, will become involved in the task of national or global governance. In poor countries, for example, they may render such services that in other countries and under different circumstances are usually provided by states. In some of the poorer countries, public institutions are often weak and inefficient. That holds true even for public services as basic as schools and health clinics. Private enterprise may run such institutions with the advantage of a more direct link to the consumers of their services. In India for example, private health clinics and private schools have been quite successful even where expressly serving the poor. Evidently though and nonetheless, this rendering of educational and health services has to be done under the auspices and the supervision of the states.

In fields other than development assistance, the borders between profit-oriented private enterprise and public service have become blurred too. Tasks are now frequently shared between these two sides. Such is the case, in particular, in the planning and the completion of large and technically complex projects. Public administrations might simply lack the appropriate tools to tackle such big and complex tasks. They also might lack the necessary financial resources, so these tasks may be shouldered by large (and frequently transnational) firms. These might then continue to operate what they have built. Or they might turn the running of the finished project over to the public administration. Such procedures are now quite common not just for national projects, but for international ones too.

Transnationals may, however, become involved in governmental functions already far removed from their immediate business interests.

Willy-nilly they have become involved in highly political tasks, such as the safeguarding of resources and environment. Doing that, they have joined up not just with governments but with international non-governmental organizations (INGOs) too. An example is provided by the establishment of the Marine Stewardship Council. It was created in 1997 by Unilever in cooperation with the World Wide Fund for Nature. Unilever is a mighty transnational corporation. Among other things, it produces processed food; and among this food also processed fish. Fish are a critical resource. As we have noted in an earlier chapter, some stocks of fish have become severely depleted and their total collapse has become a distinct danger. Not only would Unilever's image have become tainted, were it found that it had been party in causing that collapse. Such a collapse would also have dented its profits. Together with the World Wide Fund for Nature, Unilever thus established a code of conduct aimed at keeping ocean fishing sustainable. Other food processing firms had no choice but to also observe the rules established by this code of conduct. Few states would have had the same leverage as a mighty transnational corporation in creating such a worldwide regime.

This is not the only case of transnational firms supplementing states in the creation of rules of global governance. Other examples abound. When television sets began to be mass marketed, some governments tried to set the technical standards that have to be met for television to reach a broad and homogenous audience. France, for example, insisted on a specific French version of technology that would have favored its firms producing television sets and that also would have shielded the beloved *Francophonie* (community of French-speaking nations) from foreign cultural intrusion. These efforts proved in vain. Nowadays, no state would attempt to interfere with the self-regulation of the worldwide electronic industry when it develops new audio-visual media. Television is now part of daily life of billions of humans. Governments do not make it function, transnationals do.

Inevitably, all of that raises the question as to the role of diplomacy in such a new global setting where transnationals have emerged as new and potent actors. In their engagement in global governance, transnationals partly mimic institutions and procedures of diplomacy. The bigger ones among them have their own departments to assess political developments and risks. They have staff specialized in dealing with foreign governments; and other staff trained in public diplomacy. They even have their own version of protocol offices that watch over the proper form and format of encounters with public officials.

While imitating the state, transnational corporations have tended to keep the state at distance.[13] To a certain extent, historic experience provides arguments for the greater independence of transnational corporations; as history has proven states mostly ill adapted to actually run corporations.[14] Generally therefore, states are well advised to refrain from interfering with managerial decisions of private enterprise. But this is not to say that an insurmountable barrier would and should separated business from the state and its bureaucrats. As we will show in the succeeding chapter, business and the state depend on each other; and business would crumble were states not to supply those services business cannot do without. To succeed, corporations need an environment that permits them to function. This environment is shaped by the input from both sides: by input from corporations and by input from the state. This is true for the national business environment as well as for the global business environment. Notwithstanding the corporations' quest for maximal independence from the state, they still have to cooperate with the state and have to rely on services only states can provide.

Diplomats render some of these services. In their host country, they will, for example, follow the development of legislation relevant to their firms; or they will intervene if public procurements in their host country discriminate unfairly against one of their corporations. On behalf of their corporations, they also may protest against regulations that unjustly disadvantage products from their country. In case of one of their nationals planning a major investment in their host country, embassies will usually be involved in one way or another, helping to negotiate for the working permits of expatriates; or helping in negotiations with tax authorities.

But cooperation between—mostly transnational—corporations and the public administration and diplomats extends beyond such case-by-case interventions. As business has gone global, it operates in a global context; and it becomes a player on the global scene. As such it has not only gained economic advantages. Necessarily, it also had to shoulder the responsibilities ensuing from a worldwide presence. Just as firms will have to cooperate with administrators on a purely national level, they also will have to cooperate with those that administer public global goods, when they themselves go global. The circles of diplomacy and of transnational corporations will then overlap.

Notes

1. A term coined by Joseph Schumpeter.
2. Poor countries face the worst environmental problems: while their wealth permits richer countries to solve or remedy many of them.
3. The "post-material age" sociologist had predicted 30 years ago, has failed to materialize. On the contrary, compared to the "68 generation," the present one is certainly more "materialistic."
4. There is a "Marxist" explanation for that. The "capitalist" would have an interest in expanding the workforce. An ample supply of labor would depress wages and increase profits of capital. But that "Marxist" explanation fails to account for the note of moral fervor and genuine indignation that colors the US discourse on the Europeans softies that would have lost the appetite of tough and hard work, preferring to lounge in the hammock of welfare states with long vacations and short workweeks. Obviously, this moralizing has other than merely material motives. Valor is found in battle. The tougher the battle, the greater the glory of the warrior. The battlefield has shifted. One has to prove one's valor not in physical combat, but in the combat of a competitive economy and in competitive consumption. In US eyes, Europeans show too little gusto for an all-out fight on this battlefield.
5. Such an antagonism would be implied in the neoliberal notion of the "best government being the least government" and of their wish for no state interference in, or regulation of economic activity. History, and the recent world economic crisis, has proven aberrant such stipulations.
6. The German word for this competition: "Standort-Wettbewerb."
7. That is true for the majority but not all of them. Transnationals active in extractive industries frequently have a less benign effect upon their social and ecologic environment.
8. And if worse comes to worst, states will tend to "socialize" the losses of big, strategically important transnational corporations, as has been the case in the recent world economic crisis.
9. The investment rate is closely connected to the rate of overall economic growth.
10. Isn't it significant, that the tool of opinion polls was first developed for commercial purposes before becoming routine in politics? Firms seem to attach greater importance to their customers than politicians seem to attach to their voters.
11. Central Banks are top financial institutions with decisive impact on the other financial institutions of a state. I think it noteworthy and symbolic, that they are wholly exempt from political steerage and pressure; their total independence being enshrined in law and in international consensus. Governments and parliaments might declare war or abolish democracy. But they have no voice in setting interest rates at a level compatible with the economic goals and the economic situation of their country. This decision is reserved for the mandarins of central banks. The world economic crisis has prompted efforts to right this balance between politics and financial markets. Yet, the latter seem to prevail again. Their losses have been "socialized" and will be shouldered by taxpayers. The profits, growing again, remain with their shareholders and bonus-drenched executives. States continue to find themselves at the receiving end.
12. Many major banks have signed up to the so-called "Equator Principles" drafted by the World Bank. These principles provide guidelines on the ecological and social compatibility of projects the banks finance.

13.   In their majority, corporations had subscribed to the idea that the functions of state should be kept minimal; and their own scope of action should not be circumscribed. Corporations have successfully promoted the notion that the "the best government is the least government," that the state should be starved of funds so as to reduce it to a small and non-intrusive entity.

14.   Not under all circumstances do private firms outperform state-owned ones. State-owned utilities have often proved superior to private firms in their performance and in the service to their customers. They even might outperform private business in other fields. The car makers Renault and Volkswagen were state-owned for a long time, without their performance having suffered as a consequence. In the same time, many private car producers had vanished. While Volkswagen and Renault are still around, Studebaker, Humber, American Motors, Borgward, and Simca are no longer.

19

The State: Still the Crucial Hinge

"Everything that does not have a history can be defined."

—*Nietzsche*

States do have a history. Their institutions and functions have changed over times. A state of the 16th century is not a state of the 19th century, and the 19th century state again is not the same as the state of the 21st century. So we have to keep Nietzsche's quip in mind when trying to establish the role and function of the today's states in global governance.

States are no longer the only "global actors."

- Political subunits of states such as provinces or cities have come to pursue their own kind of foreign policy.
- Parliamentarians strike out on their own too. In doing so, they are more than mere mouthpieces of government.
- International Organizations are not just the smallest common denominator of their member states. They have gained varying degrees of independence and proper political weight and influence.
- Increasingly, international non-governmental organizations also impact on global governance.
- Transnational corporations have partly escaped the control of their various host states and have, on their turn, gained influence over these states. On occasions, they have a direct say in setting global rules.
- In some fields at least, globalized financial markets now challenge the claim of states to ultimate authority.
- On several issues, public opinion aggregates globally. This points toward the emergence of a global polity beyond the polity formed around the institutions of states.

This addition of new global actors, as well as the dense and growing interdependence of economies, of societies and of cultures has altered the function of states. It has affected not only their relations with the outside world but also relations to their own citizens. It has started to erode among these citizens the sense of commonality—the sense of being alike; and of being tightly bound to another in a web of unconditional solidarity.

The frantic pace of competitive consumption and the pressure of unpredictable and ever-faster change have punctured this net of solidarity and have nourished the myth of everyone being the master of his own fate. That was accompanied and promoted by the privatization of formerly public space. Services, places, occasions that had sustained commonality between citizens have shrunk or disappeared altogether. Persons commute alone in their cars to their stand alone, single family houses in the suburbs. Conscripts who did their "patriotic duty" in the army have been replaced by paid professionals drawn not from all parts of society, but from a distinct and narrow part of it. Fewer than before gather at common religious services. The public place of widely shared information and culture has shrunk, as culture and information is now mostly consumed in private homes in front of television sets and computer screens. Quality newspapers and network television lose audience to media that address small and specific groups. This will enhance commonality in this smaller group, but will subtract from the cohesion in the larger community formed by all citizens of a state.

It is not that humans would no longer need, and yearn for attachment to a group. Being genetically programmed to survive in groups, they cannot do without such attachment. In times before the Industrial Revolution, this prime attachment had been to the family, to the village community, to a guild or to another small community. Modernization had broken these liens and had substituted the *imagined community* of a state as the locus of identification. This emotional identification has been glorified and exalted. Countless monuments to soldiers that died in the two World Wars dot European landscape. All extol the supreme virtue of those who permitted themselves to be slaughtered for their state. Globalization now has weakened these ties between the state and its citizens, as these no longer feel to all be sitting in the same boat. That erodes support for state institutions as these depend in their functioning on being perceived as serving all and being useful to all.

The lesser emotional support for the state is not just due to this shrinkage of formerly public space. It is due too, to the failure of states to deliver services that citizens need and that states once could provide.

It had been the prime task of states to protect citizens from direct threats to their lives emanating from hostile states or from other hostile and foreign forces. Nowadays, states can no longer provide such a firm shield. Several countries now possess nuclear arms and missiles to deliver them across wide distances. If they explode in the targeted country, they would kill thousands, or even millions of humans. No technical ploy and no institutional/political arrangement has been found to eliminate that threat. Neither is the state able to reliably protect citizens against large-scale terrorist attacks. A drama might occur again that would duplicate the one that shook the United States on September 11, 2001 with the collapse of the World Trade Centre's Twin Towers. With all that has been done to thwart such a repeat, such an eventuality cannot be excluded. It is irresponsible to claim otherwise.

The capacity of states to provide physical security has thus been weakened. A similar erosion of capacity has also taken place in other areas where the effectiveness and autonomy of the state once had been unquestioned. It's only in theory that states still are able to tax corporations, or to tax profits and capital—gains as they see fit. In practice, this their former freedom has become limited. Capital is footloose and so are many transnational corporations. States have to fear their moving out if taxed too heavily. Therefore, tax structures and tax brackets have to conform to those of other states.[1] Individual states may no longer set taxes as they see fit.

States used to have quite some freedom in regulating their foreign trade through quotas and tariffs. By now, international agreements have abolished nearly all room for such autonomous action. Tariffs have shrunk close to insignificance.[2] Quotas on imports have been outlawed by international agreements. Neither are states free to autonomously establish a distinct regime for the entry of foreigners. Here too, they are narrowly bound by a global regime they are part of. They are restrained from acquiring all arms they like. They largely have lost the right and ability to establish technical norms for goods produced or consumed on their territory. They have to take in refugees even if they don't like to. They cannot set the external value of their currency. A state acting alone cannot cope with the consequences of the ups and downs in the world economy; and so on.

We still tend to call *international* whatever happens beyond the borders of a state; so as if this realm beyond would be governed by "*actiones inter nationes*"—that is by official transactions between states. By now though, the term "international" has become ill suited for defining this web of worldwide connectedness, of worldwide mutual dependence; and of worldwide rule-making. In particular, and as we have mentioned, the word "international" obscures the many other institutions that, next to states, also shape worldwide relations between individuals and between societies. What happens outside the borders of a country is no longer just "international"; as it is no longer determined by the interplay just of "nations."

But while states have lost their former exclusive role in shaping global order, this does not imply that they have lost all impact on it. They have not. They still have an important and even dominant role as they are the very anchors of the system of worldwide interdependence.

Whatever is said about this global system, it is clear that in order to work it still presupposes the existence and involvement of states. This becomes obvious from the counterfactual—namely from the failure and disappearance of states. If states disintegrate into anarchy and if their institutions dissolve, citizens are left to fend for themselves. They revert to a "state of nature" with everyone fighting against everyone else for mere survival. Rules and laws become irrelevant. That disregard extends to rules imposed by global governance. A dangerous gangrene comes to exist in the otherwise dense web of mutual, rule-bound inter-dependence. It spews challenges to the world order: nihilistic terrorism; unchecked pandemics, banditry and warlordism, the forced displace-ment of humans, piracy, money laundering, drug production and drug trafficking, etc.

No wonder then that the failure and dissolution of states has become the most serious and persistent challenge to a regime of world-togetherness.[3] The disintegration and disappearance of states is the counterfactual. It points to a continuing and essential role of states in keeping the global system going. States therefore continue to be important, even central in the system of global governance. Obviously though their role has changed. But in which way? And—if summed up—have the functions of states multiplied or have they shrunk?

One argument supports the latter position in claiming that states would have become *post-national*, reduced to the technical task of securing for these their citizens various services. They would have ceased to provide citizens with a firm identity as their nationals. By now, modern citizens would be bound by many ties to events, currents, news, cultures, mate-rial incentives, and constraints that originate from outside the narrow confines of their own state. Once, interactions had taken place between the citizens of one and the same state mainly. Today they do so to a lesser degree only. That would loosen the emotional ties, which bind together the citizens of one state. The flame of nationalism and of nationalistic fervor would burn less searingly. Nationalism would give way to a more prudent, ambivalent and less exclusive post-nationalism. Citizens would become more cosmopolitan.

In the very long run that might be the case. But we still have quite some way to go. Nationalism still is powerful, both in its positive form ("I am proud to be citizen of this or that state"); as well as in its negative form ("I loathe foreigners"). At present and in wealthy states, the emotional attachment to one's own state seems to become weaker. But that is under conditions of blue sky and of smooth sailing. When conditions become rougher, when feeling insecure and threatened, citizens still circle the wagons around their home country. They still perceive of the state as the strongest bulwark to preserve their interests and their identity. In time of insecurity and threat, the borders of the state again become the strong barrier separating those "in" from those "out." States and the "imagined community" they represent still function as fortresses of identity and of emotional attachment one withdraws to if the outside world becomes too incomprehensible, overwhelming, or menacing.

Cosmopolitan? Still a Long Way Off

Would citizens truly have turned cosmopolitan, it should make no difference whether they are being criticized harshly from within their own country or from other countries. But it does make a difference and that is so even in wealthy, modern states. Even there, criticism coming from outside still risks being considered illegitimate. It does not trigger serious reflection but a hostile retort and a hardening of the own position.

In the year 2000, the Austrian conservative party joined forces with a jingoistic, right-wing one to form a coalition government. Politicians in other EU countries saw that as a dangerous precedent. They warned against it. When it happened nevertheless, they imposed sanctions against their fellow EU country, Austria. With the Austrian public, that did not diminish, but it did augment the popularity of the new government. The mere fact that—not unreasonable—criticism had been addressed to Austria from abroad automatically delegitimized that criticism and subverted its intended purpose.

Nationalism, and especially nationalism in its negative form of hostility toward foreigners, is a symptom of insecurity. One might argue that insecurity wanes as people become wealthier and better educated. Indeed, strident nationalism is less prevalent in the wealthier and better-educated parts of society. On the other hand though, the process that creates greater wealth and more education implies, at the same time, an acceleration of social and economic change. It implies the erosion of local identities, a widening of social cleavages;[4] and a lessening of social solidarity.

The process of economic growth, of modernization and global-ization thus creates security and insecurity at the same time. The burden of insecurity is spread unevenly. Those well-off are affected less heavily; whereas those below them feel it more strongly. The present reemergence of nationalism in Europe and in the United States is connected, as it seems, to the unsettling impact that economic acceleration and globalization have on the less well-off part of society.

Yet notwithstanding this enduring emotional attachment to states, these have had come to share with other and new global actors their once exclusive function in the shaping of world order. Even in this reduced role, their autonomy has become circumscribed. When assessing the implications of this shift, we have to bear in mind two things:

First, we live in a world where growing homogenization among *some* states goes hand in hand with a growing diversity in the *overall family of states*. At present, states differ widely not just in per capita wealth.[5] They differ in political institutions. They differ in political culture and by the value system that prevails. Twenty years ago, Francis Fukuyama had proposed that all states would converge on a similar model of politi-cal and economic institutions. Fukuyama was proven wrong. We can no longer expect all states to ultimately share the same Western type institutions of markets and of democracy. Differences in the tasks and in the function of states will persist.

Second, even in the West, the functions of states have not remained the same over time. States, in the form we now know them today, are quite young institutions. They came into existence in the Europe of the early 16th century.[6] But even from then on, their institutional setup has changed repeatedly together with what had been defined as their prime function.

-    At first, the foremost task was the enforcement of a "state monopoly of legitimate violence." That implied safeguarding internal peace by wrenching military and police power from feudal lords.
-    The aim of maximizing war-fighting capacity then came to dominate the agenda. The double tasks thus assigned to the state were protection of the nation from external military aggression; and the waging of wars so as to expand the national territory.
-    Later on, that was followed, or supplemented, by the task of promoting a horizontal expansion of the national economy. That means an expansion of the economy not through an intensification and rationalization of production, but through wider application of existing technology. This was done both in agriculture ("physiocrats") and in manufacturing ("mercantilism").

Industrialization established new priorities. States had to facilitate and promote the accumulation of real capital invested in machinery and infrastructure. This promotion of industrialization then called for state action also in other spheres, such as:

-    the expansion and homogenization of education; the aiding of urbanization; the safeguarding of public health; and then, and going beyond that;
-    not just as a condition for higher productivity, but also as an end in itself, states had to provide a panoply of complex and costly social services. The functions of the "Sozialstaat"[7] were added to prior functions of the state.

Recent additions to the tasks of states require us to rethink the whole concept of statehood and of state functions. Traditional legal definitions are ill suited to describe that change. We have to use vague terms in their place: managing flows instead of securing a stable situation; incentives and disincentives instead of legal sanctions; plurality of actors instead of a state monopoly on action; benchmarks and targets instead of binding legal obligations; a plurality of goals instead of a dominating single one.

The Nanny State: The Case of Tobacco

It has long been common knowledge that smoking tobacco is not healthy. Yet the broader public and politics became alerted to the scope of that danger 40 years ago only, as precise data became available on the ill effects on life expectancy.

Fifty years before that, the United States had reacted to similar and well-founded concerns on the consumption of alcohol. It made it illegal in the era prohibition, with this cure creating problems worse than the ones it tried to remedy. Production, trade and consumption of alcohol continued but went underground, providing the economic basis for the rise of large-scale organized crime.[8]

In fighting tobacco smoking, one chose another strategy. Smoking was not banned outright. It was pushed back. No laws were put in place that would have criminalized tobacco smoking. But citizens were made uneasy with shocking information on the health risks they incurred themselves; and on those they inflicted on the "passive" smokers in their vicinity. No target date was set for the end-to-all smoking, but benchmarks were established; such as to reduce by this or that percentage the share of smokers in the whole population.

Courts put heavy penalties on corporations that had misled the public by hiding the ill consequences of the smoking habit. The World Health Organization (WHO) became one of the driving forces in the campaign against smoking. Transnational corporations and most eminently the tobacco firms themselves—were obliged to co-operate. Public relations and advertising firms volunteered support. Civil society became engaged. Smoking declined dramatically—an effect the rigid US "Prohibition" failed to produce in the case of alcohol.

The new tasks of states add another layer of tasks to those that remain from earlier times, as only few of the traditional state functions have vanished with the emergence of new ones. The new tasks therefore expand the list of such tasks. The more modern and wealthier a state, the longer this list; and the larger thus the share of the state in whatever is produced and consumed.

Nations of equal wealth and modernity might still differ somewhat in that respect. In the United States, for example, with their traditional distrust of the state, the state's share in the national income is smaller than in other nations at the same level of wealth and at the same stage of modernity. But overall, there is a clear correlation between rising national wealth and the rise of the state's share in a nation's wealth.

Table 19.1 Wagner's Law—State Activities Expand with Rising Wealth

Per capita gross national income and general government's fiscal consolidated expenditures

	Per capita gross national income (purchasing power adjusted)	General government fiscal consolidated expenditures as percentage of GNI
Low income countries	$ 580.00	11%
Low middle income countries	$ 1,918.00	13%
High middle income countries	$ 5,625.00	14%
High income countries	$ 35,528.00	18%

Source: World Bank, World Development Report 2007.

So—yes: the functions of the state have changed over the last four centuries. And—yes: states no longer rule exclusively in global affairs. And—yes: they no longer enjoy the undivided loyalty of their citizens. But nonetheless: both in relation to these their citizens, and also as regards their involvement in global affairs, they have not become less relevant.

Some argue that the need to keep the economy competitive would soon set limits to the expansion of state activities as, in their opinion, a rising share of the state in overall wealth would ultimately stifle economic development. Data do not support this claim. There even are good reasons for arguing the opposite: namely that a higher state share goes hand in hand with a more productive and competitive economy.

Figure 19.1 Social Expenditures and the Level of Wealth

(Social Expenditures as Share of GDP; Wealth in PPP, 1998)

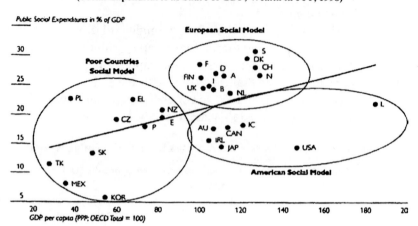

Source: OECD.

Sweden and Germany both have high social expenditures. None-theless, they are very competitive internationally, as they export more than they import and therefore have a large current account surplus. The United States has comparatively low social expenditures, but it has a huge current account deficit, as it imports more than it exports. Gauged by this indicator, the United States is not very competitive.

Whether or not encumbered by social expenditures, the economy is still central in defining the place of a state in the global chain of production and trade. It is mostly the economy that establishes the rank of a state in the world's "pecking order." Nonetheless, the relation between the state and the economy is not that one-sided. It is not just the economy that impacts on the state. Both sides impact on each other. Both sides need and support another.[9] A strong economy cannot do without a strong and efficient state.

Proof for that is provided by the rapid rise of East Asia. First Japan, then Korea, then China, and then Vietnam switched from subsistence agriculture to industrial production in a matter of a few years only. These four East Asian countries have long traditions of statehood. In these states, political/administrative institutions have evolved together with their economy. Countries lacking such tradition of statehood and of effective public institutions have failed to duplicate the success of the "Asian tigers." Countries such as Nigeria, Kenya, or Afghanistan remain mired in poverty.

The state is the crucial counterpart of enterprise in the process of economic evolution. It would not happen without the involvement of the state. Social policies, immigration policies, policies on science and research, fiscal policies, etc., all have an important economic dimension. In that sense, the state is deeply involved in the economy. This involvement has expanded with the growth and the increasing complexity of the economy.

Notwithstanding the basic complementarities of the two spheres, there is an overlap where the actions of the state and those of private enterprise merge. As we had noted in the chapter on transnational corporations, enterprise sometimes assumes functions that once were functions of states. States, on the other hand, do get involved in affairs of private enterprise. This will be the case in particular with big projects that affect all of a state's economy and where much is at stake as a consequence.

The Nabucco Pipeline from Central Asia to Central Europe: Is It a Project of Private Enterprise, or Is It a Project of States?

Europe is not self-sufficient in energy. Much of the energy it consumes has to be imported. Notwithstanding efforts of energy-saving and of attempts to tap alternate sources of primary energy, European imports of oil and gas are rising. The imports of natural gas are rising especially fast. Much of that gas comes from Russia or transits via Russia on its way to consumers in Central and Western Europe.

That makes for unease with these consumers. First, because the supply of Russian gas is limited.[10] Second, because Russia uses its position as a transit country for gas supplies not just for economic benefit, but also as a political tool. Central and Western European consumers of gas that comes from, or via Russia therefore suffer through unnerving uncertainty because a cut in the supply of natural gas would seriously disrupt their economies and societies.

The result was a project to circumvent Russia with a new pipeline (termed "Nabucco" in allusion to Verdi's opera on another hostage escape). Several major European energy companies have joined in this project and have formed a consortium, as any single one of these companies would not have been able to bring such project to completion. The leader of the consortium is the Austrian ÖMV.[11] The gas pipeline would be long, running from Central Asia through Turkey, the Balkans, and the West Balkans to Central Europe.

Members of the "Nabucco" consortium are in there for their profit and in order to safeguard a position as reliable suppliers of natural gas. But that does not detract from the eminently political character of their project.

- By its very nature, it runs counter to strong Russian economic and political interests. Russia was, in fact, not slow to react. It managed to secure, via long term contracts, the supply of Central Asian natural gas that otherwise could have been fed into the "Nabucco" pipeline.[12] In addition, Russia floated the project of a competing gas pipeline, named "Southstream," that would continue to use Russian territory while also terminating in Central Europe.

- At the moment it is not certain at all that enough gas would be available to make the use of "Nabucco" economically feasible. Iran is one of the potential, added sources of gas to be fed into the pipeline. But due to its nuclear-arms projects, Iran is under threat of economic sanctions. Co-operation with Iran on such a large-scale a project would be considered a breach of solidarity among all those many and powerful states that dangle the Damocles sword of trade restrictions over Iran in order to have it desist from developing nuclear arms. A heavy political price would have to be paid for signing a long-term gas supply agreement with Iran, as such an agreement would undercut efforts to pressure Iran by limiting economic intercourse.

- Not all problems are resolved that emerge from the projected use of Turkish territory. Some of them are political.

- Partly political is also the question as to which country would get which quota from the gas transported through the pipeline; the question as to the price of that gas; and the question as to the fees to be paid for the pipeline transiting over a state's territory.
- Last not least, the problem of energy security that the pipeline wishes to resolve is deeply political too, as a failure to provide such security is not ascribed to this or that company. Citizens will put the blame for such a failure on their own states and on their own politicians.[13]

In the Nabucco project, politics are thus interlinked intimately with economic interests and with the interests of private companies. In response, the company leading the consortium has now established its own version of a foreign ministry. With former German foreign minister Joschka Fischer it has found a politically prominent person to head that office. But nonetheless, even with those persons in charge, and even with all the clout of the powerful transnational companies involved, the project still could not do without the political support rendered by states.

The "Nabucco" project is a showpiece for the mixing of politics with the dynamics of private enterprise. But such mixing is not exceptional. Economic development and progress is not just the business of business. Given its vast consequences, it is also the project of states. That has been so already in the past. Kings in 18th century Europe went to great lengths in order to promote their manufactures and to make them equal at least to those of other European states. Overcoming economic backwardness was the prime goal of the Meji-reformers in Japan; as well as the motive of the Russian Bolsheviks when staging their revolution in 1917. The same desire motivated the Indian Congress Party after India became independent. And the same goal prompted Latin American states into the failed attempt to catch up by economically isolating their "periphery" from the "centers" formed by the already rich nations of the world.

What is new, though, is the very fierceness of this competition to move up into the ranks of economic high performers and to remain there. This has become the political top priority. It calls for mobilization across a broad spectrum of state-sponsored or state-directed activities. Few governmental agencies are by now not involved in this project of accelerating economic development. It cannot be otherwise, because success in the economic race depends on a complex set of conditions. Many things feed into economic growth. The scope of this input becomes wider, the wealthier a country has become already.

Whatever the motives for the activities of states, be they economic or others, it is clear that these activities have expanded. Many of these tasks have more than a merely national dimension. In order to accomplish them, states have no choice but to reach beyond their borders. In doing that, states effectively promote globalization as they use and enhance global interdependence.

In public discussion, this is not the image that prevails. The state is often portrayed as the victim of global forces that would have curtailed its reach and would have substituted for its legitimate power the power of other global agents. States would have been shunted aside either by those "bureaucrats in Brussels"; or by "global financial capital." For some xenophobes in the United States, it is the United Nations Organization that bullies and diminishes states with this organization aspiring to become a world government, and with its secretary-general embodying Anti-Christ and flying around in unmarked, black helicopters.

In fact though, these agents that seem to victimize states are there to fulfill functions that are necessary. Many of such functions are exercised at the behest of states, which have charged these new actors to do those things that each state, acting alone, no longer could accomplish.

That is not to everyone's liking. Extreme conservatives and the extreme Left both wish to see that process reversed. They yearn for a return to earlier times when states still could each act more independently from another. They idealize this past. They ignore that the then-existing, *rule-less anarchy* between states made for a regime of frequent violent conflict that left citizens poor, insecure and exhausted.[14]

What is so glorious about this past with the endless wars of the 18th century; with the imperial subjugation of the majority of mankind in the 19th century; with the suicidal European civil wars of the 20th century? What is so glorious about the past unchecked plundering of the earth's limited resources and the cavalier destruction of ecologically sound environment? Isn't all that rant against global interdependence nothing but the immature and unrealistic yearning for a return to the small unit and the simple village life? Doesn't this rejection of the complex and global have its parallel in sentiments that motivated the European

Romantics; sentiments which accompanied them from their beginnings in the 19th century to their late bloom in fascism and communism?

And then—What are the alternatives to economic and political interdependence? What are the alternatives to states transferring their isolated decision-making up to joint decision-making on a higher level? What are the alternatives to have other, new actors participate in such decisions? Could one recreate for the economy an exclusively national frame? As it is obvious that that is not possible, how would one organize this inevitable linkage between national economies? Could one find a substitute for worldwide markets doing this coordination? Who—what would substitute for the entrepreneurial function of transnational corporations? Would states, each acting for itself, be able to create a financial market of sufficient depth and width? Or would they be capable of shouldering each alone and each for just its own market the high costs of pharmaceutical research needed for the development of a new drug?

Inevitably, activities of financial markets do have a political dimension. Activities of transnational corporations and of pharmaceutical firms also have a political dimension. States and their citizens have a legitimate interest that these political aspects are being addressed. They have an interest, for example, in financial markets remaining grounded in the real economy, not pursuing spurious profits in stock and real estate bubbles. States and their citizens have an interest in pharmaceutical research being geared not just to serve potential patients who are wealthy and able therefore to pay high prices for new drugs. They have an interest in such drugs becoming broadly available and affordable—especially to poorer patients and in poorer countries.

States can articulate such political interests. But they will bring them to bear only if they join with other states in an organized, predictable way. Predictability implies the existences of norms and thus the existence of constraints. It implies the acceptance of a form of decision-making in which concessions have to be made; and in which the input of each individual state is only a minor part of the ultimate whole.

It is misleading to portray the acceptance of those limitations as nothing but a loss of sovereignty. We are better served by the image of sovereignty being shared between states. We thus have to get accustomed to the notion of sovereignty—the right of political decision-making—being exercised on many levels. Today sovereignty is best exercised by being there where decisions affecting one's country are being taken. This might happen on a regional or even on a global level.

Sovereignty on Many Levels

While sovereignty is being shifted upwards to joint decision-making by several states, we seem oblivious to the fact that sovereignty is also a shared in the other direction. Political decision-making takes place not just on that one level of central governments. It also takes place in communities, townships, counties, provinces. These units have varied degrees of autonomy that detracts from the full sovereignty of the central state. The central state does not interfere with towns deciding on zoning rules; or with provinces deciding on nature reserves or on secondary roads. We consider it expedient that state functions are transacted not just through the central government; but also through these sub units. Nothing seems more natural.

Long time ago and with the central authority of rulers being weak, these subunits were even politically dominant. In the High Middle Ages, towns, for example, had a great degree of independence from rulers; as had feudal vassals reigning over agricultural land. From those times on, interdependence between these political subunits became stronger. Increasingly, they came to share problems and tasks with other political units. Joint action was called for and this requirement resulted in a strengthening of the central authority. It was reflected in a shift upwards in the making of binding political decisions.

Interrelations now become more dense on a worldwide scale. This necessitates a renewed shift upwards in decision-making, with political governance becoming regional, as in the case of the European Union, or even global. But that does not imply a wholesale weakening of the political function of states. It just implies that they exert their influence no longer by standing alone and isolated from another. States join other states and they join non-state actors in making and in enforcing rules that bind all of them.

While this might be accepted, many object that in this process of joint decision-making, actors other then states would have gained too strong a role. The power of these non-state actors, such as the power of transnational corporations and of financial markets, would not be legitimized in a political process. Not controlled by politics, they would, nonetheless impact heavily upon the lives of citizens.

That is largely true. One should beware, nonetheless, of concluding that next to them states would have lost all influence. They have not. States do remain the most prominent agents in global governance. Indeed, they are the very pillars of this system of global governance. It would crumble in their absence.

States maintain that role for three reasons:

a) For institutional reasons as they have the necessary tools to effectively participate in global rule-making and in making these rules stick.

b) As they can confer legitimacy to such rule-making and to such rule-enforcement in a way no other global actor can.

c) As they more than any other group or institution[15] set the frame for individuals to define their identity.

a)   States are prominent in global governance for institutional reasons as they wield the tools necessary for an effective participation in global rule-making and rule-enforcement.

No other institution can rival states in this capacity. States have to attend to those many different interests of citizens that cannot be met by business or by the intermediate organizations of civil society. States establish the rules that govern conflicts between those interests. They have the capacity to provide a host of public services. And they have the capacity and the right to enforce compliance with rules—whether these have originated in their own narrower realm, or whether they have their origin in global governance. Other global actors can employ but few of those many instruments that are at the disposal of effective and efficient states. The toolbox of states is comprehensive and thus irreplaceable.

b)   States can confer legitimacy on global rule-making and rule-enforcement in a way no other global actor can.

To those who have been touched by it, globalization provides politically significant linkages to institutions beyond the borders of their state. They might deeply share a concern promoted by an international non-governmental organization such as Greenpeace or Amnesty International. They would be tied to such groups by relatively narrow and specific concerns and interests. This tie legitimizes a group like Greenpeace to speak in the name of its members and have an input, in this narrow field, on global governance. Greenpeace would, however, not be legitimized to address, in the name of its members, other issues such as migration or the regulation of financial markets.

The important but relatively narrow interests of Greenpeace will often conflict with interests pursued by other national or global groups. In such conflicts, Greenpeace is just a party. If this is a conflict about a decision to be passed in the realm of global governance, it will have to be resolved before such a decision can be made. There has to be a judge considered legitimate to make such an adjudication. It must be a judge who is in a position to balance against each other all the many groups and interests that are touched by a political decision. No such institution exists[16] on a global level as global institutions too, are mostly specialized and deal with just a few issues and not with all of those that are up for a political decision.

In that respect, states differ from international organizations. Agendas of international organizations are each limited to the specific and circumscribed field these organizations are active in. The agenda of states, on the contrary, is a very broad one. As a consequence, states have contact to, and influence over many, widely differing groups. All these different groups have learned to accept the state as arbiter when their interests and values clash. The judgment rendered by a state on such a clash of values and of interests is therefore accepted as legitimate.[17]

c)   *Among many institutions, states are still those that, as a rule, most strongly define the identity of an individual.*

Globalization implies that citizens attach emotionally to groupings others than the group formed by their fellow citizens. They might define themselves less exclusively as citizen of this or that state. They might add to this identity as citizens of a state an identity as employee of a transnational corporation; they might be fans of this or that foreign pop star, artist or soccer club; they might be tied to other nations by parts of their family living there; as top scientists they might largely live in a community that tends to abstract from the national background of its members.[18]

Modern humans might have acquired multiple identities and some cosmopolitan airs. But when push comes to shove, if multiple identities come into conflict, the odds are high that the emotional bond to one's own state will prevail over the liens that have been formed to groups beyond the borders.

In parts, this attachment is reflection of the privilege of political participation that states provide to their citizens and to their citizens only.

Yet the attachment to the state, to the place one is born and raised in, this emotional *embeddedness* in a home state is more basic even. It is the sum of culture, family, formative early live experience and language. This heritage translates into a strong bond to the respective state. It exists even if the ruling regime is being perceived as unjust and illegitimate.

To sum up: It has been argued that states become weaker by losing ground to other actors both in their internal and in their external tasks. The reach of internal policies would be curtailed by a loss of public space accessible equally to all citizens; by the growing individualization of life; by the expansion of the private sector into fields that had been tilled by the state before; and by a shrinking of the tax base due to concessions that have to be made to footloose corporations and to equally footloose financial capital. The economy in general would have come to dominate and reduce the state.

But there is a reverse side to this picture. Actually, the functions of the state have not shrunk. They have expanded with the expansion of the economy; not at least because a dynamically expanding economy cannot do without a dynamically growing state sector. Also, persons are still largely defined, and they still largely define themselves as citizens of this or that state. Their emotional support and attachment to a state is still strong. In sum, it thus would be wrong to claim that the state would have lost relevance in impacting on events and on persons within its borders.

It also has been argued that the state is losing ground in its capacity to impact on events beyond its borders. It is true that states have lost their former monopoly as sole global actors. They have come to share the stage with newly arrived other actors such as transnational corporations; with the extremely powerful and global financial markets; with international non-governmental organizations, *nations without a state*, and even with individuals that have become both subjects and objects of global concern and action.

While this much is obvious, states still remain the sturdiest pillars in the system of global governance. There are no substitutes for them that could enforce global rules with equal efficiency. Lastly, it is only states that can still provide the broad base of political legitimacy to decisions and rules agreed upon on a global level.

A gap between the internal and the external has always existed. It is the gap between the familiar and controllable on one side, and on the other side the distant, uncertain and strange that is difficult to gauge and to control. It has been the task of diplomacy to work in this space in-between and to connect the two sides. With the intensification of interdependence, the bridging of this gap has evolved into a complex and never-ending task, with new actors on both sides of the gap and with new issues emerging that have to be addressed. This bridging will not occur by itself in an evolutionary process that works without political interference. No such mechanism exists that would automatically produce an end result that is optimal for all. Such processes have to be guided by politics. And politics needs tools to be effective.

This is where diplomacy and diplomats come in. That, however, cannot be the old sort of diplomacy and the old sort of diplomats wedded to outdated and often counterproductive ways.

Notes

1. Triggering a race to the bottom for the lowest taxes and the most favorable conditions.
2. Among the industrial and post-industrial countries; and they have done so notwithstanding the failure of the WTO Doha Round.
3. Experience has also shown that, notwithstanding their goodwill and their mobilization of much resources, outsiders have difficulties in substituting for the institutions and services of failed states; proving that a state supported (even passively) by its citizens is irreplaceable.
4. This is a more recent development. Up until the 1970s, economic development in the rich countries had also coincided with growing equality of income. But over the last 40 years, the gap between the "haves" and the "have-nots" has become wider again.
5. It is worth recalling that in 2006, 980 million people still lived on less than one dollar a day; and that 500,000 women died annually in childbirth (UN—The 2007 Millennium Development Goals Report).
6. The case of China and Japan seems to falsify that claim, with their continued existence over 2,000–3,000 years. Being no expert on their political history, I would nonetheless surmise that like Europe, they too had a feudal order over long phases of their existence; and thus an order not compatible with the order established by and in modern states.
7. I have to use the German expression, as the English term "welfare state" does not convey the same meaning. "Welfare" is something for the derelict and poor—a charity incumbent on the rest of the population. The "Sozialstaat," on the contrary, is there for everyone. It provides everyone with services that are not well rendered by private institutions, such as health care and old-age income.
8. Just as the illegal production, trade and consumption of drugs have laid the base for a vast expansion of criminal activities and organizations; and even for the destabilization of whole states.
9. The direction of causality is not one-sided. Both realms together are imbedded in an evolutionary process.
10. At least at present, as not enough had been invested in the tapping of new gas fields.
11. Still partly owned by the Austrian government.

12.   China has managed to hook up the Central Asian sources of gas supply by a
       pipeline of its own.
13.   As proven by the precedent of a crisis that evolved in 2007 when the transport of
       Russian gas over Ukraine territory was cut for political and economic motives.
       Politicians and not private firms were held accountable for resolving that crisis.
14.   Hobbes has described the state of nature—that is the absence of a state—as
       making human existence "nasty, brutish, poor, and short." One could transfer
       that metaphor to the level of the community of states. In absence of overarching
       global or regional structures and regional or global governance, the life of states
       (and of their citizens) would also be "nasty, brutish, poor, and short."
15.   Perhaps with the exception of religious groups. But that is a proposition in
       need of closer scrutiny, as one has to ask whether the—newly increased—power
       of religion just substitutes a sense of commonality where states have failed to
       build one.
16.   Some formal international organizations, such as the UN itself, have a broader
       agenda. Its Economic and Social Council (ECOSOC) should somehow coordi-
       nate the activities of the numerous UN Specialized Agencies. ECOSOC should
       therefore function as a kind of embryonic world government—in the realm of
       economic and social affairs. But ECOSOC is far—very far—from filling that
       bill. Informal institutions such as the G-20 also have a broad agenda, but are too
       unstructured to assume quasi-governmental functions.
17.   This is one of the main reasons for the doubtful legitimacy of some decisions
       made by international organizations. Inevitably, these decisions deal with
       certain aspects of an issue that concern an international organization, while
       neglecting other aspects that are also important but inconvenient. A case in
       point are some decisions by the World Trade Organization (WTO). In one of its
       rulings, it rejected as an inappropriate hurdle to free trade attempts by importing
       states to exclude from such imports fish caught in a way endangering dolphins
       and already endangered sea turtles. One cannot blame environmentalists for
       harshly criticizing that decision. It set as absolute an interest—namely the
       interest in free trade—that should have been balanced against other interests,
       such as the interest in protecting the fauna of the oceans.
18.   The philosopher and writer Norbert Elias has defined such an acquisition of
       "multiple identities" as the essence of modernization.

20

From Government to Governance

"It is impossible to predict the future; but it may be possible to construct a partial knowledge that can be helpful in making the future; i.e., in channeling the direction of events toward a desired option from among those feasible."
—Robert Cox, 1992, p. 139

The terror of World War I spawned the Pan European Movement. So as to forestall a repeat of the war, the movement agitated for the political unification of Europe. It could mobilize substantial support, but hopes were shattered by the World War II. The experience of this new catastrophe renewed the energies of the movement. In 1948, governments were successfully pressured into participation at the Hague Congress on Europe, intended to provide the political basis for European unification, with no less an aim than the creation of a European federal state. But governments balked and made for an outcome that was modest.

The Congress resulted in nothing more than the creation of the Council of Europe. Like most other international organizations, it is only an inter-governmental body and as such under the control of its members' governments. Their decisions have to be unanimous and these decisions are therefore subject to the veto of any member state. But even if all of its members were unanimous, the Council of Europe would still be barred from dealing with issues of security policy. Furthermore, it hardly has any function in the realm of the economy and of economic relations between European countries. It therefore cannot act in the two areas that are central in European integration.

In view of the minimal results of the Hague Congress, and in view of the obvious limitations of the Council of Europe, those working for a United Europe had to search for other means to promote their cause. They had failed in an attempt to have states and their politicians act as drivers of European integration. They had to look for an alternate engine to do the job. The economy was defined as such an alternate and potent engine of European integration. Six European core states started in 1953 with the merger of their coal and steel industries. Two years later, in the Treaty of Rome, the merger was expanded into a larger project, the European Economic Community, covering not just coal and steel, but all of the economic activities of these six European states.

The European Economic Community succeeded where the Council of Europe had failed. It deepened the economic integration among its members. Over time, this process of integration came to encompass other fields; and even fields such as the police and the judiciary, that once were thought to be in the exclusive realm of internal politics. The European Economic Community mutated into the European Union. Step by step, the process expanded by involving nations other than the six original members. It now stands at 27 members and the process is still ongoing.

It was the conscious political decision of the Union's founding fathers to use the economy as a driving force for the intended political integration of Europe. History has proven them right as via the economy other than economic operators also gained a stake in it: environmentalists, consumers, farmers, persons, and groups active in assistance to poorer countries, trade unions and even the military. Globalization had touched all these groups; and they turned to the European Union to provide the political tools for protecting their interests and for balancing these interests against each other.

One cannot claim that this process of integration ran its course against the express will of the member states of the European Union. But clearly, states were not the true engines that drove that process. Were it otherwise, there is a good chance that the attempt at European integration would have stalled for a second time and that we still would have nothing more than another version of the intergovernmental Council of Europe. On the other hand, the project would also have become stuck had it not had the passive acceptance or the active support of civil society. Civil society, on its turn, would have failed to reach its objectives if it would have been blocked by the economy and by economic institutions.

European integration had therefore been promoted by several agents. It had been an evolutionary process. Like biological evolution,[1] it did not proceed in a straight, steady manner but via discontinuities. As in biological evolution, there is no master plan and no master planer to steer that process. There are many and often competing agents instead. They interact in complex ways and over various interfaces.

The European Union has no counterpart in other regions of the world. States in these other parts have not merged their sovereignty in the same way European states did. In this wider world, there is no counterpart to the European institutions, which are authorized to establish their own rules and to enforce them against the Union's members. No supreme global lawmaker exists. There is no one to pass decisions that would bind all nations of the earth.[2] No global police is in place and no worldwide army to enforce even those rules and regulations that have been agreed upon by the international community.

How come then, that we are not engulfed by chaos? How come that we have come to blindly trust the global relations and cooperation across borders to be predictable and to work with clockwork efficiency? Why we are not criminally negligent if we have come to rely on the uninterrupted import of absolute essentials like food and energy, and have tolerated native agriculture to wither and local production of energy to stagnate?

We have acquired that mindset not because we were thoughtless, but because experience has led us to trust cooperation and arrangements between states and between other global actors to have become predictable and solid. We therefore see no need to hoard food and fuel in fear that their supply from foreign places could become restricted due to hostile decisions made by supplier countries.[3] We have come to trust that even in strange places governments will try to safeguard the security of visitors. We have come to rely on the trans-border transfer of money; on aircrafts being permitted to land at foreign airports and ships to berth at foreign ports. We expect as a matter of course that we might call on the telephone someone in a faraway country. Without being aware of the many technical details, we simply expect that products and procedures have become standardized enough so as to permit such telephone calls.

Why can we trust such arrangements if there is no world government to establish rules and to enforce them if necessary? Why can we trust the stability of such rules and arrangements in absence of institutions and mechanisms such as the ones of the European Union? We trust these arrangements because, in absence of a world government, we have come to depend on a multifaceted, resilient and effective "global governance."

The European Union has evolved into a *proto federal state*. It has become endowed with a *proto government*. Yet it has come to that point by starting from, and evolving governance. Might it be that the world as such now also enters this process there where the European Union had begun it?

When seeking solutions to the problems caused by global interdependence, wouldn't we be well advised to discard the notion of some form of *government*? Should not we look instead at *governance* as a concept that can better explain how states and humans cooperate around the world in an effective and predictable manner?

In government, the ultimate and highest authority lies either with a single institution; or is divided according to the principle of a separation of powers between the legislature, the judiciary, and the executive branch. These authorities alone are entitled to pass binding rules. They alone have the right and power to enforce them. Governments rule over clearly defined territories and have the exclusive right to do so. Outsiders are forbidden to interfere. The subjects these rules are addressed to are also clearly defined as citizens or residents of a single state.

Governance is less clearly determined. Supreme authority is not lodged in one single institution (or in a legislature, an executive and a judiciary, each with clearly established functions). It is not evident, in particular, whether in governance such authority comes top-down from above; or whether, on the contrary, it derives from the express or tacit support and consent to rules that bind all to a common goal.

Under the fictions of international law, governments across the globe would all be each other's equal. They would be the sole relevant actors in the global system. If we substitute the notion of *governance* for the notion of *government* the scene becomes more diverse. It is populated not just by states of different political weight and capacity, but also by numerous other actors. It is populated with all those institutions that are capable of affecting political outcomes in more than one country.

In the preceding chapters we have dealt with many of these new global actors: international non-governmental organizations, global networks, transnational corporations, and the global financial industry. Also included are individuals who have global credibility and appeal, such as the British pop star Bono, who effectively mobilized for a debt reduction of the poorest countries, and Princess Diana, who inspired the movement to ban landmines. And then there is the most potent of all such new global actors, namely information. It now is instantly accessible all across the world with its powerful images and its implicit calls for political action.

It is clear how government works. It is evident too, how such government projects itself beyond the borders of a single state. That is defined by constitutions and by international law. But what is the mechanism of governance? Its mechanism is not so well defined. Let us therefore break this question down into a query on the three elements necessary for a new global rule to emerge and to become effective:

Figure 20.1 The Three Feedback Loops of Global Governance

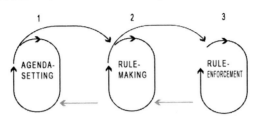

There are three of such loops, each being connected to the next one. The feedback flows within each of these three loops, but also—back and forth between them.

The first loop of *agenda setting* establishes an issue for the subsequent task of rule setting. It makes an issue an issue so to say. On occasion, states can do this. They may act as *agenda entrepreneurs* who point to a problem that, in their view, needs to be tackled. It is not just big states that assume such function as agenda entrepreneur. Quite on the contrary. This is often done by smaller states in search of an international profile and of a chance to establish a distinct global presence. It was, for example, the small state of Malta that raised awareness for the need to have a treaty that establishes a regime for the high seas that corresponds to present-day circumstances.[4]

Frequently too, the role of agenda entrepreneurs is being assumed by non-state actors. Sometimes it has been the scientific community that had put an issue on the global agenda, pointing, for example, to dangers inherent in the depletion of the world's ozone layer; or pointing to the trend of global warming caused by man-made emissions of greenhouse gases. International non-governmental organizations became agenda entrepreneurs, *inter alia*, for a number of other environmental issues that later became subject of global/international regulation, such as the rules to preserve bio-diversity, or rules that establish ecologically sound practices in forestry and fishery. Media and charitable organizations can draw attention to a looming humanitarian crisis that should be thwarted. Regular international organizations too, can raise an issue that they see in need of being dealt with. As mentioned, even single persons can slip into that role, provided they have a more than merely national presence and credibility.

In this first loop of agenda setting, an issue is being circulated between various groups and institutions. It might circulate from individuals to the scientific community, to non-governmental organizations, to international organizations and states. An issue is incubated for a certain period of gestation in this first loop before being forwarded to the next loop of rule setting.

Many of those who participate in this first loop of agenda-setting will then also participate in the *loop of rule-making*. There, their role and function will, however, be a different one. Those affected by these rules, will have a stronger role and voice. Costs and benefits of possible solutions will be assessed against another. Things will become more controversial. The first loop was an assembly of like-minded that established an agenda for global governance. In the subsequent loop of rule-making those like-minded are no longer among themselves. They have to convince those that hitherto had been mum and neutral on the question the agenda-setters had raised. They will also have to confront opponents whose material or non-material interest would be affected negatively by what the proponents of a new rule want to achieve. In this second loop of rule-setting one thus moves from discussion to negotiation with a more prominent place for those who are skilled in this task of negotiations.

Once in place, a rule has to be applied. We thus enter the third loop of *rule-enforcement*. Though commonly used, the term *enforcement* is a misleading one. Taken in its literal sense, the word would imply that compliance with a rule results from the fear of otherwise suffering the consequence of negative sanctions. But rules are being respected out of other motives mainly. This is clearly the case in the compliance of citizens with laws of their state. People do not abstain from murder just out of fear for otherwise landing in jail. In fact, deterrence by such punitive sanctions has little effect upon the level of violent crime. In their majority, people obey laws because that is expected of them and because that is the social norm.

The same holds true for international/global rules. International business norms[5] and international norms on human rights[6] are mainly respected not out of fear of otherwise suffering negative sanctions. They are mostly respected for reasons of *global socialization*; because they are perceived to be legitimate and accepted by peers in other states one wishes to emulate. Such peer pressure does not emanate solely from civil servants in other states. Franklin (2008) has shown that in bringing about a change in human rights practices in Latin America, "criticism by INGOs (such as Amnesty International) was more effective than criticism from (official) intergovernmental organizations...." Reviews, bench marks, periodic surveys are means to bring such social pressure to bear.

Those soft means of enforcement cannot completely replace all punitive sanctions. Most effective among those punitive sanctions will be those that withhold a potential benefit such as the benefit of being included in mutually advantageous economic arrangements. More dubious is the effect of economic sanctions that restrict activities that otherwise would take place, as for example sanctions that limit trade, investment, or travel. Few of these sanctions have actually worked. Some had proven counterproductive as they strengthened the uncooperative regime instead of weakening it. Equally problematic are military interventions.[7]

What then are the differences between the *global government* and the emerging reality of *global governance?*

1) "Government" would imply that a single type of actor would set the rules and have them applied too. States—either acting alone, in conjunction with others or via subservient international organizations—would hold that monopoly.

2) Unlike in "government," in "governance" the actors and their methods are *not invariable*. Action might originate in one place and the next time and on a different issue in another one. On one and the same issue, different actors might assume the leading role—each of them in one of the three realms of agenda-setting, rule-making and rule-enforcement.

3) Taking their cue from the so-called realist theory of international relations,[8] commentators have tended to characterize world order in terms of *poles of power*. In recent times, the world system thus would have changed from being *bipolar* such as it was said to have been before the demise of communism, to the *unipolar* world American neoconservatives raved about in the 1990s, and now to the *multipolar world* emerging countries would like to see arise with their powers enhanced to become equal to the one of the presently powerful. Such a worldview is wildly off the point. Where everything is connected to everything else, the very notion of some state being a "pole" becomes misleading; as does the notion of power defined as the capacity to force others to do what they otherwise would not wish to do. The notion of an autonomous "pole," able to lord over others becomes defunct as even big and wealthy states cannot reach their goals alone but only in conjunction with others. The notion of "government" abstracts from that reality. It implies that states could have their way, provided they are powerful enough. The notion of "governance" marks the demise of this illusion.

4)   A certain hierarchy between the merely local, the state-wide, the regional and the global will persist, as issues that can be dealt within a more narrow circle will in fact be dealt within the more narrow circle. But borders between these different realms have become porous and *it is no longer feasible to clearly differentiate between internal and external politics*. Political ventures into the realm of the global/international will ultimately fail if they do not have a base in internal politics.[9] Internal politics will fail on their turn, if they run up against the main stream of global politics. If one wishes for results, those two realms of the internal and the external will have to be kept in focus at the same time. The concept of "government" implies the notion of the two realms being separate; not so the notion of "governance."

5)   Changes in quantity ultimately change quality. The vastly rising quantity of international/global transactions has led to a change in the nature and quality of these relations. The issues diplomacy dealt with when created in the 17th century were limited: wars; the preparation for wars; the formation or disbandment of alliances; with occasional negotiations on the dowry thrown in that was expected at the wedding of royals. Today, global governance has to address a thousand other issues. The realm has expanded in which worldwide cooperation is inevitable if one wishes to assure the physical security of individuals and their being provided with basic goods and services. Issues such as cyber-security that were unknown still ten years ago, now demand urgent attention and they have to be addressed in worldwide context. The concept of "government" is contingent on the existence of a well-defined and stable agenda. "Governance" can deal and flourish with an open-ended agenda.

6)   It is obvious that the diversity in the nature of problems that need to be resolved also calls for differentiated remedial action.[10] Global governance cannot move on one single level only. Regulatory issues concerning the electronic industry will be dealt with in another venue, among other experts and with other tools than regulatory questions concerning finance and banking. Still vaster differences will exist between these two realms of regulatory issues and the realm of traditional security problems.

    The graphic below provides an example for this complexity as it demonstrates the plurality and diversity of actors needed for minimizing the risk of a new, worldwide influenza epidemic.

Figure 20.2 Influenza—Who Does What in Combating the Danger?

- Preparedness involves a **coordinated global effort** to make best use of resources and tools available, to help mitigate the effects of a pandemic

- A complex range of **organisations** are involved in the coordination of preparedness activities:

A snapshot of the organisations involved in pandemic preparedness and their activities

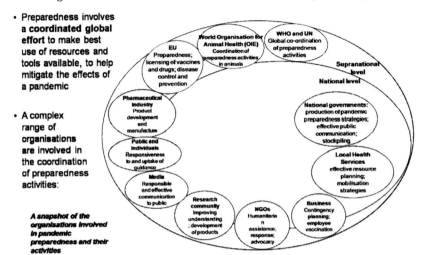

Source: the Wellcome Trust.

This inevitable diversity of actors shatters the base of one single, fully coherent "national foreign and security policy." One might be actively hostile to the Iranian government for its aspiration to acquire nuclear weapons. But that should not stand in the way of cooperation with the Teheran regime on questions such as the prevention of new pandemics or the improvement of weather forecasts. In a similar vein, it would be problematic to impose economic sanctions on China for its failure to live up to Western standards of human rights. That would not improve the situation of those in China who see their human rights curtailed. And the worsening of economic relations caused by such sanctions against China would probably hurt those that impose these sanctions more than this would hurt China itself. So it makes sense to keep the two spheres separate: to encourage better respect for human rights in China; and to deal with economic issues on their own merit. The concept of "government" implies a full integration of several issue areas into one single and coherent policy, with a clear hierarchy of goals and with security concerns coming on top.[11] Such concept can no longer be implemented. "Governance" permits the co-existence of several strains of external policies.

7) "Government" uses a limited set of tools to define issues; to negotiate the rules to address them; and to see those rules applied in practice. Discussions and the decisions by parliaments produce laws that later can be applied under the threat of punitive sanctions. In all three spheres, of agenda setting, rule-making and rule-enforcement, the tools and procedures of "governance" are more subtle and differentiated. Peer reviews, benchmarks and the powerful tools of social expectations supplement punitive sanctions that still have their place in one case or another.

The Power of Peer: Reviews and Benchmarks

The ranking of school systems through Programs for International Student Assessment (PISA) can highlight the political and operative potency of such instruments. PISA assesses the performance of students in mathematics, reading, and science according to uniform standards—agreed upon and monitored by peer-experts in the various participating countries. The results of such assessments are given below.

Table 20.1 PISA Ranking of Some OECD Countries, 2006

	Mathematics	Reading	Science
Germany	504	495	516
Austria	505	490	511
Finland	548	547	563
France	496	488	495
Italy	462	469	475
Japan	523	498	531
Canada	527	527	534
Netherlands	531	507	525
USA	474	495	489

The higher the number, the better the performance.

Source: OECD.

Some countries—such as Germany and Austria—ranked below their expectations in this PISA index. They had to accept that pride in their educational system was misplaced. That caused quite some political commotion. In Austria, it triggered efforts to search for a wholesale overhaul of the educational system. Few things in internal or external politics would have had an effect as powerful as this international peer-review. This demonstrates that this flexible tool of governance can be very effective.

All of the above arguments could tempt into the anarchist dream of the state and politics fading away and order emerging spontaneously from below and from the wishes and actions of small, rather autonomous groups. Such a conclusion would not just be wrong. It would be dangerous. It feeds into fantasies on a possible de-politization, privatization, and ultimate disappearance of a rule-bound, common public space. Such a rule-bound common public space exists between citizens of one state; it exists between the citizens of several states; and as it about to come to exist between the nearly 200 states of the world.

As in internal affairs, in global affairs too, most of the issues that call for a common response are political in their nature. Such political response cannot be captured by a neat mathematical formula nor be activated by the stroke of a pen. The answer has to be found in a process. This process of global governance is less tidy than the process that formerly had its run in internal and external politics. Things have become more complicated. The process of global governance calls for a broader political input; for more intense negotiations; for more give and take, for a greater involvement of the public; for more empathy with the views of others; and for more skills in reaching common ground.

In the following chapters we will look at the role diplomats might have in these complex political processes; and we will ask whether they are up to such new tasks.

Notes

1.   The Emanuel Kant project of a "Perpetual Peace" is frequently misrepresented as an exhortation to enlightened rulers and to an enlightened public to set up, from one day to the next, a world government. It would substitute the rule of law for endless, bloody hostility among states. Peace and prosperity would follow as by necessity. But this is not what Emanuel Kant meant. For him "Perpetual Peace" was not to be reached in just one single bold step. It would be the end product of

a long historical process. The result could not be simply willed into existence by mighty "sovereigns." "Perpetual Peace" would emerge from learning by experience and from a slow adaptation of politics. A new regime of peace could not simply be imposed from above. It would emerge from below.

2.   Safe—in rare circumstances—the UN Security Council.
3.   The Arab oil-producing countries attempted an embargo of oil exports in 1973. Given the ill consequences that this had for them, they are not very likely to repeat an embargo today.
4.   Thirty years later, it is still waiting to be ratified by the United States so as to become effective.
5.   Kollman, 2008.
6.   Adeyeva, 2007.
7.   That holds true even for interventions made for purely humanitarian reasons. For a while these might arrest murder and bloodshed. But their long-term effects are more dubious as such interventions are not likely to alter—and likely often to worsen—those facts on the ground and those tensions that had triggered the intervention in the first place. See the chapter on military power.
8.   In fact, the "realists" have been outrageously unrealistic in their assessment of the present world order.
9.   A notorious example: the peace process between Palestinians and Israelis is bound to wither and fail as long as Israeli internal politics cannot guarantee the actual dismantlement of the settlements on the West Bank. But this is something that seems very much out of reach of any Israeli government. On the other hand, Arab governments will, in the end, not be able to deliver on their peace promises if their populations remain aggressively hostile to the very notion of an Israeli state. They too will find it impossible to create in their internal politics the necessary base for an Israeli–Palestinian peace.
10.   At first sight it might seem that there is one task for which traditional proceedings of "government" and the concomitant proceedings of traditional diplomacy still retain their function. This is the task of addressing conflicts between two states or between two groups aspiring to statehood/political autonomy. But if we look at third-party interventions in such recent conflicts, we find that the picture is more complex and that here too, the process has become fractured and segmented. Traditional, third-party bilateral diplomacy shoulders just a part of such tasks of conflict resolution. In near all cases, its actions are supplemented by a set of very flexible, semi official instruments subsumed under the name of "Track Two Diplomacy." Persons from both sides that are not diplomats and who frequently are not even public officials meet in informal, mostly confidential encounters to search for common ground. Possible solutions they sketch are tested, again confidentially, by outside experts, opinion leaders, or focus groups. Such methods were applied in the search for peace among the Catholics and Protestants ("Republicans and Unionists") in Northern Ireland; in the attempt to promote a solution of the conflict between Israel and the Palestinians (in the so-called "Geneva-Process"); in conflicts in the post-Soviet area as they emerged, for example between the Ukraine and Russia, etc. This "Second Track Diplomacy" has an essential function. The moment negotiations become officially those between states, they become hostage to tactical considerations. Each party tries to enter such official negotiations with extreme positions and demands, so as to gain a tactical advantage when making concessions. As both sides wait for the other side to yield, the process might become stuck and both sides may find it increasingly difficult to "climb down" and to "lose face" in the public they rely on politically. "Track Two Diplomacy" turns the schedule around. It does not base itself on the

two starting positions; but on what may be a feasible solution. Official bilateral diplomacy cannot accept that as its own base and starting point. But it will have to be kept aware of what is going on in this "Second Track," so as to eventually wind down its own position to the compromise that has been found feasible in this "Second Track." Those active in this "Second Track" are themselves not wholly autonomous. They can only succeed if imbedded in a network of information and legitimacy such as it can be provided by civil society, by corporations, media and religious groups.

11. The world has accepted for a very long time this priority of security/foreign policy over all other realms of policies. This is Leopold von Rankes "Priorität der Außenpolitik" with "Außenpolitk" understood to be determined by security policy mainly: "Das Maß der Unabhängigkeit gibt einem Staate seine Stellung in der Welt. Es legt ihm zugleich die Notwendigkeit auf, alle inneren Verhältnisse zu dem Zweck einzurichten, sich zu behaupten. Dies ist sein oberstes Gesetz" (Ranke L, 1924, p. 37).

21

Diplomats as Facilitators of
Global Governance

"In the future there will be no diplomacy and no diplomats"
—*Count Nesselrode, Russian chancellor, 1859*[1]

Count Nesselrode had been prominent in Russian politics in the first half of the 19th century. This was a period of relative calm that followed the turmoil of the Napoleonic wars. Traditional diplomacy had safeguarded this peace through a "concert" of major European powers. As that era was about to end, Count Nesselrode seemed convinced that nothing good was to follow in a new era, when popular forces would replace authoritarian rule and traditional, big power diplomacy.

As Count Nesselrode recognized, the ground was shifting that had been the basis of traditional diplomacy. Ever since, the changes have become more massive. Count Nesselrode's world has vanished and the old concepts of governing it have become useless. It no longer suffices to balance against each other potentially antagonistic states. It no longer suffices to search for peace by creating an immutable, static order. We have to master the art of riding the wave of permanent and accelerating transformation. International prominence and power no longer derive from retaining for autonomous action a space as wide as possible. International prominence is now related to the ability to accept the inevitable shrinkage of full national independence and yet to shape this mutual dependence of states in a way that promotes national interests. The global order that once has been safeguarded by one or several big powers has now come to depend on the functioning of a multitude of more or less formal regimes and institutions. These regimes and institutions are being shaped, on their turn, not just by states, but also by a score of "new global actors."

Yet notwithstanding Count Nesselrode's forebodings on their imminent demise, diplomats are still around. They still claim a role in global affairs. In their outward appearances many of their activities still seem to be the traditional ones. And, indeed, some still are, because traditional diplomacy still has some place and function. But that function is limited. All of these traditional activities together would not support diplomacy in its claim to retain an important function in global governance. Much of this traditional diplomacy has in fact become an empty ritual; has become ineffective; and—according to my experience—even counter-productive.[2] Would they stick to such traditional functions, diplomats would therefore slowly wither away like other outdated and expensive trappings of status and prestige such as morning coats and top hats. Different agents and agencies would take their place.

Nonetheless we still find diplomats active at the levers of global governance. They are there in all of the three "loops" of global gover-nance; in the loop of agenda-setting; in the loop of rule-making; and in the loop of rule-enforcement. *Earth Summits* for example, have promoted substantial advances in the care for our planet. Their aim is to reconcile economic development—especially of the still poor countries—with the need to prevent irreplaceable resources from being depleted; and to prevent the earth's environment from being dam-aged beyond repair.[3] Given this goal, the Earth Summits are attended and shaped not just by the representatives of governments, but also by many other global actors, such as international non-governmental organizations, lobbyists for various industries, representatives of indigenous groups, etc.

The agenda of an *Earth Summit* is certainly far removed from the agenda of classical diplomacy. We therefore would assume diplomats to have little place and function in these Earth Summits. But this is not the case. Diplomats were involved, trying to bridge differences and to find common ground; or drafting a concluding text that could be accepted as guiding the actual follow-up to the conference.

The same holds true for other events and forums equally important in global governance. At the beginning of the third millennium, heads of states and governments gathered at the United Nations to define the goals they would pursue in the fight against human misery. These goals include the reduction in absolute poverty, the raising of life expectancy, the elimination of illiteracy, etc.—all issues that traditional diplomacy had not dealt with. One thus would assume that diplomats had hardly any function in the run up, in the running, and in the follow-up of this event. But they had. They were there in the background, behind the heads of states and governments. They wrote their briefing notes and their statements. Already before, they had negotiated a plausible outcome of the meeting. They were there to bridge differences that surfaced later.

In fact, venues such as these provide a welcoming habitat for diplomats. A former colleague of mine in the Austrian diplomatic service had been a mid-level, solid, but not very conspicuous, head of department in the international law section of the Ministry of Foreign Affairs. His specialty was international environmental law. He had a foot in academia, but otherwise lacked the urge to draw attention to his work and achievements. It thus came as a surprise to learn that he had been involved prominently in negotiations for the Montreal Protocol that successfully limited the emission of those gases that destroy the ozone layer in the earth's upper atmosphere and thus increase the exposure to damaging radiation. Diplomats like him were not the only ones working on that project. Scientists made decisive contributions; as did representatives of industry. Notwithstanding this multitude of other agents, diplomats were involved and theirs was a crucial contribution in tying together all these inputs and in drawing up the final instruments that were to establish the regime which, by now, has proven successful in reducing that threat to global health.

Financial experts, economists, higher civil servants from the line ministries all were active in the preparation and the follow up of the G-20 Summit held late in 2008 to deal with the world economic crisis. Military experts are prominent in negotiations on arms control and disarmament. But diplomats have a useful function even in such more technical negotiations.

We thus are faced with a paradox. How come that a profession, the practices and rites of which date back a 400 years, which may seem quixotically out of tune with modern times, how come that such a profession can nonetheless retain a key function in global governance?

We can tackle that question from two sides. We can ask whether through their training, through their on the job learning, and through adaptation to the culture of their peers, diplomats acquire skills that equip them for this function of oiling the machine of global political cooperation. We thus inquire into the nature and qualities of these actors. Political science would term that an *"actor-centered"* approach, with the outcome of a process being determined by the nature of actors involved in it.

Or we might turn the argument around and take a *systems-centered* approach. We might look at the present system of global interdependence and ask what characteristics such a system would impose on those who wish to navigate in it. Let us use this second approach first.

a)   One of the systems that determine the role of diplomats is the administrative system of their home country. Diplomats are just one of the species in the genus of civil servants. In theory, all civil servants would be nothing more than passive instruments of those at the top of the political hierarchy. But this remains fiction. Many decisions that seem to be purely administrative nonetheless imply the choice between politically charged alternatives. Even strict laws[4] and precise directives from politicians cannot eliminate that scope of discretion vested in upper-level administrators. Inevitably thus, higher civil servants do have a political function. Its extent varies from country to country. There are states with a tradition of a strong willed and self-confident civil service. There are states too, in which the role of parliaments is weak in comparison to the role of the administrative apparatus.[5] In extreme cases, politicians at the head of ministries have actually little say in the day-to-day running of affairs. They are nothing more than mere public relations agents of their bureaucracy.[6] However in other countries—such as the United States—elected officials and parliaments tend to leave to top civil servants just a narrow room for deciding matters that have political implications. Yet even if this scope for discretion in decision-making varies from country to country, it exists in all of them. Higher civil servants make decisions that are political in nature. That holds true too, for diplomats as they are members in this club of higher civil servants.

b)   Actually though, diplomats will be held at an even longer leash. Their work is of a nature that makes it difficult for parliaments or for elected officials to guide them in the same manner as they still might be able to guide other higher civil servants. Diplomats act at the divide between the realm of national politics and the realm of the global/international. To a greater or lesser degree, politicians might be in control of this first realm of internal politics. But they have much lesser impact on events taking place beyond national borders.[7]

    This is not to say that national politics has to accept passively everything that swaps over the borders. National politics can have some impact on the global system. But chances of succeeding usually depend on whether one state is able to join up with others. In negotiating with these other actors, diplomats are on a mission unto unknown and uncertain territory. They should not be bound by an injunction not to explore this or that alternative solution; or not to enter in negotiations on this or that feasible compromise. They will report back home. They will seek instructions. They will try to make the interests of their home country prevail. But they can reach common ground with other actors only if being given enough room for discretion and negotiation. When participating in global governance, diplomats will thus be more independent and less directly bound by instructions than other higher civil servants.

c) The evolution of the global system enhances the role of diplomats for the simple fact that this system is in ever-growing need of care and attendance. The densely knitted interdependence of states makes for a vast expansion of tasks that have to be addressed by common efforts. Some of these tasks are highly technical. Technical knowledge and expertise is required to tackle them. But such expertise and knowledge alone would not suffice for bringing together different views and interests. Another kind of expertise is needed in addition. This is the expertise of negotiating for positive results. Diplomats are in a good position to provide this expertise as their work trains them to accept diversity and to make the best of it. As the sheer volume of such negotiations has grown, so has the demand for the input diplomats can provide in such negotiating processes.

d) Negotiation must be based on some common understanding, on some "common sense" of the issues at stake. Negotiators have to share the same language so to say. Or—to use the technical term of social science—they have to share in the same *inter-subjectivity.* Inter-subjectivity does not imply or call for the merging of distinct cultures into a single one.[8] The world's cultures will remain distinct even under the impact of economic development and under the impact of globalization. Japan will not turn European, even if it had been tempted to try so on occasions. China will not even pretend to aim at such a profound break with its social and cultural traditions. But while cultures will remain distinct and different, the interface between them will expand nonetheless. Globalization pushes states together and forces them to work together. In order to be successful in such common work, they must be able to communicate with each other. They have to share the same inter-subjectivity.

Diplomats populate this habitat of shared meaning; of a common inter-subjectivity. This habitat of diplomatic inter-subjectivity is geared to facilitate the work of the diplomatic bridge-builders. The realm might look quaint to outsiders with its stylized forms of intercourse; with its coded language; with its blatant fictions such as the fiction of all states being equally sovereign. But this subculture exists because much of it is useful as it eases the tasks of diplomats.

At first sight it is surprising indeed, that representatives of so many different states with their many differing backgrounds are so much alike. They mostly share the same lifestyle—down to their clothing and to the kind of food served at their tables. Guests are entertained in a fashion that is pretty uniform across the whole diplomatic corps. Other outward trappings of diplomatic life are also roughly the same for all diplomats from wherever they might hail. Their professional work is structured in a way that is pretty much alike for all of them. The hierarchies are uniform with each rank being assigned distinct responsibilities. It is thus clear from the outset which diplomat in which rank should be addressed by another diplomat. Conference diplomacy is standardized in its rules and procedures. Clear rules determine what the chairperson of a meeting can and cannot do. Is well understood what is meant when a participant at such a meeting calls for a "point of order"; or when the chairperson declares that "consensus has been established."

Common and well-understood codewords facilitate communication. If a diplomat tells another diplomat, that his state would insist on something "by all means," or that talks at a meeting had been "frank and open," both sides are aware of the implications. But the common sense, the inter-subjectivity extends beyond such formalities. Underlying it all is the shared aim to come to positive results and the resolve to behave and act in a manner that makes it easier to reach that goal.

e)   While having one foot in this global habitat that they share with their colleagues from other countries, diplomats still remain servants of their home states. International non-governmental organizations can affect global governance by mobilizing their part of civil society. Transnational corporations affect global governance via their executives. Global interest groups may act through their representatives. States may participate in global governance through their heads of government or foreign ministers. But otherwise they will act through their diplomats mostly.

As we have seen, states remain the most relevant global actors by far.[9] It is to states that citizens turn when other institutions fail. Diplomats thus remain relevant as representatives of states. In global governance, diplomats provide the link to states, which still provide most of that legitimacy which ultimately must underpin all norms of global governance.

The Paradox of Global Order

A growing number of tasks and issues can no longer be tackled by single states each of them acting alone and independent from others. One should assume that this puts strong pressure on states not just to yield parts of their sovereignty upwards to a higher level of decision-making, but to ultimately merge, to unite first in confederations and then in true federal states. One would thus assume the number of independent states to dwindle.

Yet over the last century, development was in the opposite direction. The number of states has grown—dramatically so since the end of World War II and since the breakup of the European colonial empires. A further big jump in numbers occurred with the disappearance of the Soviet Union and of Yugoslavia. We have not yet seen the end of this development. Somalia has broken up in fact, if not in terms of international law. In Europe, Belgium might dissolve. With Palestine, a new Arab state is emerging in West Asia. Sudan will split in two in 2012.

Obviously, the smaller political unit provides a stronger sense of identity than a larger one, as more traits are likely to be shared in this smaller group than in a group that is bigger and that thus includes members with a wider spread of characteristics. It is obvious too, that the smaller political unit provides greater opportunity for co-determination than a bigger political unit. A single vote counts more in an electorate of 200,000 citizens than in an electorate of 200 million citizens.

So we are faced with a paradox. There should be a strong pressure toward the formation of bigger states. Yet the trend has been in the other direction toward the smaller political unit. How can that be?

The answer is that these two forces only seem to work in opposite directions. Actually, they are contingent upon each other. Some of the essential state functions have been transferred upwards and have been integrated into global or regional regimes. The state used to provide for a common economic space that set the parameters for economic activity. With the danger of big wars always present, it was states too, that could thwart the danger of such wars by warding off actual or potential enemies. To be economically successful, states had to be big enough to provide for a wide enough internal market in which firms could operate profitably. To succeed in war, states also had to be big so as to be able to raise sufficiently large armies and to carry the burden of sufficiently heavy armament.

Wealthy, democratic states no longer wage war against each other. Even small countries can expect not to be invaded by a bigger one. With the world as such having become the market for most products, the size of a purely national market has become irrelevant. Small has become feasible. Small has become "beautiful." That option for the survival and for the functioning of the smaller political unit has not opened up quasi automatically and all by itself. This option came to exist because of a change in the global regime, that is, a change in the formal and informal rules and institutions that sustain a peaceful togetherness of states and that permit economic activities to leap state borders.

Diplomacy—in its widest sense—has to build bridges between these two realms: the realm of the political unit of ever smaller states; and the realm of global regimes, rules, and institutions that safeguard those conditions which permit small political units to persist.

Diplomats therefore have their place in global governance through the function the global system assigns to them. The system as such needs those diplomatic bridge-builders. It creates room for their activities and endows diplomats with role and significance.

But let us now look at the question of the function of diplomats from the other side too. Let us use an *actor-oriented approach*. Let us look at the skills and qualities that would equip diplomats to participate in, and shape global governance.

Trying to answer this question, we face difficulties right away. There is nothing specific in the formal education required for entering the diplomatic service. In order to be admitted into the ranks of his colleagues, a medical doctor must have completed medical school. Someone aspiring to become a lawyer must have finished law school. Nobody can become a civil engineer or architect without proper academic credentials. Requirements for joining the diplomatic service are less well-defined. In Austria, one of the requirements used to be graduation from university either in law or economics. That restriction has long since been discarded. In practice, university graduates from many fields may take the entrance exam: scientists, historians, graduates in political science. Even two or three theologians had applied. Those taking the entrance exam into the US diplomatic service have an academic background that is equally broad.

So instead of looking at formal requirements such as the type of academic background, we have to look at these exams themselves and see how they sort people. How selective are they? How many apply and how many pass in the end? And which are the criteria that guide this selection?

In the United States as well as in Austria, there are three checkpoints to pass in this selection process. At the first stage, written applications are being screened with an elimination of those applicants that are less well-suited according to the documentation they had submitted.[10] The second hurdle to pass is a written examination, testing not just sheer knowledge but also skills in written articulation and argumentation. At this stage again, many applicants fall by the wayside. The third and final hurdle is the oral exam with scrutiny too, of the whole bearing and personality of a candidate. In their effect, these exams are very selective. On average, one out of ten applicants makes it in the Austrian exam.[11] In the United States the process is even more selective. There are plenty of applicants for just a few jobs and the employer can be choosey.

The fact that many apply for the few openings available proves that a diplomatic career is still considered attractive both for material and for non-material reasons. Diplomats are usually well paid—especially in their upper ranks. As civil servants, they profit from the advantages

civil servants usually enjoy such as a secure old age pension and a ro-
bust health insurance scheme. The inevitable risks and inconveniences
of postings abroad are being cushioned by generous allowances, provisions for housing; for the schooling of children; and for the benefit of
"trailing spouses."

Even more enticing are the non-material incentives for entering the
diplomatic service.[12] The main attractions of the diplomatic service are
its ever-changing challenges; the great variance of tasks and conditions
of work; the intimate connection with important decisions and events;
or—to use a grand word—the connection with "history itself."[13]

Compare this to the tedium inevitable in many other, even well-paid
positions. One may have become a generously rewarded vice president at
Unilever, responsible, all through one's career, for the sale of detergents.
With even higher salaries, one may "burn out" at 35 years of age at the
trading desk of an investment bank. As a judge one might be destined
to deal with youthful criminal offenders from the first day at the job till
the age of retirement. Compared to work in such treadmills, the work
of diplomats is privileged through its variety.

It is for all of these material and non-material motives that many
more applicants for a diplomatic career line up for the few openings that
become available each year. But there are reasons too, on the *demand
side* of the employer to keep it that way and to be in a position to select
just the few he considers best qualified.

States want diplomats to safeguard their interests and values in
global governance. States therefore have to put a premium on agents
that perform best in this task and make this state's interests and values
prevail. A state therefore has good reasons to select those well qualified
to deliver such results.

Which then are the criteria that guide states in selecting those they
think fit to provide this competitive advantage? As we have seen, these
criteria are less obvious than those criteria that qualify a doctor for a
medical job, or a civil engineer for his. The criteria for the selection and
qualification of doctors or engineers reflect the nature of the desired
outcome: a patient healed, a building well finished. In diplomacy such
end products are ill defined. The relative aptitude for the job is thus
gauged not against such an end product but against the capacity to be
effective in a process that is open-ended.

As this might seem a bit abstract, let us see how that translates into
the criteria used in the United States to judge candidates for a diplomatic

career in the final, oral exam. Let us look at some of the "skills and dimensions" that are being tested in this US exam:[14]

- To work and communicate effectively and harmoniously with persons of other cultures and value systems, political beliefs, or economic circumstances.
- To stay calm and effective in stressful and difficult situations.
- To absorb complex information from a variety of sources.
- To be honest, avoid deceit, and present issues frankly without injecting subjective bias.
- To discern what is appropriate, practical, and realistic at a given situation.
- To show flexibility in response to unanticipated circumstances.
- To interact as a team player and to gain the confidence of others.

The list of "skills and dimensions" required from aspiring US diplomats is long and we have quoted only parts of it. But all these requirements can be summed up as the capacity of being able to connect to something complex and inherently uncertain; to act in situations not under one's control; to work for an outcome that still is uncertain; and to join with others and to recruit others into this effort. These are the requirements for becoming a modern diplomat; for becoming effective in the diplomacy's new assignment as mediator and bridge-builder in global governance.

It was the function of *traditional diplomacy* to signal and promote the autonomy of each sovereign. *Modern diplomacy* is defined by its function to engage in the web of mutual dependence and to shape it. The process of selecting diplomats for their future career reflects the nature of this assignment. Diplomats become diplomats because they are selected in a way that optimizes the chances that they will be good, later on, in accomplishing this task.

The selection process does not end with the entrance exam. Training and selection continue throughout the career. Hierarchies in the diplomatic service are rather steep. The embassies of larger states are staffed by hundreds of attachés, first and second secretaries, a score of counselors, just a few minister counselors, with a lone ambassador to top it all. This might be seen as being out of tune with the present preference for flat hierarchies.[15] In many ways, such steep hierarchies might be dysfunctional in the diplomatic service too. But they serve one useful purpose. They prolong the selection process for influential positions.

The many coming from below compete for the few positions at the top. This competition is accentuated further by the mobility within the service. In a big firm, someone active in finance will usually remain in this field throughout his employment and just compete with others who also work in finance. Not so in the diplomatic service. Diplomats are expected to move around. An ambassador with credentials in the field of US-European relations might thus suddenly find himself (herself) being head of a purely administrative unit in charge of the maintenance of buildings.

This ongoing process of selection and ongoing competition honors success in the job training. It honors success of learning by doing. Such learning by doing has its place in other professions too. But it is central in the diplomatic service. The world in its complexity and fluidity is the teacher nobody and nothing can replace. In general, the selection process for top positions favors those diplomats that are best in learning and applying that teacher's lessons.

Members of the diplomatic service no longer have a monopoly in activities that are diplomatic in a wider sense. This is because the interface between internal politics and the external world has widened. Not just diplomats, others too, are being involved in global governance. Civil servants from line ministries, technical experts, representatives of interest groups now perform functions that once were assumed to be in the exclusive fief of professionals from the diplomatic corps. These others also preside over international gatherings. They too, negotiate and seek common ground in such negotiations. They too campaign for understanding and support in and by other states. But the lion's share of such activities is still being carried out by professionals from diplomatic services. This is so not just because of traditions that are slow to change. This is because the job of global governance calls for professional skills of diplomats and because they possess these skills by selection and training.

Notes

1.   As quoted in http://diplomats of the future.blogspot.com.
2.   An outdated, no longer realistic view of their own importance, accommodated by the fictions of protocol, might even tempt diplomats into becoming cartoons of themselves; as for example, the European ambassador in Washington, who in 2008 refused an invitation to the Democratic National Convention, because, unlike his EU colleagues, he thought it incompatible with his inherent dignity to have to use the bus instead of the ambassadorial limousine for the trips from the hotel to the convention center.

3. The conference produced, inter alia, the Framework Convention on Climate Change (to be followed and made more concrete by the Kyoto Protocol later on) and the United Nations Convention on Biological Diversity.

4. The fiction of "Rechtsstaatlichkeit"—the absolute rule of law—tries to negate this fact which is obvious, though, to anyone who has studied national administrations or who has been active in the upper ranks of civil service.

5. This is the case in most of the European countries. France and Austria are blatant examples.

6. Japan is the prime exhibit for this dominance of bureaucracy over politics.

7. The electorate might wish it to be otherwise. It might nourish the illusion that its politicians could extirpate all external threats and remove all incertitude arising from things "foreign." Politicians are often tempted to oblige the public and to pretend being in full control: foreign terrorists could be kept at bay, climate change could be prevented, the price of oil and gas could be stabilized, Iran would not be allowed to acquire nuclear weapons, financial markets could be regulated effectively. Such posturing for the national electorate is dangerous as it sustains illusions. When these prove to be vain, the ensuing anger and resentment is bound to undermine the legitimacy of both internal and external politics.

8. Modernization theory once would have us assume that such a fusion into uniformity would be on its way. In the meantime, we have learned that this is not going to happen.

9. As made obvious in the present world economic crisis. The world's financial institutions used to haughtily dictate their terms to public administrations, which they tended to regard as bothersome leftover from a past era, bent of obstructing their good work with useless regulation and obnoxious taxes. But lo and behold: that arrogance collapsed when the going became rougher. Financial institutions that used to lecture states on what to do now seek from states help for their sheer survival.

10. Language skills are—of course—a stringent requirement. With the ever-stronger presence of non-European countries and languages, and with a new emphasis on "public diplomacy," language skills now have become even more important. They are also being tested at the subsequent stages of the written and the oral exam.

11. At the entrance exam of autumn 2010, 120 applicants competed for the five openings for positions in the Austrian diplomatic service.

12. A few might still be attracted by some outward trappings of the job, such as the privilege of being called "Excellency" when ambassador, the privilege of living in stately residences, or the privilege of flying the home county's flag on the official limousine. But it is just a miniscule minority that wishes to join the diplomatic service for such reasons of shallow vanity.

13. Proven by the countless memoirs of diplomats that reflect their function as "witnesses of history."

14. Quoted from Kopp H, 2008.

15. While I argue for a certain functionality of hierarchies being steep in the diplomatic service, I am not oblivious to the need to flatten them; and I am certain that this is going to happen over time with the greater diversity and complexity of tasks assigned to diplomats and with information increasingly moving in a horizontal and not in a vertical pattern.

22

A New Setting for Diplomatic Activities

"Almost every international issue has a domestic consequence, more visible and direct than ever before. Almost every major domestic issue has an international component. The distinction between domestic and foreign are gone."
—Ambassador Craig Johnstone, in Korp W a.o. (2008)

No longer are diplomats exclusively engaged in the *international*—that is in relations as they exist between states, as states have ceased to be the only ones to shape worldwide politics. Today, diplomats have to deal with the wider arena of the *global*, shaped not just by states but by other actors too. Also, diplomatic activity is no longer and exclusively imbedded in a governmental mode with its top-down approach. It also has to be transacted by using the varied and more flexible tools of *governance*. Diplomats thus have to adapt to a changed environment for their work:

1) The number of states has grown. It has more than doubled since World War II. This merely quantitative change would not pose that deep a challenge to traditional diplomacy. The greater challenge derives from the *diversity* of these nearly 200 states. Traditional diplomacy evolved among states that were similar to another. Those were the states of Europe. The European offsprings in the Americas were added in the 19th century. These states defined themselves as "civilized nations" and considered the rest of the world its uncivilized part—as mere object of their policies,[1] to be missionized, exploited, educated, or exterminated.

In today's world, states:

- differ in the solidity of their statehood;
- by their wealth; and
- by their capacity to participate in global governance.

a) Some new states are solid entities[2] with governments in full control of the territory, with laws being respected and executed, and with public services of reasonable quality. But several states lack some, many, or most of these capacities. At the extreme end are failing states at the verge of disintegration. That they are quite numerous is shown in the index of failing states, inserted into chapter 12 of this book. But even states that are far from collapsing do not always live up fully to their assigned role as had been demonstrated by another chart in chapter 10 on the prevalence of corruption, with even wealthier states receiving bad grades. Corruption is more than a mere obstacle to business and just one of many minor crimes. It undermines the solidity of statehood.

b) States differ in their wealth. Today the gap between rich and poor states is as wide as it has never been before. For the foreseeable future this gap will continue to grow.

c) States differ by their political institutions and their political culture. Modernization theory would make us assume that states rank on one single scale according to their success in modernization. Those further behind would catch up eventually. In the end, all states would be alike not just in per capita income but also in their political institutions and in their political culture.

By now we know that this will not be so. Catching up in wealth can be a very drawn-out process. But even after states having become wealthy, their institutions and political culture might be very dissimilar. The example of Japan proves that point. Japan is economically successful and wealthy. The US occupation after World War II has sought to "Westernize" Japan's political institutions and culture. These might have become Western in appearance. They are not so in substance. They are shaped by Japan's long tradition of statehood. China—if successful in its continued rise—will differ even more widely from the West.

d) States differ in their vision of the present and of the future world system. As of today, global governance is still largely based on the model provided and supported by the United State and Europe, comprising a mix of democracy, rule of law, human rights, and market economics. But the hegemony of this part of the world is on the wane. The rise of South Asia and of East Asia in particular, will provide other models for world governance, and another set of values to support it. Instruments of global governance will have to adapt to this inevitable, increasing diversity.

2) Ease of communication and lower costs of transport have permitted the globalization of production and consumption. This was the prerequisite for the rapid rise in overall global wealth. But it has also has made citizens, enterprise, and states depend on events, developments, and decisions beyond their borders.

3) The rank of a country in the global pecking order is not established by military might. In fact, military might has proven not just useless but counterproductive. After their defeat in World War II, Japan and Germany have risen to world-prominence in absence of military power. The oversized military machine of North Korea cannot compensate for the terminal illness of this state. The United States is losing its preeminent position in global affairs. Its supreme military power will not cushion this slide. The true position of a state in the global pecking order is now established by its economic weight, by its capacity to add a maximum of value in the global chain of production, and by its capacity to contribute to the solution of global problems.

4) Rising wealth, a growing world population, and their growing connectedness and mutual dependence have expanded the realm of *common goods*. At the same time it also has expanded the threat emanating from *common bads*. Precious resources like an intact ozone layer, continuing biodiversity, or a sufficiently large stock of fish in the oceans, can only be preserved by common efforts. Common efforts are also needed for the aversion of common bads: such as global pandemics; the proliferation of weapons of mass destruction; wild gyrations of the global capital markets; or a worldwide rise in temperature caused by the emission of heat-trapping greenhouse gases.

5) In response to these common challenges, international organizations have multiplied. They have extended their reach and authority. They have ceased to be merely passive instruments of their nation-state members and have gained authority of their own. In some cases, they have assumed enough power and legitimacy to impose their decisions on unwilling member states. The European Union has gone farthest in this direction.

But decisions by the Security Council of the much-maligned United Nations also establish binding norms that supersede merely national norms and wishes. Some international organizations that are not formally governmental—like the International Standard Organization (ISO) or the International Committee of the Red Cross (ICRC), have similar authority.

6)   States never held the absolute monopoly in establishing and shaping relations with economic, civic, or political entities beyond their borders. Other agents had always been active in this field too. By now though, this presence of non-state-actors has gained a wholly new dimension. The most potent among these new, non-state actors are transnational corporations. Over the last decades their direct investment in other countries has grown by leaps and bounds. Transnational firms have thus become crucial partners of governments in the race for economic prominence. Frequently, they are the dominant partners in this relationship. Sometimes they are simply dominant without much partnership.

7)   The rise of transnational enterprise and a denser global interconnectedness is accompanied by a rise in numbers and relevance of international non-governmental organizations (INGOs). States and other political institutions shaping global governance cannot ignore them. The involvement of some major INGOs in global governance has, in fact, become institutionalized. Next to such well-organized and well- recognized global groups, there are those that emerge spontaneously in reaction to certain events or issues. This development has been accelerated by the wide use of the Internet.

8)   Quite a number of issues that once could be addressed effectively on a purely national level can now be tackled but in cooperation with other states and with other global actors. Fiscal and monetary policies; policies ensuring food and drug safety; efforts of environmental protection; measures to fight organized crime and terrorisms, and many other policies can only be designed and implemented with the help of other states and of other global actors. Such cooperation is often mediated by international organizations, by less formal groups like the G-20, or by other facilitators like INGOs that set the agenda and then act as catalysts for its implementation.

9)   It has been argued that world governance would continue to be based on political arrangements that never could amount to more

than a mere sum of purely national politics. This argument assumed the absence of any polity on a more than merely national level. A polity is a politically constituted group. By now it is hard to ignore that such groups have formed also on a transnational or even on a global level. Persons represented by INGOs are members of such a polity. But beyond that, all political actions that reach into the transnational and global, and that bypass states automatically imply the existence of a more than merely national polity. These polity groups may either initiate actions; or they may become their object. The so-called Millennium Targets, for example, have humans, not states, as their addressees. The targets are not set in terms of what states do, or don't do. The targets are defined in terms of human fates: such as the absence of hunger; the prevention of premature death; the promotion of literacy.[3] A further proof for the existence of a global polity are norms, that have gained universal acceptance and the power to directly bind not just states but groups and individuals too. Rules that sanction massive, persistent gross violation of basic human rights or wholesale genocide have become stringent enough to permit their being applied against individuals that have become guilty of such crimes.

10) Relations of things within the borders of a state with things beyond these borders have become so intense that the line dividing these two realms has blurred to the extent of making it impossible to classify many events, developments, or policies as either purely internal or purely external. An increasing number of internal policies have an external dimension, vice versa; many affairs that once had been external only, now translate also into internal ones.

11) This has made it impossible to shield the politics of external affairs from the pressure of public opinion. Bureaucratic mandarins engaged in external affairs can no longer ignore the wishes and sentiments of ordinary citizens. The public, on the other hand, has yet to fully come to terms with the fact that its wishes, and the leaders elected to uphold these wishes, often will not prevail against some unyielding force of the external.

12) The blurring of the borders between internal and external affairs is also reflected in a changing institutional setup for those administrative and political transactions that cut across borders. Diplomats and ministries of foreign affairs once ruled exclusively in

this domain. Now, many other administrative public institutions have also entered the field. They too, deal directly with partners in other countries. There are fields of global interaction, and important ones at that, such as the global monetary regime, in which diplomats hardly have any say at all.

13) As a consequence, it has become difficult to subsume all these official trans-border transactions under a single and coherent foreign policy. Many types of foreign policies co-exist that are conducted on many different levels. There is the foreign policy of central bankers and of ministers of finance. There is the foreign policy of the ministries of the interior and of the police. There is the foreign policy of public cultural institutions, etc. On rare occasions, some coordination among these many different chains of foreign policy might become possible or inevitable. But such coordination cannot be achieved by administrative fiat. The task has to be accomplished by flexible, mutual accommodation.

14) Administrative public institutions and the diplomatic service in particular, are at the service of the state. Their status and actual influence thus depends on the status, power and effectiveness of the state. It is widely assumed that this power of states is in decline. Other institutions would have curtailed their freedom of action. Transnational corporations, financial institutions, and the financial markets in particular are not just passive subjects to the dictates of a state. Often they may turn the table and have their wishes and interests prevail over the wishes and interests of states.

15) But such a view takes account of one side of the equation only. States may have come to depend on transnational enterprise. But, on the other hand, transnational corporations need states and depend on them for the delivery of essential inputs such as law and order, basic education, infrastructure, vocational education or higher education, and research. The state thus gains status and influence as provider of essential inputs into a dynamic economy.

16) The state has also expanded its realm by having been charged with the delivery of a large number of sometimes costly services: old age and unemployment insurance, control of immigration and integration of those immigrated, promotion of entrepreneurship, support of cultural activities, protection of the privacy of personal data, etc. Many of these new tasks of the state have a dimension transgressing national borders.

17) This growth and change in the task of states has been accompanied by changes in the methods of delivering state services. In some fields, traditional, hierarchical command and control methods persist. But in other fields, more flexible methods are being used: enticement, persuasion, peer pressure, benchmarks, etc. Such methods are also used in programs that transcend the borders of states. Rigid, legally founded *government* is complemented by less rigid *governance*, with the state functioning as catalyst, animator and facilitator.

18) For its citizens, the state is no longer the sole and exclusive source of identity. That bond has loosened with the ongoing individualization of life and with shrinkage of the sphere that once was considered communal. These changes also affect the external posture of states. They make, for example, for reduced readiness to sacrifice life or money in the uncertain adventure of war.[4]

19) That said, nationality, that is identification with a state, is still high on the list of characteristics that define a person to himself and to others.[5] Democracy, as it is now prevalent in the world, also ties individuals to their states because voters have a say in the decisions and thus can identify with them. These links sustain states in their function as the still sturdiest anchors of global governance. In fact it is through participation in global governance that states now have to fulfill many of their functions.

To be effective in this task, they cannot do without diplomats.

Notes

1. Even at that times, diplomatic missions had been dispatched to place like Edo or Beijing. But they were meant to establish contact to something exotic. They were not conceived as an element in a relationship between equals.
2. The three elements of stable "stateness": autonomy, capacity, legitimacy.
3. The complex of these and similar goals can be subsumed under the term "human security" as opposed to the term "state security."
4. In most mature and wealthy democracies, the army of conscripts has thus been replaced (by the more costly) army staffed by professional soldiers.
5. Fifty years after the start of European integration; and with "70 percent of all politically relevant decisions being made in Brussels," still a very small percentage of citizens of the European Union define themselves primarily as such; with the vast majority seeing themselves primarily or even exclusively as citizens of this or that EU member country.

23

The Diplomatic Service Needs to Adapt

"There is a complexity to human affairs which science and analysis simply stands mute.
—*David Brooks,* New York Times, *May 12, 2009*

The task of global governance implies dealing with diversity, uncertainty, and risks. It implies the search for cooperation on many levels and with many players. Diplomats are not wholly unprepared for that task. Seeking cooperation and common ground in an uncertain environment had been part of their assignment already in the past. That part of their heritage continues to be useful in their new function in global governance. Otherwise though, they will have to adapt. The field they now have to till is not the one they used to till. Massive changes have intervened. Diplomats need new tools for these new tasks. Their institutions have to adapt, as have their methods of work.

This challenge did not arrive overnight and some such adaptations to a new reality have taken place already. They should be noted because in general, bureaucracies are loath to change. Like individuals, they do so only under the pressure of challenges they could not meet otherwise. The fact that in foreign services such bureaucratic inertia had begun to melt is thus proof of the exceptionally strong pressure exerted upon these services. They are among those state bureaucracies that are most intensely exposed to the necessity to adapt to a transformed work environment.

Even treasured traditions were discarded. When I entered the Austrian Foreign Service in the early 1960s, the defining output of embassies was still the *political report* on their host country.[1] Literary critics might bemoan its demise. But in the meantime, this exhibit of subtle wit, couched arrogance, greater or lesser writing skill has quietly died of its uselessness.

The pressure resulting from the changed nature of its work also made the Ministry of Foreign Affairs embrace modern technology at an early date. This ministry was the first among the Austrian ministries to use fax machines. Later on, it became the first to broadly use e-mail. It also was the first among the Austrian ministries to have gone fully electronic with paper files just as backups.

But more important than these merely technical changes were those in institutional culture. The working culture and the formal and informal bureaucratic structures used to be very hierarchic. Only those diplomats at the top had full knowledge on an issue, with their underlings just holding bits and pieces. This changed with the introduction of photocopiers. It was not ordered or even sanctioned from above, but ambitious officers in subordinate position started using photocopiers to distribute copies of interesting papers to their peers. E-mails have accentuated this trend toward a more horizontal flow of information. Together with such horizontal distribution of information, and with otherwise also easier access to information, hierarchies have flattened. This has facilitated the rise of young diplomats.

While still sticking to the ideal of the diplomatic generalist, the actual practice has proven specialization inevitable. The base of recruitment has been broadened with the prior near-monopoly of lawyers being broken.

All these changes have made the old bureaucratic machine function more smoothly. They have not yet altered the innate sense of mission of the ministry and of its diplomats. They have not yet caused a wholesale transformation of the internal arrangements and they have not prompted the ministry to redefine its role versus other public institutions. The present setup has not been evaluated against the necessity to become useful and functional in the new setting of *global governance*.

(1) *A very selective gathering, processing, and analysis of policy relevant information* remains one of the core tasks of diplomats. But the diplomatic service is far from being the sole agent in this realm. It has many competitors. It has to take account of them; cooperate with them and use them; or yield its place to them in cases where these other services can provide superior results.

   a) In some instances, diplomats might still have a relative advantage over other gatherers and processors of information. This may be the case when they can provide insights into official policies and actions of their host state in those fields that are directly relevant to the relations between this host state and their home country.

b) Diplomatic services will, however, already be less adept at gathering and processing information on global actors that are *not states* and that nonetheless impact heavily on the outcome of political processes which touch their own country. This holds true, in particular for information on economic and financial issues.

c) There is little, in house, ex post evaluation of the information gathering, of the information processing and of the information analysis done by the diplomatic service. Most other institutions that deal in information have to tolerate such an ex post evaluation and have to learn from it. A report by a newspaper, by a wire service or by a television network has to be retracted and or corrected if proven misleading. Wrong and not corrected information might even trigger punitive legal action. This constant feedback keeps other information providers alert and teaches them to avoid errors. In the self-enclosed sphere of diplomatic information gathering and information processing, such valuable feedback is rare. It has to become routine and it has to become institutionalized.

d) The diplomatic service is still far from being able to make full use of *policy-relevant information that does not originate in its own narrow circle*. A score of institutions can provide information that should be considered in foreign policy decisions. Some of my colleagues in the Austrian diplomatic service have managed to acquire the know-how for using such external sources of information. But such skills have to be taught on a broader scale and more systematically. They also should be updated periodically. A pointer to such targeted, operational information gathering is the "Situation Centre and Crisis Room" which will be part of the newly created European Union diplomatic service—the "European External Action Service." The staff of the Situation Center and Crisis Room includes IT experts, scientists, and statisticians. Among their tools is special software that permits them to scan global TV broadcasts for names and key words.

e) Diplomatic generalist can go only so far in accessing and in using such external sources of information. This is because searches for relevant pieces information have to be targeted narrowly. They have to be based on some prior knowledge of the issues at stake. In a second phase, the information thus gathered will have to be evaluated in its proper context. In many instances, the expertise of specialists will be required for both of these steps. Such specialists might be found in academia, in think tanks and in foreign policy research institutes. Or they might be scientists when only they can provide the technical expertise needed in decision-making on some complex issues. Only scientists, for example, can furnish diplomats with the necessary know-how on the effects of chemical weapons; or on the contribution of greenhouse gases to global warming; or on the depletion of the fishing stock in the oceans. Diplomats will have to learn to use, and to work with such specialists. As a rule, these will have to be given a formal status as consultants and/or members of official delegations.[2]

f) The Austrian diplomatic service—and I surmise that of other countries too—is not very good in managing information that is imbedded in its members (*knowledge management*). Only bits of the information, for example, gathered by one diplomat on the post she or he is about to leave is transferred to his (or her) successor.[3] Other institutions avoid such loss of information by providing for a period of overlap between the outgoing and the incoming functionary.[4] Neither is the knowledge an Austrian diplomat has gathered in a foreign posting handed on by debriefing when he or she returns. Knowledge vested in diplomats is also wasted by posting them to places in which their prior knowledge is of no use—as is the case when one of the rare Arab speakers in a small foreign ministry is not posted to an Arab country.

g) The way ministries of foreign affairs are organized inhibits the internal sharing of information and an open internal discussion on options in critical areas of foreign policy. One section of the ministry might ignore the priorities of another section. The two sections even might come to work at cross-purposes. Hence the need to encourage the flow of information across these sections; and the need for internal discussion to resolve differences on policies. The US Department of State has set up special websites for informal internal discussion. But it is doubtful whether these have fed into actual policies. Neither can such electronic platform substitute for personal, face to face encounters. Not only should there be place for them. They should be encouraged and given a firm institutional base; and such encounters should involve more than just those on the very top-level of the ministry.

h) Rigid hierarchies also inhibit the articulation of dissenting opinions and of their fair-minded evaluation. A superior can easily squash suggestions of a subordinate, yet that superior is not infallible. Ideas may therefore be buried that would have merited closer scrutiny.[5] To prevent such losses, the corporate giant IBM has instituted a procedure that allows subordinates to "appeal," so to say, to someone higher in rank than the immediate superior. Similar arrangements might be helpful in the diplomatic service.

i) One should consider an extension of the duration of each tour of duty served in a foreign country (or at an international organization). Arguments against this proposition are well rehearsed. Too long a sojourn on a foreign post would tempt diplomats to "go local."[6] It would let them lose sight of their own country and of its interests. The risk is there, but it has to be balanced against the fact that—according to the shared experience of my colleagues—it takes two years on the average to gain a firm footing in a foreign post and to become fully operative. Four years is the average duration of a posting abroad.[7] That implies that up to 50 percent of the money invested in sending a diplomat abroad is being wasted. Extending the duration of foreign postings would reduce such waste.

j) In recruiting diplomats, the former near monopoly of graduates from law schools has been broken in Austria. The base of recruitment has been expanded, but it is narrow still. Few of the new entrants have a background as historians or as empirical economists. Even more surprising is the dearth of entrants with a background in area studies—such as Latin American or Chinese studies. Entrants with backgrounds in science could also usefully expand the stock of expertise.

The changing tasks of diplomacy would call for a greater diversification of skills acquired in the prior education and/or prior occupation. Efforts must be made to further broaden the base of recruitment.

(2)   Recruitment and career development privilege the diplomatic generalist. Such generalists still have their use. Yet, greater specialization is needed. A standard diplomatic task that would be the same all over the world no longer exists. Diplomatic work has become differentiated according the regions of the world and according the issues that are being addressed. A different set of skills is required for dealing either with wealthy countries; or with crisis-ridden countries; or with very poor countries. The same holds true for the differentiation according to the issues addressed by diplomacy. There is the diplomacy adapted to the task of nation building and of crisis management. There is the diplomacy on security and military issues. There is the diplomacy on global regulatory issues and on global governance. There is the diplomacy among EU member states, etc.

Diplomatic generalists will have difficulties in becoming fully efficient in one of these different areas. If states wish to impact on political decisions and developments, they need their diplomatic representatives to specialize in one of these divergent tasks. Such specialization will impose administrative burdens on ministries of foreign affairs and especially on the ministries of medium-sized and smaller countries. They will find it difficult to administer five or more different career paths for diplomatic officers, if the total number of such officers is just in the low hundreds. Nonetheless, they will have to find solutions to this dilemma.

(3)   The most trenchant divide in diplomatic service is the one *separating bilateral from multilateral diplomacy.* The latter is expanding by leaps and bounds—both in volume and in relevance, while traditional bilateral diplomacy is loosing much of its former standing. Though still the archetype of diplomatic activity, bilateral diplomacy is obviously ill equipped to address most of those tasks that have to be tackled in global governance.

Bilateral double taxation agreements were, for example, a staple product in bilateral diplomacy. By now, those bilateral tax-treaties have become inadequate. The issues they address call for broader solutions, as it is only in the context of multilateral cooperation that the fight against tax fraud and tax evasion can be successful. Multilateral diplomacy was once considered a mere adjunct to bilateral diplomacy. Now it should be the other way round. Bilateral diplomacy should have its function in support of multilateral diplomacy mainly.

a) Ministries of foreign affairs will have to *shift resources from bilateral to multilateral diplomacy* and they will have to adjust the career paths of their staff accordingly. The specialization of diplomats in multilateral diplomacy alone will not suffice, as diplomats active in multilateral diplomacy need more than a superficial knowledge of the subjects they will have to address in such multilateral settings. These subjects vary widely as does the institutional setup and the institutional culture of those international organizations that deal with these widely differing clusters of issues.

- There is the multilateral diplomacy concerned with questions of security—as for example, the diplomacy surrounding the Organization for Cooperation and Security in Europe—the OSCE, or the North Atlantic Treaty Organization—NATO.
- There is the multilateral diplomacy that promotes the development of still poorer countries—such as the multilateral diplomacy that surrounds organizations like the Food and Agricultural Organization—FAO, the United Nations Industrial Development Organization—UNIDO, the United Nations Development Program—UNDP or the United Nations Conference on Trade and Development—UNCTAD.
- There are the worldwide or the merely regional, general-purpose organizations, like the United Nations—UNO, or the African Union—AU.

  Inevitably thus, diplomats will have to specialize not just in multilateral diplomacy, but also in one of these different clusters of issues addressed by multilateral diplomacy. Such specialization can be promoted by keeping diplomats on the same track during their career. But even diplomats thus trained will frequently need the support of technical experts, and—as mentioned—diplomatic services will have to integrate such experts into their ranks.

b) Serious engagement in multilateral diplomacy is not compatible with battles over shallow prestige. Disproportionate political energy is still being spent by some countries in bilateral interventions to get one of their diplomats assume the presidency of this or that committee of the United Nations General Assembly; or on being elected to a non-permanent seat of the UN Security Council; or to the UN Human Rights Council. Such efforts are justified only if the country competing for such positions is willing and able to promote an agenda that is of benefit to the organizations as such and to the majority of its members. But those are rarely the motives, and most of such battles therefore involve nothing more than the search for visibility and status among insiders. Much political capital is thus misspent in such fights over empty glory.

If used to other ends, however, bilateral diplomacy may very well supplement and support multilateral diplomacy. In fact, support for multilateral diplomacy has by now become a major, if not the most relevant task of bilateral diplomacy. Interventions by bilateral diplomacy will thus commonly accompany multilateral negotiations on weighty and contentious issues,[8] such as they take place in the Security Council of the United Nations, in the World Trade Organization (WTO), or in the Organization for Security and Cooperation in Europe (OSCE).

c) This calls for *stronger, automatic and institutionalized linkage between multilateral and bilateral diplomacy.*

Keep the Multilateral Agenda on Your Desk

In relating his experience in an EU member country, a US ambassador mentioned that he had always at his desk the agenda for the upcoming meetings of the EU General Affairs Council. The European Union is ruled by councils. The most prominent is *the* "EU Council," composed of heads of state and government. It assembles four times a year in formal session.[9] In the hierarchic order of councils, the General Affairs Council sits just below this august body. It is attended by the ministers of foreign affairs.

Charged with overall coordination, it ranks above other EU councils that are attended by the line ministers of EU member states. In practical terms, it is the General Affairs Council that prepares the agenda for the EU Council and also controls the other EU Councils. Decisions of the General Affairs Council are therefore important not just to the EU member states, but also to countries outside the European Union that have close relations with the European Union.

The US ambassador was thus well advised to keep track of the agenda of the General Affairs Councils so that he could intervene with the authorities of the EU country he was posted in, in order to present the US position on a topic that would be discussed in that EU Council.

Bilateral diplomacy needs to be mobilized in support of multilateral diplomacy in a *systematic manner.* Multilateral and bilateral diplomacy should not run in two distinct spheres and with separate lines of communication. This is not to imply that every bit of information and all instructions pertinent to multilateral diplomacy need to reach bilateral diplomatic representations too. There has to be a filter. But bilateral diplomatic representations should be made aware of those issues at stake in multilateral diplomacy that are relevant to the home country and that would profit from a support—or lack of hostility—by the country a bilateral ambassador resides in.

d) Much of the *work with international organizations will be done by national officials that are not part of the diplomatic service.* That is inevitable. It makes no sense to have diplomats take the lead in transactions with the World Meteorological Organization—WMO or with the World Health Organization—WHO. This is a task of specialists from the relevant public institutions. Nonetheless, a certain risk is inherent in completely dissociating these experts from the diplomatic service. Even at merely technical international organizations, political issues might pop up though they have no real place and no connection to the actual tasks of that organization. The World Health Organization—WHO is not there to rule on relations between the People's Republic of China and Taiwan. The

Food and Agricultural Organization—FAO is not the place to
seek solutions for the thorny Arab-Israeli conflict. Nonetheless such issues have been grafted unto their proceedings. Yet
even in absence of such misuse, a foreign policy component
might become attached to questions that seem to be technical
only:[10] how to allocate resources between countries; how to
realign voting shares in the bodies that direct such technical
organizations; how deeply to interfere in internal affairs, etc. A
way has to be found to deal with such political questions in the
context of a country's wider foreign/global policy. Diplomats
have routine in tackling like tasks. When such political issues
pop up, they therefore should become involved even if that
international organization deals with merely technical issues
otherwise.

How can that be done? It could be done by including
diplomats in the delegations to meetings of purely technical international organizations. But for most countries that
solution will not be feasible, given a rather small diplomatic
staff; and given also the strong proprietary instincts of some
of the line ministries that wish their own representatives to
have the say over all parts of an agenda. The dilemma thus
has to be tackled in a way less rigid and formal. It could be
done in periodic inter-ministerial meetings of all those civil
servants who deal with international organizations;[11] and it
could be done by including diplomats in the routine internal
exchange of information on issues a line ministry will have
to address in an international gathering.

Irrespective of such more or less formal arrangements, it is the
administrative culture of a state which, in the end, will decide on
the scope and depth of cooperation between the Ministry of Foreign Affairs and other ministries. In some states, and especially
in states with a record of clientilism, ministries are regarded as
fiefs to be defended against all intruders. The interest of the state
will suffer from such atavistic attitudes. But these are difficult to
alter. The administrative and political cultures of states change
slowly at best.[12]

(4)   The shift from bilateral to multilateral diplomacy is paralleled
by a *shift in relative weight away from embassies and in favor
of the administrative centers* in the capital. This is facilitated by
the revolutionary developments in communication, transport, and

travel. It makes no sense, for example, to charge an ambassador with negotiating with his host country an issue he is ill equipped to handle due to his lack of expertise. His own ministry of foreign affairs is more likely to have someone in command of such expert knowledge. The costs of air travel having become minimal, it is more expedient to send this expert to substitute for the ambassador in the dialogue with authorities of the host country.

Proper processing and analysis of information also demands expert knowledge. In analyzing some pieces of information on the internal politics of the host country, an embassy might still have an advantage. But in most other cases the advantage will be with the ministry back home, because it can compare and evaluate against each other the information it has received from several embassies; and because it is better placed to mobilize expert knowledge from other sources. The necessity to coordinate with other public authorities is an added reason for this shift of relative weight and influence away from embassies. An embassy is not well placed to coordinate its own position with entities like its home ministry of finance or its home ministry of the interior. This is a task for the foreign ministry which has a much better chance to be successful in such an endeavor.

(5)   A generously staffed, qualified, and efficient diplomatic service with a dense net of representations all over the world is a national asset. Such qualified and efficient diplomatic service keeps a country engaged in the task of global governance. It enables that country to seize leadership in global political processes.

This is not because prestige might be attached to such leadership. More relevant is the ability of an efficient diplomatic service to steer the process that leads up to decisions in a way that is advantageous to the home country.

The Advantages of a Highly Qualified and Large Foreign Service

The diplomatic service of the United Kingdom is sizeable with a dense net of generously staffed diplomatic representations. This caused quite some discussion in the 1970s, when this big apparatus was perceived as an outsized, no longer required leftover from the times of the British Empire. A Royal Commission was therefore established with the mandate to judge whether this criticism was justified. The commission was also charged with sketching the outlines of a future, less costly way of safeguarding British interests in the wider world. The Commission came up with radical proposals: the diplomatic service in its present form should be abolished. The bulk of the staff should be dispersed among the British line ministries there to attend the foreign relations that each of these ministries was bound to entertain. The smaller part of the staff should be transferred to the prime minister's office. Representations abroad should be reduced drastically. As in the eyes of this Commission, much of the consular work would have been redundant. It should be reduced too.

These radical proposals were not heeded. The British Foreign and Commonwealth Office reacted with an expertise of its own, suggesting a preservation of the status quo. It prevailed and the British diplomatic apparatus continues to be big if seen in relation to the now reduced global status of the United Kingdom.

Was this outcome just the consequence of bureaucratic inertia? Are the expenses for this relatively big diplomatic service justified by its work and its actual impact on international/global politics?

Several of my friends were employed in Brussels at the Secretariat of the EU Council; at its Political Committee, or in the nascent "Cell" for a future EU diplomatic service. These are institutions that work closely with diplomatic services of member countries. To a large extent, they even depend on their input. All of my friends in these EU institutions agree in their evaluation of the British input. It is of unequalled quality. The crisp and well-written British papers are usually the first ones to arrive. British diplomats are the best in summing up meetings. They are the first to submit draft proposals for resolutions or other decisions. Only trained observers will detect the tilt in favor of British interests contained in such documents. This advantage to Britain is bought at a price that is just a fraction of what the United Kingdom expends on armament like submarines or supersonic attack aircrafts. The advantages that such military expenditures have purchased are questionable. Not so the advantages of the less costly and highly professional British diplomatic services.

A narrow circle of insiders only views the diplomatic service in such positive a light. The broad public usually does not share that view. Ministers of finance see no reason why not to yield to this pressure of public opinion. Farmers, teachers, or policemen can mobilize a supportive lobby for claiming a bigger share from the state's budget. Their lobbying prevents cuts in the public expenditures for farmers, teachers, and the police. Diplomats have no such lobby.

As a consequence, their service is usually the first in line to suffer budget cuts. That the tasks of diplomacy are expanding in parallel with growing global interdependence is to little avail in this context and neither will diplomatic services be able to thwart budget cuts by pointing to their political usefulness. While prompted by shortsightedness and concessions to populism, the budgetary constraints imposed on diplomatic services will continue and are likely to become worse. Diplomatic services will be confronted with the necessity of doing more with less. How can that be achieved?

a) Costs may be cut by getting rid of some expensive trappings of diplomatic presence in foreign countries. Not everything can be or should be chipped away. Outward signs of status will continue to have their function as they ease the work of diplomats. Guests should feel honored by being invited to the residence. Food and wine do not need to be the one of five star restaurants. But they still should be above the average and a certain aura has to be maintained. Serving hamburgers and beer wouldn't do. But that being said, there still is scope for some savings by having less expensive residences and office buildings. One even could do without chauffeurs. Such savings might quell misgivings about the alleged high life and extravagance of diplomats. But these savings will not be substantial, because keeping an embassy is cost-intensive under all circumstances. It will remain expensive notwithstanding all efforts to curtail unnecessary splendor.

b) More substantial savings might accrue from several states using joint embassies with overhead costs shared. EU countries had attempted to proceed in that direction. They have not gone very far yet, as bigger EU member countries are loath still to share facilities. As of now, this is just a pilot project, with some smaller EU countries having established such joint facilities in Asana, the new capital of Kazakhstan, in Moldova, and in Montenegro.

c)   Greater savings can be realized by closing a few embassies and *substituting other forms of diplomatic presence*. When travel was expensive, long and dangerous, the permanent physical presence in a foreign capital might have been more expedient and cost efficient that doing business by travelling envoys. Travel is now fast, safe, and cheap. This shift in relative costs opens the option for a non-permanent diplomatic presence though roving ambassadors, and/or—for specific tasks and issues—through special envoys. In most cases, these are second best solutions. Yet they are better still than the void of having no presence in a foreign country at all.

d)   This form of a periodic presence can be supplemented by a very low-cost permanent presence;[13] such as the one provided by a small local office, staffed by a few locally employed persons. That office would do administrative work; would arrange for the periodic visits of the roving ambassador and for visits of other officials.

e)   The work of roving ambassadors could also be complemented by interactive virtual embassies. These would have to function under supervision from professional diplomats at the ministry of foreign affairs and/or from diplomats posted at a nearby embassy. To be effective, those sites would have to be truly interactive. They would have to be attended to on a daily basis.

f)   Costs could be reduced somewhat by a still wider outsourcing of non-core functions, such as the administration of personnel, or the maintenance of buildings.

(6)   Much is now being made of *public diplomacy* as a new and important task of diplomats. Such emphasis is not wholly unjustified. The opinion of the public and attitudes of opinion leaders do impact on foreign policy decisions of a state. Diplomats have to reach out to the public of their host country also because this public—on its turn—may also bypass its own national government and might become directly engaged in international/global affairs.[14] Inevitably thus, diplomats will have to deal with that part of the public in their host country that has gained such influence in global governance.

Embassies with ambition, time, and resources to spend, tend to enter this field with relish, with a hodge-podge of mostly untargeted activities; with social events; with the sponsoring of cultural projects; with lecturing all over the place; with advertisements in widely circulating media, etc.

In such enthusiasm for public diplomacy, one risks to overestimate the capacity of diplomats to actually influence public opinion.[15]

Official authorities of all kind have limited impact on public perceptions.[16] As outsiders, diplomats are at an added disadvantage. Embassies may have nonetheless some minor influence on how the public of the host country views their home country. As outlined in a previous chapter, embassies and diplomats also function as symbols of their state. They have to perform as such, representing their country in a symbolic way and in a way that recognizes the susceptibilities and interest of their host country. At a minimum, their behavior and bearing should not diminish respect for their home state. But public diplomacy certainly implies more than the stricture to avoid such damage. It implies efforts to actively seek changes in the opinion and attitudes of their host country. For that, simply spouting out messages will not suffice. In order for these messages to be accepted, they have to *meet* the *interests* of their intended *recipients.* Therefore, one has to know these interests of the other side so as to shape the message accordingly. Of course, the content of messages will be shaped by the policies of the home country, and it is the home country too, where most of the "raw material" for such messages will originate from. But embassies can be helpful by adjusting a message to the specific interests of the intended recipients in their host country.

When confronting critical voices, greater credibility and better effect will be usually obtained by diplomats acting not themselves but via highly visible and respected citizen of the respective country.

In public diplomacy, the aim of influencing political decision has to be kept in mind. Public diplomacy has therefore to be tied to a few policy priorities. It has to be targeted to precisely reach that audience that is relevant in shaping a decision on such politically relevant issues. Public diplomacy activities of embassies have therefore to be guided closely by their own ministries of foreign affairs.

While limited and not as extensive as often proposed, public diplomacy is nonetheless an activity diplomats should be qualified to perform. They have to learn some of the tricks of the trade: public speaking, methods to hold one's own in controversial public discussions, what to do and not to do when on television, etc. One of the most useful tools is the perfect fluency in the language of the host country. That latter requirement is not that easy to meet, especially by smaller diplomatic services with too limited a staff to permit a career specialization based on language skills.

An opinion once in place is not easy to alter. If one wishes to influence it, one should better intervene in the process that creates a definite opinion. In the shaping of public opinion on global affairs an important role accrues to think tanks, research institutes, and academic institutions. Public diplomacy should therefore engage with such institutions. That calls for persons qualified for such interventions. Ministries of foreign affairs should have on their staff some that have credibility in those settings and who can be accepted as peers by academics, researchers and analysts. If diplomats thus qualified cannot be found, experts should be brought in from the outside.

Special attention has to be given to data now stored in electronic form as such data now have become the prime source of information for a wide public.[17] Data banks and electronic documentation have to be scrutinized routinely in order to update information they contain. There should be monthly checks, for example, on information provided by Wikipedia and on information contained in widely used, credible online political documentations.

By now, all ministries of foreign affairs have their own website. Most of the embassies have them too. Keeping the general website of the ministry updated and relevant is a task incumbent upon the whole diplomatic corps of a country. At embassies, each diplomatic officer should be held responsible for the information contained on his or her subject on the website of the embassy. She or he should be accountable too, for keeping interactive sites truly interactive.

(7)   The pressure to do more with less is especially acute in the realm of consular activities. These are bound to expand. US consular officers issue 6.5 million non-immigrant visas per year. The Moscow embassy of Austria—a country of no more than 8 million inhabitants and of a mere 84,000 square kilometers—had granted 100,000 visas to Russians in 2008 and had to purchase a separate building to accommodate the vast coming and going of visa applicants. Together with the quantity, the *complexity* of consular work is growing too. In issuing visas, for example, precaution against illegal immigration or against the inflow of criminals and terrorists has complicated procedures. Other consular work has also become more time consuming. Notwithstanding such pressures, consuls' work must remain customer-friendly. Basic interests of citizens both of the home country and of the host country have to be respected.

In face of continuing budgetary constraints that inhibit an expansion of consular staff, how may foreign ministries cope?

a)   One option is to outsource or franchise consular work. That would have its precedents in history when much of that work had been off- loaded on private persons—often expatriates of stature, who financed their consular activities with fees from those that had requested such consular services. Can that precedent set the pattern for the future? To my knowledge, the United Kingdom has outsourced the issuing of visas—at least in the United States. But with the issuing of visas now that closely intertwined with national security considerations and with other basic state-interests, such outsourcing is highly problematic. If done at all, the franchise takers have to be kept under close supervision. Outsourcing would also require consular work to become self-financing through sufficiently high consular fees. That would create its problems too; not the least of the dangers being a commercialization of such a basic state service. Consular work has to be conducted according to principles that generally guide administrative activities of the state. Such work must not become subject to the search for a maximum of return on capital invested by some private entrepreneur. If a state decides to outsource consular work, it should do so with great caution. It will be prudent to first start with some closely monitored pilot projects.

It is enticing to believe that greater use could be made of information technology in contacts between consular officers and their clients. That seems to promise some savings and to also expedite procedures. But that would also involve risks. In view of the notoriously porous nature of the Internet, it would be difficult to effectively guarantee the privacy of personal data. Also, such wider use of electronic processing would disadvantage citizens of countries with still sparse access to the Internet. Furthermore, one should not ignore that a fuller use of information technology in the contact between consular officers and their clients would also subtract from the human element that needs to enter in any work with so heavy an impact on the fate of individual persons. One thus should use great precaution when expanding the use of information technology in contacts between consuls and their clients. Information technology can be useful in the administrative processing of visa applications and in administrative transactions connected to other consular tasks. But that source of savings has already been exploited. Little additional headway will be possible in this field.

b) As in the case of embassies, more substantial savings could be realized by several countries—and especially several EU countries—sharing consular facilities.[18] In consular work, questions of prestige weigh less heavily than they do in diplomatic work. It should therefore be easier to establish such offices that are common to several states. Some EU countries have already seized that option.

c) Savings might finally be realized by lowering the overheads of consular offices; by locating such offices in less expensive parts of a city; or by employing more local staff.

d) Most states have an extensive network of honorary consulates. These are not run by career staff but by local dignitaries who volunteer for that position and who usually have some connection to the country that appoints them. Their actual workload varies widely. The majority of them are not engaged in the heaviest burden—namely the issuing of passports and visas. This could be changed and honorary consuls could become involved in that kind of work too. This should not cause major problems, as the final decision on visa applications does not rest with them anyhow. (Such decisions also do not rest with consuls employed abroad by the ministries of foreign affairs.) The Ministry of the Interior has the final say (in the United States, the Department of Homeland Security).

(8) a) New actors now deal in global affairs. Among those are various public authorities and some of them have even come to establish their own kind of foreign ministry. They communicate directly with partners in other countries. Doing so, they tend to bypass their own national diplomatic services. Diplomats thus have no longer the monopoly of being in charge of all official relations to other international actors. This development is irreversible and it seems to reduce the realm and relevance of diplomatic services, as one would assume that diplomatic services must lose what others gain. In a certain sense, that holds true. The diplomatic service may no longer claim to control all of these official relations. It has to accept that it has neither the expertise for such a role; nor the authority to enforce such a claim.

It thus should be obvious that diplomatic services and diplomats no longer hold that unique and exclusive function in relations between states and in global governance that public perception and their own professional ethos once ascribed to them. But this development has, on the other hand, assigned them with a potential new function. This is the function of assisting these other public authorities in *their* relations with foreign partners. Diplomatic services are well-equipped for that task. Among all public authorities, they have the broadest net of foreign contacts. They command over an infrastructure which they can put at the disposal of such other authorities. And while they lack technical expertise in many fields, their skills and traditions adapt easily to a large variety of tasks.

Other national authorities are well advised to use these services and have their representatives work in tandem with diplomats. Acting alone might create trouble for them and for the country as a whole. Line ministries, for example, tend to overestimate their capacity to shape the outcome of negotiations. They tend to attach too great significance to the political interests and impulses of their own countries and they tend to underestimate the political constraints imposed on their foreign negotiating partners.[19] Line ministries entering the field of international negotiations tend to become too self-confident, believing themselves to be in full command of those technical skills in negotiations that diplomats have acquired and internalized in a long historic process. The culture and tradition of diplomats and their experience from a constant on the job training will make diplomats more prudent and effective in circumnavigating difficulties when dealing with other global actors.

b) While the scope of diplomatic activity expands through this service function to other public authorities, diplomats will, on the other hand, have to yield some ground and to accept into their ranks civil servants that come from such other public authorities. Since long, military attachés[20]—and their usually vast retinue—have been part of embassy staff. By now, they have been joined by officers of numerous other public authorities. In US embassies, diplomats from the State Department are now a distinct minority. That is not the case yet for the Austrian embassies. But in the case of Austria too, quite a number of special attachés have found shelter at its embassies as: attachés for social affairs, for science and technology, for agriculture, for the ministry of the interior, for commerce, etc.

c) In theory, the ambassador should be entitled to rule over this multitude of representatives from different public authorities. In practice, this is not automatically the case, as these other representatives will tend to follow the instructions provided by their own home authorities, just as the ambassador will tend to follow the instructions and general policies of his ministry of foreign affairs. Generally, though, the problems that might arise from such diversity seem bigger than they actually are. The sense of being on board of a common ship in the sometimes treacherous waters of a foreign country creates an ésprit de corps even among the representatives of so many different public authorities. Of course, there is no avail if the authorities back home work themselves at cross-purposes. Their underlings posted as attaches at embassies abroad can do little to bridge such cleavage.[21]

    d) At home, conflicts between different public bodies all engaged in managing international/global relations cannot be resolved by a simple administrative fiat. Efforts by the ministries of foreign affairs in particular would backfire were they to attempt to regain a monopoly in dealing with foreign public institutions. It would prompt those other authorities of the home country to continue as before, but without an even marginal involvement of the ministry of foreign affairs and of its diplomats. Solutions to the dilemma have to be sought in a pragmatic way through steps both at home and at embassies abroad.

Ministries of foreign affairs could strengthen their linkages to the other ministries and to other public authorities. If these authorities are about to build their version of a small diplomatic apparatus, the ministries of foreign affairs could be helpful in seconding some of their own officers to assist in that endeavor, thereby creating personal links that more than formal rules assure coordination, mutual information, and common purpose. Also, interagency/inter-ministerial working groups on international/global affairs could be created or upgraded so as to endow them with a truly operative instead of a merely decorative function.

Informal methods, more than any strict legal prescriptions, will also facilitate at embassies the cooperation and coordination between diplomats and the representatives of other public authorities that serve as attachés at these embassies. It is the task of the ambassador to become the catalyst of such informal sharing of information and cooperation. Ambassadors will have to learn that they cannot simply impose themselves and their views, and that any formal authority assigned to them to rule by stern command all of the diverse attachés, would be that—namely formal only and not real.

    (9) Heads of governments have secured a prominent and often dominant role in the shaping of the external relations of their countries. This is so for two reasons. We have touched on the first one just before. It is no longer just the Ministry of Foreign Affairs that deals with partners in foreign countries. Many other ministries also do. In most cases it is neither necessary nor possible to meld all these different relations into one coherent policy. In some instances, that has to be done nonetheless. Being just one among many ministries, ministries of foreign affairs are not

well-placed to do that job—especially when divergent views of ministries reflect starkly different interests. So someone has to intervene who is above ministers in rank and political clout. The task accrues to the head of government.

The inflationary multiplication of summits is the second reason for heads of government becoming involved more deeply in foreign relations. This "summitry" is more than a mere fashion. It has become so widespread because of the need to back up international cooperation with the full weight of politics. This powerful backup cannot be provided just by foreign ministers. Prime ministers are in a better position to deliver it.

This shift of function from the ministers of foreign affairs to heads of government has not proceeded without friction. Accounts of rivalries between foreign ministers and their prime ministers are in fact part of the shared diplomatic folklore. Dealing in foreign affairs makes for enhanced political visibility. That is something a politician is loath to share with another politician—be it the prime minister or the foreign minister. Such rivalries gain greater political weight when, in coalition governments, foreign ministers and prime ministers do not belong to the same party and do not share the same basic outlook on foreign affairs.[22]

One could try to resolve the problem by attaching the diplomatic apparatus of a state to the office of the prime minister.[23] But that still would not eliminate the need for a foreign minister. A head of government has to attend to many questions. She or he simply does not have the spare time and capacity to also run the foreign ministry with its hundreds of decisions that have to be made every day; with its incessant travelling and with its heavy load of protocol. So even if the bureaucracy of the foreign ministry were attached to the bureaucracy of the prime minister's office, there would still be a need for someone to hold the formal rank of a foreign minister so as to shoulder all those tasks in foreign relations the head of government simply could not take care of.

And then there would be the question as to the relationship between these two bureaucracies—the one from the prime minister's office and the one from the foreign ministry largely composed of diplomats. The latter have their own, distinct bureaucratic culture, their separate career path, their stringent entrance exams. The bureaucracy of the ministry of foreign affairs and the bureaucracy of the prime minister's office thus cannot be simply merged.

But if one has to retain a separate foreign minister anyhow, and if one has to maintain a diplomatic service that is distinct from the rest of the bureaucracy, why do away with the ministry of foreign affairs as a separate entity by integrating it into the prime minister's office? Attempting such a solution would not make sense. One could leave the situation where it is with a separate ministry of foreign affairs—provided however, that the prime minister and his staff then can fully use the diplomatic service for their own international activities which have expanded so very much and which are by now so essential in global governance.

I wonder whether this condition is fully met at present. I surmise that the foreign ministries and the prime ministers offices still tend to move in their own universe, with the bonds between them being haphazard and not organic. The G-7 and G-20 summits demonstrate the need to improve upon the status quo. Among the many summits they certainly are one of the more consequential ones. They are being prepared by so-called "sherpas"[24] who then also monitor the follow-up. The sherpas have their main and direct contacts to the sherpas of other summit participants. It is this network mainly, that provides the backup for the summits. Obviously though, summits would profit from a broader administrative base in their preparation and in their follow-up. Such a broader base could be provided by an involvement of ministries of foreign affairs, which thus would gain the added function of being the "sherpas of the sherpas."

The effectiveness of summits, and the effectiveness of heads of governments in foreign affairs in general, is also endangered by another tendency. While some of the heads of government enter the realm of foreign affairs with trepidations, most seem to quickly become enamored of this subject. Having climbed the many steps to the top position in national politics, they are sure of themselves and soon become overconfident when dealing in foreign affairs; not at least because in this sphere opposition both from internal and from foreign actors seems to be less direct and brutal. Criticism and opposition is thus ignored or brushed aside more easily.

Diplomatic advisors to heads of government picked from among the ranks of the diplomatic services will alleviate parts of the problem. Yet the heads of government still would need a broader base for their foreign policy activities and it can only be provided by the ministries of foreign affairs. Cooperation between their offices and the foreign services should therefore not be left to accident. It has to have a firm institutional—and if necessary legal—basis. It should, for example, be obligatory to include the prime minister's office in the list of addressees that receive the more relevant foreign policy papers. The prime minister and his office will have to be involved as per routine in the preparation of important foreign policy decisions. A firm political will, but also firm institutional arrangements should safeguard such flow of information.

(10) The most dramatic change of diplomatic services is, however in store for the member countries of the European Union. They will have to adapt their services and the whole mode of operation to the work of the newly created "European External Action Service." As with many other institutions of the European Union, future developments only will ascribe to this new service its precise function und weight. But it is clear as of now already that this weight will be considerable and that it will absorb and/or overshadow much of the foreign policy activities of member states. That holds true, in particular, for the foreign policy activities of medium sized and of smaller EU member countries.

The legal base of this European Service is Article 13 a–III of the "Lisbon Treaty" (the successor to the failed "EU Constitution"). It puts that Service under the leadership of the EU "High Representative"—at present Catherine Ashton from the United Kingdom. She and the Service will prepare and implement decisions on EU foreign relations and on common security and defense policies. It is true that the decisions themselves will be made by the "Foreign Affairs Council." This Council meets monthly. It is presided over by the "High Representative" and attended by the ministers of foreign affairs of member countries—and if necessary—by ministers of defense, trade, or development. In a merely formal sense, decisions over foreign and security policy will therefore be made by the member countries and not by the "High Representative" and her External Action Service. But the setup is such that member countries will actually have to yield much of that formal authority to the new, joint institution.

The internal organization of the European External Action Service confirms that conclusions. It will be staffed by civil servants of the European Commission; and by diplomats seconded from the member countries. The latter, however, may make for no more than 40 percent of the total staff. Staff from the Commission will thus dominate and also set the tone for the administrative "culture" of the new Service, which will have embassies in most countries of the earth.

Two further factors will de-emphasize the inter-governmental nature of the setup and will underline its "federal" nature. Much power will be vested in the secretary-general, charged with the day-to-day running of the organization. And the directly elected European Parliament may wield powerful tools of control and oversight.

What remains of the diplomatic services of European Union member countries (and especially of those of small and medium sized states) will thus have their main function in feeding into, and working with this new and powerful European diplomatic Service.

(11) Diplomatic protocol and its basis in international law should be adjusted to present-day conditions. Traditional diplomatic protocol has its usefulness, as has the 1961 Vienna Diplomatic Convention, which provides the basis in international law for the status and function of diplomats and a firm corset to a professional setting that otherwise might be rife with rivalry and friction. These formal, legal rules help keep diplomacy functioning even under the adverse circumstances of hostile relations.[25] They provide for a certain uniformity that, as does any standardization, facilitates orientation. Those advantages should not be belittled. Nonetheless, in many other ways, these rules have become dysfunctional. One should consider their updating.

That concerns, for instance, the so-called diplomatic immunity that exempts diplomats from being subject to the actual application of the law of their host state.[26] This privilege has been justified by the need to shield diplomats from undue pressure of their host states, some of whom might otherwise feel tempted to drum up charges against diplomats they dislike. But that privilege of immunity is sometimes abused and such abuse fuels disproportionate animosity toward the profession as such. One has wisely agreed *not* to apply immunity in real estate dealings. When diplomats fail to pay the rent for an apartment or the price for a property purchased, they can very well be prosecuted and made to comply with the terms of their contracts. In view of that precedent, there should be no reason to exclude them from sanctions against minor violations of road traffic rules. The work of diplomats will not be impaired by their having to pay parking fines. There is no reason either, to exempt them from paying value added taxes or excise taxes in a way any other resident of their host country is obliged to do. As they use the same roads as these other residents, there is no evident reason for them to pay less for gasoline. Their being exempt from providing social security insurance to their household staff has caused some human tragedies and finds little understanding in countries where such insurance is obligatory.

All those shortcomings might seem trivial. But it is clear that they add neither to the status of diplomats nor do they facilitate their task. Other legal provisions pose more substantial obstacles to modern diplomatic work. Article 41 of the Vienna Diplomatic Convention, stipulates that... *"they have the duty not to intervene in the internal affairs of the receiving state."* If narrowly defined and applied, that provision would limit contacts of diplomats to contacts with the ministry of foreign affairs of the host state. A few of the remaining totalitarian regimes might welcome such an interpretation. But such a narrow interpretation would inhibit most activities diplomats now actually perform. These activities therefore lack any basis in international law; or even seem to contravene international law as defined by Vienna Diplomatic Convention of 1961.

In fact, there is no binding, universally agreed upon legal basis for quite a number of other functions and tools of modern diplomacy. As we have remarked, roving ambassadors and special envoys might need some local staff in places they visit but on occasion. What is the status of such staff? What rules should apply to Internet-based virtual embassies that will become more common over the next few years? How to treat consular activities that are outsourced to private firms? What about the common and tacitly accepted practice of some major states to spy by intercepting and decoding electronic messages of embassies?[27] What legal provisions for the status of international non-governmental organizations and for their dealings with states and with diplomats? Is a diplomat posted in a difficult foreign country within his rights, for example, to pass information on human rights abuse to the local branch of Amnesty International?

Those open questions do not lend themselves to be resolved quickly by the community of all states. The Vienna Convention codified practices that had evolved over centuries. It codified a consensus that had evolved over this long period. But it would be extremely difficult to find consensus on how to tackle the new issues that have emerged just recently. By now, states differ too widely to permit finding a common denominator that would allow a thorough overhaul of such outdated rules. The views and interests of nations like Nepal, China, Singapore, Germany and the United States are too incompatible for that.

Change will thus come in small steps and from the fringes. The obligation not to interfere in internal affairs, for example, is now being balanced by the "responsibility to protect"[28] when an immediate and serious humanitarian crisis calls for such an intervention. Few ministries of foreign affairs will by now dare, or bother to object to a foreign ambassador giving an interview in media of his host country exactly with the intent to "interfere in its internal affairs." International organizations have *de facto* acquired authority beyond the one provided by their charters. It is not possible yet to find a legal basis for most of these changes. It is clear though, on the other hand, that the absence of a firm legal basis might endanger and/or complicate activities that otherwise have become quite standard. Diplomats and their service will have to live with that dilemma.

(12) What for the diplomats themselves—their status and function?

    a)   Several decades ago, there were few with a post-graduate degree. The upper ranks of the bureaucracy were in need of their services. Strong demand and limited supply made for good salaries and solid prestige. By now, supply and demand have changed. Job seekers with post graduate university degrees and with some more skills added are in ample supply. The pool of available candidates for positions in the upper ranks of the civil service is further enhanced by prospects of a secure position with lots of fringe benefits. In times of permanent change and uncertainty on the job market, this is no small attraction. That holds true also for the diplomatic service with its need for qualified and well-educated personnel. It still is very attractive as is confirmed by the long-waiting lines for diplomatic entrance exams. A vast supply of qualified personnel thus meets limited demand. That is expressed in salaries no longer that superior to average salaries and to the salaries of other civil servants.

b) Travel to foreign countries is now commonplace; as is the exposure to foreign cultures which has become near inevitable in modern societies. Knowledge of foreign languages has expanded.[29] Many persons other than diplomats now spend part of their professional life abroad. The foreign is no longer that exotic and the aura of the exotic that diplomats could bathe in has lost some of its glimmer.

c) Diplomats are no longer the only ones in civil service who deal with public institutions in foreign countries. They have got company through higher civil servants from other governmental bodies who also ply that field. To a large extent, these other civil servants use the same skills as diplomats. That detracts from the claim for a uniqueness of diplomats that before had been widely accepted.

d) The diplomats' fief frays at the fringes. At the core are still those who pass the entrance exams and then follow a lifetime career in the diplomatic service. But these *core diplomats* have to accept as colleagues persons with other career paths, who will join them for a limited time or for good. Experts, consultants, advisers will become attached to the diplomatic corps in order to be helpful with technical issues. Diplomats, on the other hand, will increasingly leave their position under the ministry of foreign affairs and start work in other public institutions where they, on their turn, will serve as experts who can provide know-how for the international activities of these other institutions.

e) Nonetheless, there will be continuing demand for the services of core diplomats. They will retain a relatively high status not at least because of a continuing need to select them from among the best. That is so not only because diplomats still are seen as symbols of their state. It is also and mainly because of the nature of their substantive work which calls for a broad base of knowledge, skills, and aptitudes.

Coda

The world and global governance is burdened by diverging developments:

-   States have become more unequal, while facing at the same time a growing number of common tasks, problems, and risks.
-   Links across the borders of states have grown in number and intensity. Dividing lines between the internal and the external blur. Yet it is states that retain a near monopoly in conferring political legitimation on solutions to problems that transcend borders. The non-national, the global as such does not (yet??) have its own powerful constituency and potent base of political legitimation.
-   The agenda of global governance and its methods are complex. Issues are being dealt with in different venues, and on different political levels. Many public and private institutions now share in the task of global governance. They provide necessary but narrow technical knowledge and technical skills on subjects they are engaged in. These many transactions can no longer be subsumed under one single and coherent national foreign policy. Nonetheless there is a need for overall political guidance and political input into these many different levels and fields of global governance.
-   Order is more easily maintained with rules that are firm and durable. But the multitude of actors and the wide variance of transactions between them make for a rather fluid and unsteady system of global governance. Steering has to be done by hand. One cannot rely on an autopilot.

Such contradictions have to be accommodated. Bridges have to be built between what seem to be irreconcilable opposites. That has to be done in negotiations, which are political by their very nature. Political bridge-builders engaged in that task need helpers who can reach out to both of these conflicting sides. Diplomats are such helpers.

How can that be, given that their profession took its shape in times and circumstances that differ profoundly from those in place today? Diplomats will only retain such function if they embrace change. As we have argued, a continuing functionality and usefulness of diplomats and of diplomatic services is contingent on reforms in the methods of work; and contingent on the reform of institutions that underpin this work.

In a very critical review of my own involvement in bilateral and multilateral diplomacy, I have shown in the first part of this book that such necessary changes have been slow to arrive. Nonetheless, they are under way, being promoted by the sheer necessity of adapting to challenges of the dramatically transformed environment global governance has to shape. Not ignoring the distance a reform of diplomatic services still needs to cover, there is no doubt that such an adaptation has progressed over the last years.

But why, one could be prompted to ask, should one still call diplomacy a work that, since it got its name, has been changed so profoundly and that is bound to undergo even further changes in the future? One would not call a metallurgist a smith just because both are working with metal. Their jobs are not the same. What a smith did 500 years ago has no counterpart in what a metallurgist does today.

We may, however, still use the old name of "diplomacy" for this work though it has changed so very much in nature and methods. We may do so because some crucial aptitudes, because the guiding ethos are still alike in both old fashioned diplomacy and in its modern version.

Diplomacy still is the art of dealing with the uncertain, the unknown and unknowable; it is the art of dealing with the foreign, it is the art of reaching out and of seeking understanding, trust, and compromise. The growing interconnectedness and interdependence of persons, societies, and states has not lessened to the need for such skills. It has heightened it.

Notes

1.   With a close monitoring of whether embassies had dutifully met their quota of such political reports.
2.   I still am proud of having broken ground in my former capacity as head of the policy planning department in bringing aboard scientists from Austrian universities for negotiations on the Comprehensive Nuclear Test Ban Treaty, and on the negotiations for the elimination of chemical weapons.
3.   This is particularly dysfunctional with the information concerning the contacts a diplomat has acquired over his tour of duty in a foreign country. His secretary might have a list of at least some of these contacts and will stand ready to provide

it to the successor. But such lists are useless without comments that provide additional information on these persons. The knowledge that Mister So-and-So can be reached under a certain telephone number does not help very much in a search for a contact that might be of use on a certain issue. As Austrian consul general in New York, I had, for example, quite good and extensive contacts to groups of Jews that had been displaced from Austria to the United States in the Nazi era; and good contacts too, to Jewish organizations. No mechanism existed to have my successor benefit from these contacts. That information was thus lost.

4. Providing for such an overlap between incoming and outgoing diplomats will put additional strains on the diplomatic service, already under the pressure to cut jobs and expenditures. But in the choice between quantity and quality of personnel, one is generally well advised to opt for quality. Better some well-informed diplomats than a slightly larger number of them that enter a new position without a hunch about the activities of their predecessor. The idea of such an overlap also would run counter to deeply embedded routine and diplomatic folklore. According to a well-circulated quip by the diplomat's "patron saint," French foreign minister Talleyrand, "ambassadors would tend to perceive of their predecessors as criminals; and of the successors as idiots."

5. The highest order awarded in the military of the old Austro-Hungarian Empire was the Order of Empress Mary Therese. It was given for the successful *disregard* of a command given from above!

6. Catching "localities"—in the insider parlance of the service.

7. In some diplomatic services, such as the one of the United Kingdom, the duration is even shorter.

8. Many diplomatic representations at international organizations and especially many of those from poorer countries tend to act very much on their own, with scant oversight by their head office. Interventions at this head office are therefore useless.

9. In addition, the EU Council convenes each year for at least one informal meeting .

10. Two salient examples from the World Bank. The Bank had to make some highly political decisions on whether and how to become active in Kosovo after it declared its independence from Serbia, with some states accepting that declaration, some staying neutral, and some opposing it. The World Bank had also to decide on how to continue its substantial support for the population in Gaza after the electoral victory of Hamas, which many of its Western members had branded as a "terrorist organization." Such decisions should not be left to bankers. They have to be made in view of the overall political context of the Kosovo conflict or of the process of finding peace in the Middle East.

11. Higher civil servants from Austrian ministries that deal with international organizations meet, if not frequently, at least regularly. As these meetings are ritualized, they add very little to actual foreign policy coordination.

12. As shown by the difficulties of Romania and Bulgaria to live up to the promises made at their entry into the European Union to rid their administrations of clientilism and rampant corruption.

13. When I worked at the OECD office for "Cooperation with Countries in Transition," we had such "anchors" in some of the most important "Transition Countries," such as Russia. They served us very well; and they were low-cost.

14. Some such interventions might be more effective than intervention by governments. Franklin J. (2008) presents a study showing that interventions of organizations like Amnesty International are more likely to have an effect on countries violating human rights than do interventions by governments or by official international institutions (like the UN Human Rights Council).

15. Counterproductive was, for example, the arrogant attempt by the US administration of President George W. Bush to use "public diplomacy" not just for conveying information. The aim was set higher. "Public Diplomacy" was seen as a tool of "transformative diplomacy" with the assigned mission to change, from the outside, the whole internal regime of a state.

16. The general image of a country is rather resistant to change. For the foreseeable future, the Netherlands is saddled with the image of hemp being openly sold in Amsterdam. Austria remains the country of Mozart, Hitler, and Freud with some ski instructors thrown in. Italians like to sing and the French would hate Americans.

17. Attention has also to be given to some more old-fashioned media that provide basic information on a country. I was always disturbed by the fact that my country, Austria, did not register in some of the most salient international statistics. And it is statistics that most analyst and opinion leaders will look at first when forming a judgment on a country.

18. That suggestion finds support in a recent, 2010, recommendation of "EU Sages" on the next ten years of the EU integration process. They recommended a wholesale merge of the consular services of EU member countries.

19. This conclusion is substantiated by Austria's experience with membership in the European Union. After having driven negotiations into a ditch, line ministries had often to be rescued by the Ministry of Foreign Affairs and its diplomats.

20. The size of those offices of military attachés still reflects the outsize importance ascribed to military matters over the last two centuries.

21. A warning example for the damage that might ensue both at home and abroad was the profound policy difference between the US Department of State and its head, Secretary of State Colin Powell on one side, and of Vice President Cheney and Defense Secretary Rumsfeld on the other. The conflict very much damaged the already precarious role of the United States as a global "benign hegemon." I was traveling in Serbia at a time when Secretary Powell put Serbia under strong pressure to sign on to the International Court on War Crimes in Yugoslavia. Secretary of Defense Rumsfeld, at Powell's side, put exorbitant pressure on Serbia *not* to sign up to the International Criminal Court. The Serbs were not amused.

22. In Austria, that had serious consequences in the early 1990s during the break up of former Yugoslavia. The foreign minister rooted for an early recognition of states that had seceded from Yugoslavia. The head of government called for greater prudence. This conflict complicated Austria's foreign policy at the critical moment of war between two of its neighbors.

23. A smaller version of a separate foreign service (minus representations abroad) has been attached as the National Security Council to the office of the US president. In its role as foreign policy instrument, this office is handicapped by its function to mainly coordinate foreign and military policies. It thus has contributed to the "militarization" of US foreign policy that has had its share in undermining the US position in the world.

24. This alludes to the "sherpas" that lead mountaineers up to the summits of the Himalayas.

25. It is exactly under these circumstances of hostile relations that diplomacy is most urgently needed.

26. Contrary to public perception, diplomats are not except from the law as such. Diplomats are actually held to respect it.

27. The acceptance of that practice—or at least of the current US practice—is reflected in the acceptance by OECD countries of an obligation *not* to develop a cryptology that could encode messages in such a way that they could no longer be read through ECHELON—the US electronic spying system.
28. The international community has even agreed upon a "responsibility to protect," that is the duty to intervene in exceptional settings such as those of an ongoing genocide.
29. With the exception perhaps of the English-speaking countries, which feel comfortable with the adoption of their language as the universal *lingua franca*.

Bibliography

Adams H., 1995, The Collected Works of Henry Adams, London.

Anderson B., 1991, Imagined Communities: Reflections on the Origins and the Spread of Nationalism, London.

Angel N., 1910, The Great Illusion: Studying Military Power in Its Relation to Their Common Social Advantages, London.

Annan K., 1997, Opening Address to the Fifth Annual Department of Public Information/Non-Governmental Organization Conference, United Nations Press Release, SG/SM/6320, PI/1027, September 10, 1997.

Avdeyeva O., 2007, "Why Do States Comply With International Treaties—Politics of Violence Against Women in Post-Communist Countries," in International Studies Quarterly, 2007/51, pp. 877–900.

Axelrod R., 1984, The Evolution of Cooperation, New York.

Barnett M., M. Finnemore, 2004, Rules for the World: International Organizations in Global Politics, London.

Baumann Z., (ed.) 1998, Globalization—The Human Consequences, Oxford.

Baylis J., S. Smith, P. Owens, (eds.) 2006, The Globalizations of World Politics, Oxford.

Beck U., 1997, Was ist Globalisierung, Frankfurt.

Becker M., S. John, S. Schirm, 2007, Globalisierung und Global Governance, München.

Bischof G., 2007, "US Public Diplomacy—Past and Present," paper for the panel New Forms of Public Diplomacy, Europäisches Forum Alpbach, August 2007.

Boghossian P., 2006, Fear of Knowledge—Against Relativism and Constructivism, New York.

Brand U., 2001, Nichtregierungsorganisationen in der Transformation des Staates, Münster.

Brand U., 2007, The Internationalization of the State as the Reconstitution of Hegemony, WP 1, IPW University of Vienna.

Breen R., 2004, Kim Jong-il: North Korea's Dear Leader, Singapore.

Brooks S., W. Wohlforth, 2009, Re-Shaping World Order, in Foreign Affairs, 88/2, pp. 49–63.

Bürger C., F. Gadinger, 2007, "Re-Assembling and Dissecting: International Studies Practice from a Science Perspective," in International Studies Perspectives, 2007/8, pp. 90–110.

Bull H., A. Watson, 1984, The Expansion of International Society, Oxford.

Calhoun C. (ed.) 2002, Dictionary of Social Sciences, Oxford.

Calliers F., La manière de négocier avec les souverains, de l'utilité des négociations, du choix des ambassadeurs et des envoyés, et des qualités nécessaires pour réussir dans ces emploies. Its English language version: Keens-Soper H, K Schweizer, (eds.) 1983, The Art of Diplomacy, Leicester.

Chicago Council on Global Affairs. Public Opinions Study, 2008 http://www. thechicagoscouncil.org/dynamic_page.php?id=76.

Cohen S., 2006, The Resilience of the State: Democracy and the Challenges of Globalization, Boulder: Colorado.

Cooper A., J. English, R. Thakur, 2002, Enhancing Global Governance— Towards a New Diplomacy, Tokyo.

Cooper A., 2005, Stretching the Model of Coalitions of the Willing, Working Paper, Centre for International Governance and Innovation, University of Waterloo, Ontario.

Cox R., 1992, "Towards a Post-Hegemonic Conceptualization of World Order: Reflections on the Relevance of Ibn Khaldun," in Rosenau J/E Czempiel, 1992, op. cit.

Creveld M., 2009, Gesichter des Krieges: der Wandel bewaffneter Konflikte von 1900 bis Heute, München.

Deutsch K., 1953, Nationalism and Social Communication, Cambridge, USA.

Dicken P., 2007, Global Shift: Mapping the Changing Contours of the World Economy, 5th ed., London.

Dickie J., 2004, The New Mandarins: How British Foreign Policy Works, London.

Dixon J., 2009, "What Causes Civil Wars? Integrating Quantitative Research Findings," in International Studies Review, Vol. 11/4, pp. 707–735.

Dorff R., 2005, "Failed States after 9/11: What Did We Know and What Have We Learned," in International Studies Perspectives, 2005/6, pp. 20–34.

Drezner D., 2007, All Politics Is Global: Explaining International Regulatory Regimes, Princeton.

Duke S., 2002, "Preparing for European Diplomacy," Journal of Common Market Studies, Vol. 40, pp. 849–870.

Ehrenberg A., 2010, La societé du malaise—le mental et le social, Paris.

Eichler E., 2006, The Role of Identity in European-US Relations, in (eds.) Gustenau G., O. Höll, T. Nowotny, Europe-USA: Diverging Partners, Wien, pp. 245–264.

Eldon S., 1994, From Quilt Pen to Satellite, Royal Institute of International Affairs, London.

Enterline A., M. Greig, 2008, "Against All Odds: The History of Imposed Democracy and the Future of Iraq and Afghanistan," in Foreign Policy Analysis, 2008/4, pp. 321–347.

Falk R., 1999, "World Prisms: The Future of Sovereign States and International Order," Harvard International Review, Summer 1999, pp. 30–35.

Fehr E., S. Gächter, 2000, "Fairness and Retaliation: The Economics of Reciprocity," Journal of Economic Perspectives 14(3), pp. 159–181.

Foreign and Commonwealth Office, (Whitepaper), 2006, Active Diplomacy in a Changing World, London.

Franklin J., 2008, "Shame on You: The Impact of Human Rights Criticism on Political Repression" in Latin America, in International Studies Quarterly 2008/52, pp. 187–211.

Frum D., 2004, An End to Evil, The War on Terror, Ballantine.

Giddens A., 1999, Runaway World: How Globalization Is Re-Shaping Our Lives, London.

Glasius M., M. Kaldor, H. Anheimer, (eds.), 2007, Global Civil Society, London.

Goldstone J., 2010, "The New Population Bomb: The Four Mega Trends that Will Shape the World," in Foreign Affairs, Jan/Feb 2010, pp. 31–43.

Gstöl S., 2007, "Governance Through Governance Networks. The G-8 and International Organizations," in Review of International Organizations, 2007/2, pp. 1–37.

Guehenno J-M., 1994, Das Ende der Demokratie, München.

Haas R., 2008, "The Age of Nonpolarity," Foreign Affairs, May-June 2008.

Hamilton A., J. Madison, J. Jay, 1788, The Federalist Papers, edition 1989, New York.

Held D., 2000, Regulating Globalization? "The Re-Invention of Politics," in International Sociology, June 2000, Vol. 15/2, pp. 399–408.

Henderson S., 2002, "Selling Civil Society: Western Aid and the Non-Governmental Organization Sector in Russia," in Comparative Political Studies, Vol. 35/2, March 2002.

Hinteregger G., 2008, Im Auftrag Österreichs, Wien.

Hocking B., 2004, "Privatizing Diplomacy," in International Studies Perspectives 2004/5 pp. 147–152.

Hoffmann S., 1981, Duties Beyond Borders, Syracuse.

Holmes J. A., 2009, "Where are the Civilians?" in Foreign Affairs, January-February 2009, pp. 130–148.

Hood L., 2007, "The Education of Carne Ross: From Outrage to Opportunity," in Foreign Service Journal, May 2007, pp. 42–45.

Hooghe C., G. Marks, 2003, Unraveling the Central State—But How; Types of Multi-Level Government, WP 87, IHS, Vienna.

Houghton D., 2009, "The Role of Self-Fulfilling and Self-Negating Prophecies in International Relations," International Studies Review, Vol. 11/3, pp. 552–584.

Huntington S., 2004, Who Are We? The Challenge to America's National Identity, New York.

Ingelhart R., C. Welzel, 2009, "How Development Leads to Democracy—What We Know About Modernization," in Foreign Affairs, 88/2, pp. 32–48.

Jazbec M., 2006, Diplomacy and Security after the End of the Cold War: The Change of Paradigm, in 41. Jahrbuch des Diplomatischen Akademie, Wien, pp. 163–177.

Kaufmann J., 1996, Conference Diplomacy, 3rd ed., London.

Kaul I., I. Grünberg, M. Stern, (eds.) 1999, Global Public Goods—International Cooperation in the 21st Century, New York.

Kegely S., 2008, World Politics: Trends and Transformations, Claremont: Florida.

Kelly K., 1994, Out of Control—The New Biology of Machines, Social Systems and the Economic World, New York.

Kennan G., 1997, "Diplomacy without Diplomats," in Foreign Affairs, September 1997.

Kennedy P., D. Messner, F. Nuschler, (eds.) 2002, Global Trends and Global Governance, London.

Keohane R., 2002, Power and Interdependence in a Partly Globalized World, New York.

Keohane R., 1975, "International Organizations and the Crisis of Interdependence," in International Organization, Vol. 29/2, Spring 1975, pp. 357–365.

Kessler O., 2009, "Towards a Sociology of the International? International Relations between Anarchy and World Society," in International Political Sociology, Vol. 3/1, pp. 87–108.

Keynes J. M., 1936, The General Theory of Employment, Interest and Money, London.

Kille K., 2007, The UN Secretary General and Moral Authority: Ethics, Religion and International Leadership, Washington DC.

Kissinger H., 1994, Diplomacy, New York.

Koch M., 2009, "Autonomization of IGOs," in International Political Sociology, Vol. 3–4, pp. 431–448.

Kollman K., 2008, "The Regulatory Power of Business Norms—A Call for a Research Agenda," in International Studies Review, 2008/10, pp. 397–419.

Kopp H., C. Gillespie, 2008, Career Diplomacy—Life and Work in the US Foreign Service, Washington DC.

Kramer H., 2000, Politische Kompetenz und Demokratie, in : Zilian J (ed.): Politische Teilhabe-Politische Entfremdung. Graz-Wien, pp. 33–52.

Kuperman A., 2008, "The Moral Hazards of Humanitarian Interventions: Lessons from the Balkans," in International Studies Quarterly, 2008/52, pp. 49–80.

Ladeur K-H., 2004, Public Governance in the Age of Globalization, Hants, England.

Lane A., 2007, "Modernising the Management of British Diplomacy: Towards a Foreign Office Policy on Policy-making," in Cambridge Review of International Affairs, Vol. 20/1, pp. 179–193.

Langhorne R., 1997, "Developments in contemporary diplomatic practice," in Diplomacy and Statecraft, 1997–1998.

Lebessis N., J. Paterson, 1997, The Evolution of Governance: What lessons for the Commission? A First Assessment, EC Forward Studies Unit, Working Paper, Brussels.

Lipschitz R., 2008, "Imperial Warfare and the Naked City—Sociality As Critical Infrastructure," in International Political Sociology, Vol. 2/3, pp. 204–218.

Lisa L., 1999, The Political Economy of International Cooperation, in Kaul I, et alia, op cit, pp. 51–63.

Livre blanc sur la politique étrangère et européenne de la France, 2009, www. diplomatie.gouv.fr/ministere_817/modernisation.

Lovelock J., 2009, The Vanishing Face of Gaia—A Final Warning, New York.

Marshall P., 1997, Positive Diplomacy, London.

Mathews J., 1997, "Power Shift," in Foreign Affairs, January/February 1997.

McMillan P., 2008, "Subnational Foreign Policy Actors: How and Why Governors Participate in US Foreign Policy," in Foreign Policy Analysis, 2008/4, pp. 227–253.

Mearsheimer J., 2001, The Tragedy of Great Power Politics, New York.

Miller J., 2008, "Soft Power and the State-Firm Diplomacy: Congress and IT Corporate Activity in China," in International Studies Perspectives, Vol. 10/3, pp. 285–302.

Morgenthau H., 1948, Politics among Nations, New York.

Moynihan P., 1998, Secrecy—The American Experience, Newhaven.

Moynihan P., 1980, A Dangerous Place, New York.

Muldoon Jr J., 2005, "The Diplomacy of Business," in Diplomacy and Statecraft 16/2, pp. 333–359.

Muldoon Jr J., 2007, The New "New Diplomacy": The Changing Character of Multilateral Diplomacy at the United Nations; paper for the Dec 2007 annual conference of the British International Studies Association, Cambridge UK.

National Security Strategy of the United States, September 2002, www.gloabl saecurity.org/military/library/policy/national/nss-020920.pdf.

Neumann I., 2007, "A Speech that the Ministry Might Stand For—Or Why Diplomats Never Produce Anything New," in International Political Sociology, 2007/1, pp. 183–200.

Neumann I., E. Overland, 2004, "International Relations and Policy Planning: The Method of Perspective Scenario Building," in International Studies Perspectives 5/3, pp. 258–277.

Newsom D., 1988, Diplomacy and the American Dream, Indiana University Press.

Nicolson H., 1954, The Evolution of the Diplomatic Method, London.

Nowotny E., 2005, "Diplomats: Symbols of Sovereignty Become Managers of Interdependence: The Transformation of the Austrian Diplomatic Service," in Contemporary Austrian Studies, Vol. 14, London, pp. 25–38.

Nowotny T., 2005, Strawberries in Winter: On Global Trends and Global Governance, New York.

Nowotny T., 1991, Die grenzüberschreitende Tätigkeit der österreichischen Bundesländer, in Österreichischen Aussenpolitische Dokumentation, Wien.

Nowotny T., 1988, Identitätskrise der Diplomaten, Österreichische Zeitschrift für Politikwissenschaft, 1988, Heft 2.

Nowotny T., 1986, Anmerkungen zur multifunktionellen Standardrede über die österreichische Außenpolitik, Österreichisches Jahrbuch für Internationale Politik, Jg 1986, Wien.

Olson M., 1965, The Logic of Collective Action: Public Goods and the Theory of Groups, Cambridge, US.

Oye K., 1986, Cooperation under Anarchy, Princeton.

Paine T., 1791–1969, Age of Reason, in: The Writings of Thomas Paine, Vol. 4, re-edited, New York.

Pape W., 1998, From uni-bi-multi-lateral systems to omnilateral systems, EC Forward Studies Unit, Brussels.

Paschke K., 2000, Report on the Special Inspection of the German Embassies in the Countries of the European Union, Berlin, Sept 2000.

Petritsch W., 2009, Globalisierung, Weltinnenpolitik und das Dilemma der Demokratie, in: Vranitzky F., (Hsg) Themen der Zeit II, Passagenverlag Wien, pp. 147–171.

Peyrefitte R., 1951, Les Ambassades, Paris.

Ragazzi F., 2009, "Governing Diasporas," in International Political Sociology, Vol. 3/4, pp. 370–397.

Ramo J., 2009, The Age of the Unthinkable: Why the New World Disorder Constantly Surprises Us and What We Can Do About it, New York.

Ranke L. V., 1924, Politisches Gespräch, München.

Rauch J., 1994, Demosclerosis, New York.

Reimann K., 2006, "A View from the Top: International Politics, Norms and the Worldwide Growth of NGOs," in International Studies Quarterly, /50.

Reinisch P., 1911, Public International Unions: Their Work and Organization— A Study in International Administrative Law, Boston.

Review of Overseas Representation: Report by the Central Policy Review Staff ("The Think Tank Report"); 1977, HMSO, London; and the reply from the British FCO: The United Kingdoms Overseas Representation. 1978, HMSO, London.

Rittberger V., (ed.), 2002, Global Governance and the United Nations System, Tokyo.

Robertson D., (ed.), 2007, A Dictionary of Modern Politics, New York.

Rosenau J., 2003, Distant Proximities: Dynamics beyond Globalization, Princeton.

Rosenau J., E. Czempiel (eds.), 1992, Governance Without Government: Order and Change in World Politics, Cambridge, UK.

Ross C., 2007, The Independent Diplomat—Dispatches from an Unaccountable Elite, Cornell University Press.

Satow E., 1979, A Guide to Diplomatic Practice, 5th ed., London.

Schiff A., 2009, "Quasi Track One Diplomacy: An Analysis of the Geneva Process," in International Studies Perspectives, Vol. 11/2, pp. 93–111.

Singh J., 2007, "Culture or Commerce? A Comparative Assessment of International Interactions and Developing Countries at UNESCO, WTO and Beyond," in International Studies Perspectives, 200/8, pp. 36–53.

Skelsbaek K., 1971, The Growth of International Non-Governmental Organizations in the 20th Century, Wisconsin.

Slaughter A. M., 2009, "The American Edge," Foreign Affairs, Jan.–Feb. 2009, pp. 94–114.

Smith K., 2003, European Union Foreign Policy in a Changing World, Cambridge, UK.

Sofar S., 2005, "Guardians of the Practitioners Virtue—Diplomats in the Warriors Den," in Diplomacy and Statecraft 16/1, pp. 1–10.

Steel R., 1990, Walter Lippmann and the American Century, London.

Steiner B., 2000, Another Uneasy Middle: Diplomacy and International Theory, Paper at the Annual ISA Convention, March 2000.

Stiglitz J., 2002, Globalization and its Discontents, London.

Stourzh G., 1969, in Bracher K-D, E. Fraenkel (eds.) Internationale Beziehungen, das Fischer Lexikon, Frankfurt.

Stourzh G., 1977, Außenpolitik, Diplomatie, Gesandtschaftswesen: zur Begriffserklärung und historischen Einführung, in Zöllner E (Hsg) Diplomatie und Außenpolitik Österreichs, Wien.

Strange S., 1992, "States, Firms and Diplomacy," in International Affairs, 1992/1, pp. 1–15.

Sucharipa E., M. Reinprecht, 2000, The Future of European Diplomacy, Diplomatische Akademie, Wien.

Taedong L., 2007, The Rise of International Nongovernmental Organizations: Influences of Globalization or Domestic Political Economic Structure; www.allacademic.com/meta/p179523_index.html.

Talbott S., 1997, "Globalization and Diplomacy: A Practitioners Perspective," in Foreign Policy, No. 108, Autumn 1997, pp. 68–83.

The American Academy for Diplomacy, Oct 2008, A Foreign Affairs Budget for the Future—Fixing the Crisis in Diplomatic Readiness, Washington.

Trevelyan H., 1974, Diplomatic Channels, London.

Tschofen H., 2002, Die große Welt in greifbar nahen Räumen, Wien.

Tuchman B., 1984, The March of Folly, New York.

Waldheim K., 1985, Im Glashaus der Weltpolitik, München.

Walker T., 2008, "Two Faces of Liberalism: Kant, Paine and the Question of Intervention," in International Studies Quarterly, 52/3, pp. 449–468.

Wallerstein I., 1983, Historical Capitalism, London.

Weart S., 1998, Never at War: Why Democracies Will not Fight Another, Newhaven.

Weiss T., S. Davis, 2007, The Oxford Handbook of the United Nations, Oxford.

Wheeler N., 2003, Saving Strangers, Oxford.

Wildner H., 1959, Die Technik der Diplomatie—l'Art de négocier, Wien.

Wilson D. S., 2008, How Darwin's Theory Can Change the Way We Think About Our Lives, New York.

World Bank, 1997, The State in a Changing World, Washington, DC.

www.americandiplomacy.org—an electronic journal published by retired US Foreign Service Officers, hosted by the University of Chapel Hill NC, USA.

www.usdiplomacy.org: Website of the Association for Diplomatic Studies and Training (ADST).

Zacharia F., 2008, Post American World, New York.
Zacher H., 2001, International Organizations; in The Oxford Companion to the
    Politics of the World, 2nd ed., Oxford.
Zeng K., J. Easten, 2007, "International Economic Integration and Environmen-
    tal Protection—The Case of China," in International Studies Quarterly,
    2007/51, pp. 971–995.

Index

CPSIA information can be obtained at www.ICGtesting.com
Printed in the USA
BVOW080036121212

307880BV00004B/9/P